Treating the
Multiproblem Family:
A Casebook

Treating the Multiproblem Family: A Casebook

Kjell Erik Rudestam
York University

Mark Frankel
The Dellcrest Children's Centre

Brooks/Cole Publishing Company
Monterey, California

Brooks/Cole Publishing Company
A Division of Wadsworth, Inc.

Printed in the United States of America

10 9 8 7 6 5 4 3 2 1

Library of Congress Cataloging in Publication Data

Rudestam, Kjell Erik.
    Treating the multiproblem family.

    Bibliography: p.
    1. Family psychotherapy—Case studies. 2. Problem
        family—Case studies.   I. Frankel, Mark, 1945–
II. Title.
RC488.5.R826   1983   616.89'156   82-19739
ISBN 0-534-01300-7

Subject Editor: *Claire Verduin*
Manuscript Editor: *Barbara Burton*
Production Editor: *Fiorella Ljunggren*
Interior and Cover Design: *Victoria Van Deventer*
Illustrations: *Cyndi Sumner*
Typesetting: *Instant Type, Monterey, California*

To our fathers, Edvin Rudestam and Herbert Frankel

About the Authors

Kjell Erik Rudestam received his Ph.D. in clinical psychology from the University of Oregon in 1969. He is Professor of Psychology at York University, a Diplomate of the American Board of Examiners in Professional Psychology, and the author of two other books, both published by Brooks/Cole Publishing Company: *Methods of Self-Change* (1980) and *Experiential Groups in Theory and Practice* (1982).

Mark Frankel is Director of Mental Health Services at The Dellcrest Children's Centre in Downsview, Ontario. He has worked as a clinician, consultant, and administrator since completing his Ph.D. in clinical psychology at the University of Rochester in 1970.

About the Consultants

Gerald Beckerle, Ph.D., is Chief Psychologist at Toronto East General Hospital. After studying clinical psychology at Michigan State University, he worked as a staff psychologist at Fort Logan Mental Health Center, Denver, Colorado. His clinical interests include family, marital, and group therapy, hypnosis, and neuropsychology.

Richard Berry, Ph.D., is Director of Adolescent Services at Thistletown Regional Centre for Children and Adolescents in Toronto. His graduate degree is from York University, and his special clinical interests include the treatment of antisocial adolescents and the study of infant/mother attachment.

Sandra Birenbaum, M.S.W., is Director of the Youthdale Centre for Individual and Family Therapy in Toronto. Since obtaining her degree from the University of Toronto, she has worked in a variety of programs specializing in the treatment of adolescents and families.

Michael Blugerman, M.S.W., is President of the Toronto Centre for Personal and Organizational Development, Inc. Since obtaining his graduate degree from Waterloo Lutheran University, he has worked as a marital and family therapist and as a consultant to a variety of children's service agencies. His professional interests include the training of mental health staff and family therapy.

William G. Carty, B.A., is the Residence Supervisor at Oolagen Community Services in Toronto. He was trained as a child care worker at Browndale Residential Treatment Centre. His special interests include the treatment of adolescents and their families and the uses of residential treatment for adolescents.

Gerald A. Casey, Ph.D., is Senior Psychologist at C. M. Hincks Treatment Centre in Toronto. His clinical interests include strategic family therapy and hypnosis. His graduate degree is from Michigan State University, and he has worked at Portland State University and the Ontario Institute for Studies in Education.

Barbara J. Dydyk, Ph.D., is Director of Children's Services at Thistletown Regional Centre for Children. She received her graduate degrees from Loyola University, Chicago. Dr. Dydyk has done postdoctoral training in family therapy at Chedoke Child and Family Centre in Hamilton and has clinical experience with both emotionally disturbed and mentally retarded children. Her professional interests include structural family therapy, systems interventions, and program evaluation.

Gregor J. Finlayson, Ph.D., is Chief Psychologist at Earlscourt Child and Family Centre in Toronto. His graduate degree is from the University of Toronto, and he has worked as both a therapist and a trainer in the field of family therapy, in addition to managing a day treatment program for children. His professional interests include family therapy and children's learning problems.

Esther Gelcer, Ph.D., is Chief Psychologist at the Child and Family Studies Centre, Clarke Institute of Psychiatry, in Toronto. She has worked as a therapist, lecturer, consultant, and administrator and is currently Director of the Toronto Family Therapy Training Programme. Her clinical interests include family therapy, play therapy, and projective testing.

Cynthia Gertsman, M.D., F.R.C.P.(C), is a child and family psychiatrist in private practice and consultant to several mental health agencies. After receiving her medical degree from the University of Ottawa, she studied child psychiatry at the University of Toronto. In addition to her consultation and private-practice activities, she is active in the supervision and training of residents in child psychiatry. Her clinical interests include both the practice and the teaching of family therapy.

Howard Irving, D.S.W., is Professor in the Faculties of Social Work and Law at the University of Toronto. He obtained his M.S.W. from the University of Connecticut and his doctorate from the University of Toronto. He is the author of several books and many journal articles on the subject of divorce mediation and family law and is the Research Director of the Toronto Family Court Project. In addition, he maintains a private practice in marital and family therapy. His current interests include conciliation counseling, joint custody, and family therapy.

Catherine Jackel, C.C.W., is a faculty member of The Child Care Work Program of Centennial College in Toronto. She has had a wide range of professional experiences in mental health centers serving emotionally disturbed children, adolescents, and families. Her interests include family treatment, parent education, and group work with adolescents.

Joseph H. Kluger, Ph.D., is a psychologist with the Child Development and Counselling Services, North York General Hospital, in Toronto. His doctorate is from Queen's University, and he has received advanced training in clinical child psychology as a postdoctoral fellow at the University of Rochester Medical Center. In addition to his primary position, he consults to several treatment centers for children and maintains a part-time private practice. His clinical interests include individual and group psychotherapy with children, mental health consultation to schools, and parent counseling.

Harvey Mandel, Ph.D., is an Associate Professor of Psychology at York University and past Chairperson of the York Counselling Centre. His graduate degree is from the Illinois Institute of Technology. He consults and has an independent practice, specializing in brief forms of treatment with couples and adolescents and their families.

Peter Marton, Ph.D., is Coordinator of Research at C. M. Hincks Treatment Centre in Toronto. His graduate degree is from the State University of New York at Stony Brook. He has worked as a Research Associate in the Psychiatric Research Unit of Toronto's Hospital for Sick Children and as a consultant to several child and family treatment centers. His professional interests include high-risk infants and family treatment.

Rudolph L. Philipp, Ph.D., is Supervising Psychologist at Thistletown Regional Centre. Since receiving his degree, he has worked with emotionally and behaviorally disturbed children, run many parent education groups, and done research on psychosomatic problems, family relations, and hard-to-serve adolescents. His clinical interests include parent education, behavior modification, and family therapy.

Elizabeth Ridgley, M.S.W., is Director of Community Services at Thistletown Regional Centre in Toronto. She received her M.S.W. from Columbia University and has taken extern training in family therapy at the Philadelphia Child Guidance Clinic. Before assuming her current position, she was Clinical Director of Oolagen Community Services in Toronto and has been a family therapy consultant to a variety of treatment agencies. Her major current clinical interest is the family treatment of symptomatic children.

Julian S. Rubinstein, M.D., F.R.C.P.(C), is a psychiatrist in the Adolescent Services of Thistletown Regional Centre for Children and Adolescents. His medical training was done at the University of the Witwatersrand in Johannesburg, South Africa, and his psychiatric residence at McMaster University. He established the Parent-Therapist Program at Chedoke-McMaster Hospital and has worked extensively as a clinical supervisor and teacher of medical students and mental health professionals. He is active as a family therapist, and his clinical interests include family psychiatry and program development for treatment of emotional and learning disorders in children and adolescents.

Marjorie Shore, M.S.W., is a social worker in private practice in Toronto. She received her degree from the University of Toronto and additional training at the Chedoke Child and Family Centre. Mrs. Shore specializes in the practice of family therapy.

Paul Spring, M.D., F.R.C.P.(C), is a child psychiatrist in private practice. He completed his medical training at the University of Toronto and holds a Certificate in Psychiatry from New York Medical College. He is also a Diplomate of the American Board of Psychiatry and Neurology. In addition to maintaining a private practice, he is a university lecturer and psychiatric consultant. His professional interests include play therapy, adolescent psychiatry, and family therapy.

Bruce Stam, C.C.W., is Director of Group Homes (Niagara Region) for Ausable Springs Ranch in Kleinburg, Ontario. He received his child care degree from George Brown College and has worked in group homes as a supervisor at The Dellcrest Children's Centre in Toronto and as a parent educator. His primary current clinical interest is the use of community homes for the treatment of severely disturbed children.

Steven Stein, Ph.D., is Coordinator of Research at Thistletown Regional Centre for Children and Adolescents. His doctorate, in clinical psychology, is from the University of Ottawa. He conducts clinical research and practices behavior therapy, with special emphasis on the treatment of couples and adolescents.

Mary Pat Tillman, M.S.W., is a psychiatric social worker with the Family Therapy Unit of Toronto East General Hospital. She obtained her graduate degree from Wilfred Laurier University. In addition to her primary position, she is a faculty member of the Toronto Family Therapy Institute. Her clinical interests include family therapy and individual psychotherapy.

William Wetzel, M.S.W., is a psychiatric social worker at Toronto East General Hospital. His graduate degree is from the University of Toronto. He maintains a private practice in family and marital therapy and teaches at a community college. His major clinical interests are family and marital therapy.

Preface

The education of a therapist typically begins in the classroom and progresses to the real world. We have learned, over the course of our own development as educators and clinicians, that there is a substantial difference between the "academic" and the "actual" in clinical practice. This book is intended to help reconcile that difference. From our experience as consultants to mental health settings that specialize in the treatment of children and their families, we have noted that too many workers have prepared for professional activity by learning about single, isolated treatment problems and methods. Unfortunately, the children and families who present themselves for treatment rarely fit neatly into simple formulations. The effort to adjust to working with real families, with their complex problems, can then be intimidating—even overwhelming—for the beginning clinician. As consultants, we have reflected on this situation and asked students and therapists what kinds of skill training might be most useful to them. One answer we have consistently received is: increased exposure to a wide range of realistic, multiproblem cases, together with the vicarious learning that comes from observing or listening to more experienced therapists discuss and perform their craft. This book provides both; it is the product of our search for a useful training tool and offers a provocative glimpse into the conceptualizing and strategic planning of 24 expert clinicians.

Treating the Multiproblem Family contains 24 cases exemplifying problems that are typical of those brought to child-oriented community mental health settings. The presenting problems range from bedwetting to child abuse, from truancy to delinquency, from school phobias to thinking disorders.

Children and families are described in "three-dimensional" terms that allow the reader to sample their many different and important facets. Each case is presented according to a standardized format and is followed by the conceptualizations and treatment recommendations of two or three invited consultants. Their comments were recorded from mock case conferences moderated by the authors. Because we wanted our book to be truly eclectic and interdisciplinary, the consultants—selected on the basis of their experience and reputations in the professional community—consist of psychiatrists, psychologists, social workers, and child care workers. Their orientations are also varied and include psychodynamic theory, behavioral psychology, and family systems theory. Regardless of the theoretical constructs that underlie their thinking, the consultants were always encouraged to provide down-to-earth, *practical* suggestions for the aspiring clinician.

The book begins with an introductory chapter that provides suggestions on how to use the material for instructional purposes and an overview of primary treatment modalities for working with children. In addition to the cases and the consultants' dialogues, each chapter includes a summary and a set of discussion questions. There is also a glossary at the end of the book, which includes all technical terms found within the text.

Treating the Multiproblem Family should be useful as a text for undergraduate or graduate students in training to become caseworkers or therapists working with children and families. The book may also be helpful to practicing psychotherapists and caseworkers who wish to develop a broader repertoire of clinical skills. We have found the use of the cases to be a highly engaging activity in both the classroom and the clinic because it stimulates creative thinking as students and professionals compare their observations and suggestions to those of the experienced (but fallible) consultants. Consequently, the book can serve as a companion text to more theoretical writings in academic settings, as well as a sourcebook for training and supervision in mental health settings.

We would like to thank our own teachers and professional models, beginning with the clinical psychology faculties of the University of Oregon and the University of Rochester. Special gratitude is due to The Dellcrest Children's Centre in Toronto, whose staff's devotion to children and families has provided much of the inspiration for the completion of this project. The enthusiasm, professionalism, and generous efforts of our 24 consultants have, of course, been critical to this volume. We also wish to acknowledge the ongoing support and expertise of the Brooks/Cole family, especially Claire Verduin, Fiorella Ljunggren, and Joe Guzaitis, and the helpful comments of four conscientious reviewers: Gerald Erickson of York University, David Foat of the University of Minnesota, Craig Gilbert of the University of Nevada at Las Vegas, and James P. Trotzer of the University of Wisconsin–River Falls.

The manuscript was expertly typed by Dulcis Prendergast and the staff of the York University Secretarial Services. Finally, we want to give special thanks to our wives and children whose support and caring provide us with constant reminders of the meaning and importance of families.

Kjell E. Rudestam
Mark Frankel

Contents

8
Beyond the Nuclear Family   224

Glossary   258

Treating the
Multiproblem Family:
A Casebook

1

Introduction

Clinicians who treat the psychological problems of children and adolescents are seldom prepared for the severity and profundity of their clients' real life problems. The problem behaviors of children described in the university classroom tend to be simpler than those arising from real life in the community. It is one thing to learn specific techniques to treat a bedwetter or a phobic child, particularly when these difficulties are presented by a well-motivated, economically stable family free of marital strife, sibling problems, and school and community complications. It is altogether different to treat a problem child whose mother is jobless and depressed, whose estranged father is assaultive, and whose siblings are running unsupervised through the community. In the real world, family problems are often complex and demanding. The clinician working in a community-based setting is most likely to face such complicated families.

Family problems encountered in community agencies are often so complex because of the process by which the client came to the agency's attention in the first place. Some families, of course, are self-referred and well-motivated to accept recommendations and make changes. More often, however, families are persuaded or coerced to seek professional intervention when a family member, usually a child, has become particularly bothersome to people outside the family unit. The family's arrival at the clinic is the last step in an unsuccessful problem-solving process. The professional clinician is consulted only after the family has failed to solve the problem on its own or by enlisting the aid of friends, teachers, family physicians, and clergy.

Furthermore, in many community mental health centers and out-patient clinics, the more desirable cases, in which the family is interesting, likeable, and motivated and the prognosis is excellent, tend to be grabbed by workers with the most skill, experience, and professional status. The more onerous cases often filter down to workers with the least training, experience, and expertise. Moreover, these caseworkers may not stay on the job long. Often they begin with enthusiasm and a certain naive idealism but shortly burn out and become depressed, disillusioned, and cynical.

It has also been our experience that many therapists who have case responsibility, including child care workers, social workers, psychologists, and psychiatrists, have expertise within a relatively narrow range of interventions derived from a particular theoretical orientation. Likewise, supervisors who offer ongoing consultation have their own individualized ways of conceptualizing a case or treating the family. These consultations may be of high quality but still not provide the most effective approach to dealing with a wide variety of complex cases. These factors may "conspire" to make the clinician's task (and the family's task, as well) frustrating or overwhelming. We intend to offer the clinical student an opportunity to reduce this frustration through early exposure to the complexities of real families. In addition to providing examples of realistic clinical problems, we are also seeking to portray the complexity and richness of clinical responses and strategies that can be used to address those problems. We hope that such a "sample" of complex problems and clinical methods can be used as a tool in preparation for the treatment of the multiproblem family.

The casebook approach

This casebook presents a number of families representative of those who come or are referred to child-oriented community mental health clinics. The cases themselves are fictitious but are patterned after cases that we and our colleagues have seen in mental health centers. They were carefully selected to cover a large variety of the cases that workers encounter within child agencies. Though there are a number of variables along which one can categorize cases, we considered the following dimensions to be of primary importance:

1. Age of patient
2. Family factors:
   Socioeconomic status (SES)
   Marital status
   Sibling status
   Extended family status
3. Referral source:
   Self-referral
   Court referral
   Family doctor referral
   Other agency referral
4. Situational factors:
   Home
   School
   Community

The cases reflect the way in which these variables are distributed among families typically encountered at community agencies. The children range from age 3 to age 16. More cases are of low and low-middle than high-middle and high socioeconomic status. The families have from one to four children. In some instances, extended family members are living with the designated family. A few families are self-referred, but most are sent by other agencies, most often the school system. Finally, the multiproblem nature of these families implies that difficulties are often identified in the school and community as well as in the home.

We have defined cases according to the ostensible problem of the child who brought the family to the clinic's attention. The cases cover a wide and comprehensive range of problems, with one notable exception. We have not included blatantly psychotic or autistic children because they typically demand considerable professional expertise and concentrated effort and many clinics avoid treating such severely disturbed children. In multiproblem families, of course, more than one significant behavioral difficulty may exist in the family or in the same individual. The following problems are emphasized in one or more cases:

Adolescent pregnancy	Depression
Sexual acting-out	Suicide
School behavior problem	Learning problems
School phobia	Withdrawal, isolation
Stealing	Bizarre behaviors
Aggression or violence	Fire setting
Running away	Physical disability
Negativism	Enuresis and encopresis
Obsessive-compulsive behavior	Incest
Child abuse	Exhibitionism
Drugs and alcohol	Divorce
Hyperactivity	Dependency and immaturity

We invited 24 professional psychotherapists and consultants with expertise in child and family practice to participate in this project. Our experts represent diverse professional disciplines, including child care, social work, clinical psychology, and psychiatry. Our lack of allegiance to any one discipline is based on an impressive research literature which suggests that the variables that define effective therapists cut across the helping professions (see Meltzoff & Kornreich, 1970). We deliberately invited consultants who could give down-to-earth, specific recommendations. It is our impression that too many texts (and consultants) make a formal diagnosis of a child problem using an abstract, theoretical framework (for example, "This child is low in ego strength"), giving the worker very little in the way of practical suggestions. Our consultants were asked to participate in conferences focusing on specific cases. The material presented in each case is similar to the information a caseworker might obtain from an initial assessment interview or from a referral source. The format consists of:

1. Identifying Information—including composition of the family and nature of the presenting problem.
2. History of Problem—including previous professional contacts.

3. Marital and Family History—including the families of origin of the parents.
4. Characteristics of Family Members—including personality characteristics of each family member and how members interact.
5. School and Community—including difficulties in the school and/or community and other support systems.
6. Special Assessments (optional)—including tests administered to the identified child, if any.

At the end of each case description is a transcript of a case conference conducted by one of the authors with three (or in a few instances, two) consultants. The consultants were asked to make sense of the case material on the basis of their own belief systems and their experience with problem families and to offer specific pragmatic suggestions to the worker or workers who have primary case responsibility. The basic issues around which we guided the case discussions include:

1. What other information, if any, should the worker gather before treating this case or during treatment?
2. Who should be seen in treatment?
3. What kind(s) of treatment formats are recommended?
4. What treatment strategies are recommended?
5. What kinds of worker characteristics and skills are important?
6. What special problems are envisaged with this kind of case?
7. What is the prognosis or likely outcome?

In some instances there was consensus among the consulting experts on how to conceptualize and address a problem. In other instances there was disagreement. This divergence of opinion should not be surprising in view of the fact that no one school or person has *the* solution to any of these admittedly difficult sets of psychological problems. Treatment strategies have to be evaluated in light of their face validity and their adherence to existing theories of child development and behavioral change. They have to be judged in regard to their promise of eliminating the designated problems while aiding the family to mature and better cope with new problems they may face in the future. Most important, treatment strategies have to be assessed in regard to their likelihood of being effectively implemented. A central purpose for providing this collection of cases is to broaden the reader's scope of conceptualizations and strategies.

The input of the consultants is, of course, a product of their own training as well as of their clinical experience in the field. At present there seem to be three predominant theoretical orientations for intervening in the problems of children: psychoanalytic, behavioral, and family systems theory.

Psychoanalytic orientation

The attempt to extend psychoanalytic principles to the treatment of children began more than 50 years ago with the pioneering efforts of therapists such as Freud's daughter Anna, Melanie Klein (1948), and August Aichhorn (1967). Psychoanalytic theory assumes that children develop disorders because of deficits in their psychosexual development caused by faulty interactions with significant parenting figures. Children face the task of satisfying basic human drives and needs while simultaneously operating within the limits imposed by external reality and their own internalized moral standards. On an unconscious level, they learn that expressing their drives may lead to punishment from the environment and anxiety from within. When the environment is unfavorable, in terms of overly indulgent, harsh, inconsistent, or unavailable family members, the child will not learn adequate mechanisms for channeling anxiety and coping with drives (Lichtenstein, 1980). Instead, the child will have unresolved conflicts and socially objectionable ways of dealing with impulses.

Positive change in the child and the family is a function of intellectual understanding, including the understanding of feelings, as well as of an accepting therapeutic relationship. Since the parent-child relationship has led to internal conflicts, the antidote is to explore their origins. The child who steals, for example, might be acting-out unconscious, angry feelings toward a parent or sibling. Treatment tends to be child-centered and aims to uncover the unconscious emotions underlying maladaptive behavior. Sessions with the child would consist of suggestions, clarifications, and interpretations to enable understanding and change to take place within a nonjudgmental environment. With young children, the analytic counterpart to verbal analysis with adults is play therapy (Axline, 1947), a popular approach in which the child is encouraged to act out conflicts and life themes with toys and games. Through play, the child may become aware of the source of problems and learn to express needs more appropriately.

Behavioral orientation

A second dominant orientation in working with children and their parents is behavior therapy. Behavior therapy applies the principles of learning and behavioral change derived from experimental research in psychology, including the pioneering efforts of John B. Watson in classical conditioning and B. F. Skinner in operant conditioning. Classical conditioning is the model exemplified by Pavlov's dogs, in which a response becomes elicited by a previously neutral stimulus that has been paired with a stimulus event that typically elicits this response. Many fear and anxiety responses are regarded as acquired in just this way. The operant model, on the other hand, assumes that the reinforcing consequences of a behavior help to develop and maintain it. Most learning deficits and unsocialized behaviors are attributed to the operant conditioning process.

The behavior therapist views maladaptive behaviors as having been created by the same laws of learning as adaptive behaviors. Basically, "abnormality" and "normality" are determined by social norms concerning the consequences of behavior. The behavior therapist is less concerned with historical causes than with the child's immediate social environment. Thus, the behaviorist orientation is more educational than medical, and traditional diagnosis is eschewed in favor of direct observation and description of unwanted behaviors. The behaviorist is interested in objectively measuring problem behaviors but not in interpreting them as expressions of unconscious needs.

After carefully identifying the target of therapy, direct approaches are used to discourage unwanted behaviors and encourage desirable behaviors. Since parents have considerable potential control over the actions of their children, the behavior therapist would be more likely to work with the adults than to address the problem child directly. Treatment focuses on teaching parents to ignore or punish inappropriate behavior and to reward desirable behavior consistently (Patterson, 1971). Specific techniques from the behavior therapist's repertoire might include using contingency management, contracts, and token systems, teaching and modeling more appropriate parenting skills, and manipulating the environment to change responses that are a function of specific situational cues.

Systems orientation

Family systems theory has gained popularity in recent years because of the efforts of therapists and teachers such as Nathan Ackerman (1958), Salvador Minuchin (1974), Virginia Satir (1964), and Jay Haley (1976, 1980). There are many different schools of thought within family systems theory. The key element differentiating systems theory from traditional, individual theories about child problems is that symptoms are viewed as reflecting disturbances in the "balance of emotional forces in that individual's important relationship systems, most particularly the family system" (Kerr, 1981, p. 234). Consequently, the family systems therapist does not deal with the problems expressed by one family member without acknowledging that behavior as expressing something meaningful in the functioning of the entire family. The family therapist treats the child's problem by instituting changes in the way family members relate to one another. In short, the family is the client, and no single individual is at fault.

Most family therapists are concerned about the family's structural organization: how the members' relationship patterns meet the family's functional and emotional requirements in living. The therapist's specific interventions commonly aim to realign family members and create well-defined yet flexible boundaries between them. Systems-oriented family therapists rarely use interpretations or explore the feelings of family members. Some family therapists are particularly interested in designing strategic interventions that directly attack the problem behavior. Such interventions may include "reframing" problems to reduce blame and encourage empathy and using directives and tasks that paradoxically encourage symptoms so that members can no longer use them to maintain the status quo in the family. Other family therapists want to improve family communication and make use of such techniques as role-playing, sculpting, and problem-solving exercises.

Resource-based interventions

This abbreviated excursion through three distinct conceptualizations of the problems of childhood and adolescence cannot do justice to the array of theories and techniques that exist in the field. The purpose of this overview is to provide a context for the commentaries of the consultants. Some of their recommendations, of course, do not emerge clearly out of one of the three major theoretical orientations. Moreover, their treatment recommendations include referrals to hospitals, public nurses, group programs, adoption agencies, welfare departments, residential placements, or the court and consequently go beyond psychotherapy per se.

In spite of differing theoretical and professional backgrounds, however, our consultants do share an ecological perspective—that is, viewing problems in the context of extended relationships, social systems, and the community rather than in isolation. Hence, many of their suggestions seek to utilize available community resources or to modify environmental circumstances in order to alleviate both child and family problems. The ecological perspective indeed may be emerging as a metatheory within which major approaches to treatment can be contained (Salzinger, Antrobus, & Glick, 1980).

The other common bias that our consultants share is an emphasis on identifying the strengths and competencies in children and families seeking treatment. Such an orientation is crucial, especially when engaging a multi-problem family that seems to bristle with deficits and pathology. Throughout the case conference transcripts, the reader will find consultants speculating about, identifying, and building on what children and families have achieved or have shown the potential to achieve.

How to approach the cases

We hope that these cases will be read reflectively and in a spirit of inquiry. The successful clinician is able to think through a problem in an organized fashion. Developing a systematic approach to a case means gathering sufficient information to make an intelligent formulation of the problem, then choosing treatment modalities and strategies based on that conceptualization, as well as on the availability of alternative resources. Use the cases as an active learning tool by struggling with the same information the consultants were given and compare your reasoning with theirs. Read the case descriptions and respond to the seven issues the consultants addressed before you read the transcripts:

1. What additional information would you solicit? Why? How would you go about doing so?
2. Whom do you identify as the client? Whom would you see in treatment? Why?
3. What treatment format(s) would you use? Individual therapy? Marital therapy? Family therapy? Which people would you see together? Why?
4. What strategies would you use? Psychodynamic? Behavioral theory? Systems theory? How would you initiate treatment and enlist the client's cooperation? What specific interventions would you use to deal with particular problems? What other resources would you draw on?
5. Which worker skills and characteristics are important? What kind of worker would you ideally recommend?
6. What specific problems do you foresee at the outset? What could go wrong during the treatment?
7. What do you envisage as the likeliest outcome for this case? Where would you go from there?

After you have answered these questions by yourself or in "case conference" with others, read the opinions of our consultants, comparing them with your impressions. Remember that the consultants' contributions are primarily intended as a stimulus for thought and discussion rather than as infallible recommendations.

The case conference method, including the use of a consultant, for planning and reviewing treatment can be extremely powerful and helpful. The approach allows for the interaction of several points of view which can stimulate and enrich the clinician's own insight into the family and enhance his or her objectivity. Traditional case conferences have important limitations, however, of which the most critical is that a conference must occur at a specific point in time. On the other hand, good clinical work is an ongoing, continuing process between clinician and client. Such a process requires treatment to proceed by formulating hypotheses, by testing them with the client, by evaluating the effectiveness of specific interventions, and then by formulating new or modified hypotheses about the problem and how it can be solved. Furthermore, unless consultation is "live" (that is, involving the client as a participant or the consultant as a witness to treatment), important information may be overlooked. We suggest that a group of clinical students role-play a case conference ("live" or traditional), using one of the cases described, in order to appreciate both the strengths and limitations of the method.

Ethical considerations

Finally, we urge you to keep in mind the ethical responsibilities of therapists and caseworkers. Ethical standards are particularly important in the treatment of children, who are often victims to the wishes of adults and unable to defend their own rights. It is incumbent on the worker to be fully informed regarding legal statutes in the area of child treatment and the principles espoused by one's professional affiliation. Although ethical considerations are critically important, they are generally assumed and not made explicit in the case discussions. The following text is intended to highlight what we regard as compelling ethical concerns in this field. Much of the discussion is derived from articles by Rosen, Rekers, and Bentler (1978) and Walker, Ulissi, and Thurber (1980).

Community mental health workers need to examine their value systems and recognize that values will continually influence the decisions they make in designing and conducting treatment strategies. Since there are no absolute rules for judging how to proceed with a given case, how we decide to move will be deeply colored by our own judgments regarding good and bad procedures and desirable and undesirable outcomes.

During initial contact with a child and family, certain ethical issues predominate. The first issue concerns who will be seen and who will be defined as the client. The American Psychological Association (1977), for example, maintains that a therapist must make clear whether he or she is primarily serving the child, the parents, an agency, or the broader community. Sometimes, of course, these groups will not agree, as when a child insists on fewer restrictions and the parents seek to become tougher, or when the local community complains about an abusive child-rearing practice and the parents draw on the sanctity of their home boundaries. The worker needs to balance a respect for the wishes of the child and family with a sensible regard for the community's moral and legal standards.

The general ground rule in dealing with all clients is to seek their voluntary participation in treatment based on informed consent. Informed consent implies that a person has competence and sufficient information on which to make a proper decision and does so voluntarily (Martin, 1975). The problem is that children, particularly under the age of 12, cannot offer fully informed and competent consent for all kinds of treatment decisions. The worker must therefore consider a person's decision-making capacity. This becomes important, for instance, in deciding whether to yield to a child's lack of consent. Of course, life-threatening behaviors, such as severe anorexia or potential violence, demand immediate action. One useful guideline to treating a person against his or her will is the presumed long-range effect of a problem behavior. For example, a severely phobic child or a 7-year-old who has not been toilet-trained may not welcome professional intervention, but the likely long-term effect of nonintervention is increased problems and misery for the child. A worker must consider the consequences of not treating the child if the child cannot act on his or her own best interests.

Of course, one would then seek the consent of a parent or surrogate to protect the child's rights.

Another ingredient in deciding whether to accept a client is the probability of success of a given treatment. Workers have an ethical responsibility to define the limits of their competence to clients and refuse to offer a service that they are not qualified to offer. The client must be made aware of both the risks and potential benefits of an approach. Certainly, aversive techniques are methods of last resort. The therapist must not knowingly harm clients of any age.

After a client or client system has been accepted for treatment, other ethical issues move forward. Confidentiality is a strong value in the psychotherapy context, and any limits to it must be fully discussed with the client. In working with children and families, there are times when community and legal statutes compromise absolute confidentiality. If so, the client has the right to know this beforehand and under what circumstances you, the worker, would divulge confidential information to community agencies, courts, or other family members.

Selection of treatment goals is another task colored by value considerations. Treatment goals may involve data from parents, the therapist, and the community, as well as the child. Generally, one works within the value system of the child and the child's caregivers. The question is usually "What do *they* want changed?" rather than "What do *I* want changed?"—a particularly important focus when dealing with clients from minority cultural groups within the larger community. The therapist must continually weigh the scales between the rights of an individual to freedom of expression and the rights of others to expect conformity. The client's welfare must be integrated with community needs. For instance, in most communities parents do not have the right to keep young children out of school. When clients are not directly involved in the determination of treatment goals, because of hospitalization or incarceration, for example, they need more protection, not less. The best strategy is for the worker to help the client look at both the short-term and long-term consequences of various behaviors. Workers, of course, draw on their own expertise to make judgments regarding pathology and prognosis. Selected treatment goals should be explicit so that all parties understand the purpose of the working agreement.

Other ethical judgments arise during later stages of treatment. A therapist who has begun working with a family is obligated to carry treatment to a logical conclusion and to be available to the family on a reasonable basis throughout that period. Likewise, if treatment is not moving forward satisfactorily, the therapist has a responsibility to evaluate the case, reconsider whether to continue or terminate, and ensure that appropriate referrals are conducted if they are deemed advisable.

Ethical guidelines are important because of the power differential that exists when a relatively uninformed member of the public relies on the presumed expertise of a certified professional. Attention to these ethical considerations and working within a humane code of ethics is a prerequisite for treating families and their problems.

REFERENCES

Ackerman, N. W. *The psychodynamics of family life.* New York: Basic Books, 1958.

Aichhorn, A. *Delinquency and child guidance: Selected papers of August Aichhorn.* New York: International Universities Press, 1967.

American Psychological Association. Standards for providers of psychological services. *American Psychologist,* 1977, *32*(6), 495–505.

Axline, V. M. *Play therapy.* Boston: Houghton Mifflin, 1947.

Haley, J. *Problem-solving therapy.* San Francisco: Jossey-Bass, 1976.

Haley, J. *Leaving home: The therapy of disturbed young people.* New York: McGraw-Hill, 1980.

Kerr, M. E. Family systems theory and therapy. In A. S. Gurman & D. P. Kniskern (Eds.), *Handbook of family therapy.* New York: Brunner/Mazel, 1981.

Klein, M. *Psychoanalysis of children.* Honolulu: Hogarth, 1948.

Lichtenstein, E. *Psychotherapy: Approaches and applications.* Monterey, Calif.: Brooks/Cole, 1980.

Martin, R. *Legal challenges to behavior modification.* Champaign, Ill.: Research Press, 1975.

Meltzoff, J., & Kornreich, M. *Research in psychotherapy.* New York: Atherton Press, 1970.

Minuchin, S. *Families and family therapy.* Cambridge, Mass.: Harvard University Press, 1974.

Patterson, G. R. *Families: Applications of social learning to family life.* Champaign, Ill.: Research Press, 1971.

Rosen, A. C., Rekers, G. A., & Bentler, P. M. Ethical issues in the treatment of children. *Journal of Social Issues,* 1978, *34*, 122–136.

Salzinger, S., Antrobus, J., & Glick, J. *The ecosystem of the "sick" child.* New York: Academic Press, 1980.

Satir, V. *Conjoint family therapy.* Palo Alto, Calif.: Science & Behavior Books, 1964.

Walker, C. E., Ulissi, S. M., & Thurber, S. Values in behavior therapy with children. *Psychotherapy: Theory, Research, and Practice,* 1980, *17*, 431–439.

2

Fragmented Families

The four cases presented in this chapter provide examples of families that can be characterized by such words as *disengaged, underorganized, unstable,* or *chaotic*. These adjectives describe groups of people who fit the legal or biological definitions of a family but who do not function as a cohesive living unit.

Such families appear to have weak emotional bonds and/or to lack common agreements and understandings about how they might cooperate as a unit. One is struck, when meeting them, by a sense of isolated individuals living private lives with little apparent awareness of how they affect one another. Consequently, any challenge to the family system (for example, financial problems, a member in trouble) is met with a series of uncoordinated and unrelated responses by family members.

A child may react to this milieu with uncertainty and anxiety or with alienation and anger. It is generally agreed that children require some stability and predictability in their significant relationships and life spaces and that denial of these needs is harmful and stressful. The therapist is often faced with helping the family to build a more stable and intimate family unit while immediate practical problems pressure them. Treatment efforts with such families usually place substantial emphasis on improved communication, problem solving, and structuring of family life.

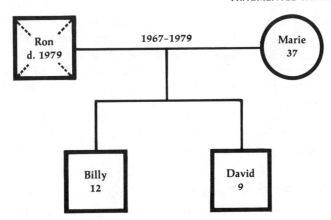

THE ALLEN FAMILY

Identifying information

The Allen family consists of Mrs. Allen and her two sons. Mr. Allen is dead. Mrs. Allen finds both boys hard to handle and complains of their constant fighting with each other. She sees Billy as unhappy, withdrawn, friendless, and lacking in confidence. David is more of a school problem and is reported to be aggressive with peers, disruptive, a boy who rarely completes his schoolwork. David's teacher and the school's guidance counselor both encouraged the mother to seek treatment.

History of the problem

Mrs. Allen had been concerned about the boys in the past. When Billy entered school, it was found that he had a mild to moderate hearing impairment in both ears and was given a hearing aid. He must sit at the front of his classes, near the teacher, and his speech remains immature. Billy never seemed to have many friends and now spends a good deal of time in his room or watching TV. At school, his work is erratic. David was a behavior problem in the third grade and now, in fourth grade, is being considered for possible placement in a special education class. Mrs. Allen has not sought help from mental health professionals for herself or the boys in the past. She yells at the boys when their fighting "gets on her nerves."

Marital and family history

Mrs. Allen's family of origin consisted of her parents, two older sisters, a younger brother, and herself. Her parents separated when she was 12, and she lived with her mother and siblings until her marriage to Mr. Allen at age 21. She describes her father as a cold, perfectionistic, and distant man to whom she never felt close. Her mother was subject to frequent periods of depression, and her older sisters, especially Angela (two years older than

Mrs. Allen), functioned as parents for Mrs. Allen and their younger brother.

Mr. Allen was a machinist of age 27 when he and Mrs. Allen married. He grew up in an intact family including three older brothers. Mrs. Allen reports that Mr. Allen was not close to his family before his death. She describes the marriage as having no major problems nor any separations. Mr. Allen died of a heart attack at age 40 with no previous history of serious illness. Mrs. Allen reported that he got along well with both boys but was especially close to David.

Characteristics of family members

Mrs. Allen works as a full-time secretary in a large business firm. The boys stay with a neighbor after school until mother arrives home. The family lives in a small one-bedroom apartment in which Billy and David share the bedroom and mother sleeps in the living room.

Mrs. Allen appears to be a warm, committed mother who nevertheless lacks confidence in her ability to parent. She describes difficulties in managing her sons in a helpless tone and cannot explain their conflicts and other problems. She admits that she often feels depressed. She seems to have few social or emotional involvements outside the home. Mrs. Allen's mother died four years ago, and her siblings are living in other cities. Billy, as noted, is withdrawn, closed, and guarded. He distrusts others and shows little ability to express feelings. He seems worried about his mother's happiness, health, and money problems. Efforts to have him discuss his feelings about his hearing problem are nonproductive. He is often expected to supervise and be responsible for his younger brother, David. David is somewhat more accessible to relationships. He approaches adults in a defiant, testing manner, maintaining a "tough guy" front. He feels picked on and persecuted in school by peers and teachers alike.

The family as a group appears disorganized and leaderless. Warm feelings are expressed openly and easily from mother to both boys and reciprocated by David. Mother relies heavily on her sons for support and decisions. Despite their obvious bonds, however, the family engages infrequently in family activities, aside from daily routines and occasional outings (bowling, visit to zoo). There is a quality of isolation about all three lives.

School and community

Billy is described as quiet and isolated at school. His academic work is low average. His teacher remarks that he has shown some special interests in science projects and in mathematics and that he seems to enjoy reading. But he is not a behavior problem and seems neither strongly liked nor disliked by other children. Classmates pay little attention to his hearing impairment. He spends little time in the community, although he has one male friend with whom he does spend time.

David frequently appears sullen and angry in school. He is aggressive with other children, especially smaller children whom he can bully. He is negative about trying new academic work, and what work he does tends to be sloppy and incomplete. His teacher finds him disruptive and attention-seeking in class. In a one-to-one situation he is responsive to firm limits and much more cooperative. He enjoys sports and shows good athletic skills. He often spends time playing with peers but doesn't maintain relationships over time and often gets into fights.

Special assessments

David is currently undergoing psychological assessment regarding need for placement in a special behavioral class. The testing has not yet been completed, but the school psychologist reports David's intelligence is average and his academic skills are about one year behind.

Billy has not had any special assessment except for speech and hearing but is reported to be in good health by the Allens' family doctor.

Case discussion

Consultants: Dr. Harvey Mandel, Mrs. Marjorie Shore, Dr. Steven Stein

Interviewer: To begin, is there any other information that you'd like the worker to obtain?

Shore: We really need a very thorough school report on both kids. I would want to keep in touch with the family doctor, and I'd want to hear from him. This case concerns a mother who feels incompetent as a parent, and I would want to know how she deals with the G.P. Does she bring her kids to him, does she talk with him, is she requesting certain techniques from him? I may want to use the G.P. to give support to her, since a good G.P. can be a very good support to a single parent.

Interviewer: Steve, would you like any additional information?

Stein: I'd want to know more about what the family sees as its problem. I want to know what David feels—does he see himself as having problems, or does he see the world as rosy and he's just doing his thing? I want to know what Billy thinks, how he's doing, how he sees himself, sees his brother and the kind of relationship that exists between them. And I'd get more information about the way the mother is feeling about what's going on. One of the issues mentioned is control of the family. I would want to know if she brings that up as an issue, if she sees that as a problem. Who's making the decisions, who's running the family?

Interviewer: Harvey, anything missing to you?

Mandel: We're talking about a single-parent family, and one of the things that's happened here is that David is expressing the loss of his relationship with his father through aggression and acting-out behavior, and Billy has been, in a sense, asked to substitute in the family as a parent. He's the one who supervises his younger brother and is responsible for his younger brother, and yet he has a reaction too, in that he's withdrawn. There is a depressive reaction in this kid. So I would want to know more about the nature and the quality of the relationship the father had with both of them. That's number one. Number two is to take a look at what changes occurred in the behavior patterns of the kids when the father died and disappeared. What did the family try to do to support these kids or deal with the loss? I'd also like to know what resources, if any, are available to the mother. That includes the G.P., any group in the community, any relatives in the community, single-parent groups or a babysitting network, any self-help kinds of networking. It also appears that we're dealing with a multiproblem family in the sense that I don't know exactly what the major problem is. Is it the aggressive behavior that David's showing? Is it the withdrawn behavior that Billy is showing? I would want some sense of prioritizing from the family. I would first ask mother about it, then I would ask the kids about it. What are the things they want to see change?

Stein: That's important. My suspicion is that they will say that they're here because of David, that the school told them to come. We'd have to dig to get something out of that.

Mandel: They may not stay with that, but at least that would be the beginning. But I see other things floating around here, and I'm not sure where to begin the intervention until I have some sense of where they are.

Interviewer: Where might you go from that point in terms of how you conceptualize this case?

Shore: Well, first of all, one would have to see this as a single-parent family that was floundering, and to that end there'd be a number of cautions. For instance, that the therapist not come in and be the second parent, which is a very easy role to assume. That's very dangerous because it only supports mother's incompetence. So before going in, there has to be some understanding that the initial goal would be to help mother to feel more confident. The second thing that I would want to do is develop a strategy, which would also be a part of the assessment, which would include the school. I would want a meeting between mother, the school, and myself. I would want mother to be more involved with the school, and I would use that relationship as the first kind of stroking that I could give her—that she could go to the school, that she could ask the appropriate questions, that she could cooperate with them and be successful. I would start by helping her to feel that she's more in control of the parenting, even to the extent of being more in control of what was happening with regard to the school. And I would use that intervention as an assessment, because I would want to see if they were able to use that kind of concrete, structural approach. I would then use that approach to look at other problems they were presenting, like bedtimes, breakfasts, wake-ups, and other issues that a single mother needs to be very organized around.

Interviewer: What kinds of questions would you ask the school?

Mandel: To begin intervention without involving the two main parties, I think, would be an error. So, for me, meeting with the school is critical. Just by virtue of the fact that the meeting occurs, you would be defining the school and mother as having a joint difficulty. I think it should be presented that way to the school as well as the mother. They do have a joint problem—namely, the boy's aggressive behavior—rather than the school labeling mother as having total responsibility for his difficulty. So the strategic aim of that meeting is to try to get some kind of partnership going with the school and mother in dealing with the boy's behavior. It may involve an agreement that every two or three days the teacher phones mother and shares particular information about how he is doing. And mother would have specific tasks that involve schoolwork at home, so that mother begins to join the school and the school begins to feel that mother is involved. Mother would be encouraged to ask questions about how her son is doing in school and to share any similarities between how he behaves at home and how he behaves in school. This would also show that this boy is not dramatically different in school, he's not a tyrant at school and an angel at home—that, in fact, both adults share the same kind of difficulties with him. So those are some of the kinds of strategies that I would start with. The assumption is that I don't see this initially as a family therapy issue, but as a systems issue: the problem of school difficulty with an aggressive child.

Shore: The other thing that happens when the therapist, the school, and the parents meet is that both school and parents feel they have a consultant and therefore are not going to struggle through this alone. There's going to be some outside support that would be offered to both if a systems approach is going to work.

Interviewer: Would you also take a systems approach, Steve?

Stein: I agree largely with what's been mentioned. I may differ a bit in terms of going another step further. I think the mother needs some behavior management skills. She's got to know that she's in charge of this family, and I would teach her about controlling the kids using time-out or using contingency contracting, reinforcing appropriate behavior. In terms of a systems intervention, I might work with the teacher to set up some kind of token systems for David in the classroom, having the teacher reinforce his appropriate behavior and completing daily cards relating to his performance in academics as well as to his behavior in the classroom, that David would have to take home.

Mandel: That's interesting because you would then be acting as a consultant to the school, which gives them a structure that would be consistent with the new structures that have been put in place at home. I would do the management thing with mother alone. I would not deal with the kid in a family therapy scene and somehow try to model for this mother how to deal with these kids. First of all, I think that's pompous as hell. If mother can learn through a discussion of some of the worst difficulties she has in controlling a particular kid, then you don't need to bring the kids in, you don't need to start modeling, you don't need play therapy with the kids, etcetera.

Interviewer: So if you were teaching management skills, you would have the worker be there with mother, but you wouldn't have the child included?

Mandel: Correct. My feeling is that if mother can be concrete about the different kinds of situations that drive her nuts, and you talk about the alternatives that she hasn't tried, and you give her some homework and let her follow through on it, and *if* she has the energy and strength to follow through, I don't see the need for a higher level intervention.

Interviewer: Steve, I wonder if you'd be willing to describe some of those behavior management techniques you were talking about?

Stein: I would probably start with tracking, teaching the parent to track behaviors and differentiate between positive and negative ones. She knows what they are, but she would have to be very specific about them—such as whining, beating, kicking, and fighting other kids. The next step would be teaching her how to record those behaviors in a consistent manner when they occur so that they can be presented to the therapist afterwards. And then setting up some contracts with, in this case, David, who is the more aggressive child. Setting up a contract or an agreement—at first giving him a behavior that's incompatible with the one that constitutes the problem. For example, if he gets into fights with Billy over the TV, teaching him an alternative strategy for dealing with watching the show he wants to watch. I'd want very concrete examples from them and make some kind of contract with David that if he deals appropriately with a particular situation, he would get such and such a reward or privilege that he obviously likes. It seems to be very difficult for this parent to be consistent with him, so I would make sure that she learns to be consistent. The time-out procedure would be used whenever David is extremely noncompliant with certain commands or requests. He will know in advance that when that happens, he will spend five minutes in a quiet room or quiet place where there are no activities for him to do.

Interviewer: Are there any other aspects to the time-out procedure that are important for the worker to keep in mind?

Stein: Several. It's not to be done excessively, the child needs to understand the procedure fully beforehand, and the worker needs to know how to deal with noncompliance to time-out.

Mandel: I've also seen that a group can be very effective with single parents. Group support adds the dimension that mother is not the only one who's floundering with kids, that others are having the same kind of difficulty. If it appears within the group that one or two people can't follow through, then a more structured one-to-one approach may be necessary. I would try to determine her highest level of functioning and support her at that level, and if she can't gain something from the group, I would consider a one-to-one situation.

Shore: I have a different approach. I would see the kids together with the mother once so that I could have a better understanding of the subtleties of their behavior and help mother to understand the messages that she's reacting to. I'd find that very difficult to do without having those messages in front of me. Usually when you get a family together and encourage them to interact, within two minutes they present that kind of behavior, so that you can help mother become more aware of it. The other reason I would want to bring this family together is that I would be very interested in their affective expression. I would have an initial hypothesis that the experience of having gone through a parent's death has been stifled and has become a covert expression. So one of the things I would want to do is go back and talk with this family about their mourning. I would want to talk about how mother dealt with having two babies, two young children. Perhaps she didn't have a job then and had to go out and start a whole life for herself. I would want to know who supported them, how they cried together, whether the children went to the funeral. Then I would want to make an assessment whether they are still in mourning and help them to work that through. For a period of time I might take mother out and work with her, so that she could then go back and work with the boys, so that I would not become the parent working with the boys.

Another thing that I've become more and more aware of lately is the extent to which children will go to keep their parent from acting depressed. I've seen a number of cases where the acting-out keeps the parent alive in the children's mind. And that acting-out is a tool they use to keep their parents there. There is an underlying fear that when a parent is depressed and perhaps apathetic and sleeping and tired, they're going to die. Some children will go to any length to keep that parent awake and thus alive. I would want to explore that hypothesis in this family's life.

Interviewer: What might you do if you found that to be the case?

Shore: I would want all of them aware of it. To become aware, I would do the same kind of thing that Steve talked about. I would want to know where everybody was before the acting-out occurred—if, for example, mother was on the couch sleeping and all of a sudden the kids were fighting over the TV. Or do they do the same thing when mother is actively watching TV with them? I want to help them to differentiate the times when mother's awake and thus alive from the times when she's depressed and perhaps dead. My hope would be to make them aware that parents do go through these periods and that children are obviously scared and have a right to be scared. Hopefully, they could help their mother to understand their fear in a way that would keep her awake, without being destructive to them and being aggressive in school, and so on. I would know that I wasn't going to change that pattern because it is a very basic, primal pattern to keep a parent alive. But how they keep that parent alive and how that parent keeps himself or herself alive can begin to change. It's also very striking for a parent to hear that behavior in that way because it reframes it from a naughty child to a very caring child.

Interviewer: Would either of you recommend individual therapy for either or both of these kids?

Mandel: That's interesting. I thought about play therapy, for example, for the younger one. I don't mean in terms of playing with dolls necessarily, but some avenue of expression for the anger, because I'm assuming that some of the aggressive behavior involves anger.

Shore: And probably a lot of sadness.

Mandel: I see the sadness more. You can see the aggressive behavior as an agitated depression. I see the two boys as almost expressing two sides of the same coin. So, some avenue of getting the family to discuss this—it can be done within the family as a unit, it can also be done for each child individually. Optimally, I would help mother to express her own sorrow and anger at this man for leaving her, and then give her the task of working with the children around that issue. If that can't happen, I would have to use other inputs. That would be my first goal. This is always an ethical question for me. If a parent can do it, do we have a right to take that away from him or her? Many times we go in and take it away without ever testing the hypothesis that they're quite capable of doing it for themselves.

Stein: I differ a bit on some of these issues. I wouldn't spend as much time on the death issue and the loss unless that came up in the course of therapy as a current concern to someone in the family. In terms of seeing anyone for individual therapy, I would base that decision on the first session or two when I see them as a group. I would also want to know about David. How bright is he for a 9½-year old? Some 9½- and 10-year-olds can be taught what kinds of trouble their aggressive behaviors can get them into. So I would want to get a quick assessment of how appropriate a candidate David would be for a cognitive-behavioral approach. In terms of Billy, my questions would again evolve around whether he sees himself as having a problem, whether he sees himself as being depressed, how communicative he is. I wouldn't be too worried if the two boys couldn't identify their problems at this point, if mother is engaged in some behavioral management.

Interviewer: When you're talking about the use of a cognitive-behavioral approach, are you talking about something more than pointing out some disadvantages of the boy's behavior?

Stein: On the first level, I'd be pointing out some of the disadvantages and also getting him to realize what those disadvantages are. On another level, it would also involve filling in alternatives, having him see what the alternatives are, and changing his behavior because he realizes the consequences of his behavior.

Interviewer: We're moving into strategies. Are there other strategies that occur to you here?

Stein: To back up a bit, nobody has mentioned the hearing impairment of the older child.

Mandel: I made the assumption that when Margie mentioned a much more detailed school report, that included a detailed work-up of the boy's functioning in the school, especially as it relates to the impairment.

Shore: And that would also include the G.P.'s report.

Mandel: I would agree. I would assume we had information about that. I'm interested if his withdrawal or any of his unhappy behaviors are related to the fact that he has an impairment. And are we talking about some speech impairment related to the hearing impairment? Things like that would hopefully come out on the report or as part of the initial assessment. I was wondering what you would do with this information, if in fact he has a significant hearing impairment. How would that influence your therapy? Are there specific strategies you would use in treatment?

Shore: One of the things that often happens with hearing-impaired children is that they don't take part in activities. One of my cases was a hearing-impaired child who wore a hearing aid and never wore his hearing aid to sessions. That kind of acting-out would have to be dealt with. That would also help mother to take on more of a parenting role. This write-up only says that any discussion of his hearing problem is nonproductive. That could be because he doesn't hear things.

Stein: Or it could mean determining ways to get him to accept his problem and not feel sorry for himself.

Mandel: I made an assumption when I read that he had been given the role of the more responsible one who wanted to supervise his younger brother. I didn't get a sense of overprotection on mother's part of a kid who has a physical disability. I got the impression that this boy was expecting it. If he had continued with the impairment and his father had lived, this boy might not have been asked to be as responsible as he is. I think there's a positive aspect to that. So I made the assumption that this boy is not quite as protected as one might expect with a boy with a physical impairment.

Interviewer: Would any of you attempt to deal with the relationship between the boys?

Stein: I don't think that was brought out too much. There was some fighting. One of the ways I would deal with it is through the mother's behavior management with the kids. If the worker saw any of the kids individually, or if they came in as family, it could be dealt with by showing them the disadvantages of fighting with each other and developing other ways of getting what they want.

Interviewer: Do any other strategies come to mind?

Stein: One other thing that may again relate to David, the younger son. He might benefit from a good social skills training group. He obviously has problems relating to peers.

Interviewer: In terms of potential obstacles, what might you want to advise or warn your worker to be on the lookout for here?

Mandel: Well, one thing that Margie has already identified as very important is the issue of a therapist/worker charging in on a white horse and somehow becoming the second parent—the better parent. Because the worker has more energy, supposedly more stability, more background, more support, etc., etc., what happens when the worker takes over is that one is left for a period of time with the illusion of new stability and new strength. All you have to do is pull back a little bit and the constellation of factors and problems begins to show up again.

Interviewer: Any others?

Mandel: Yes, I think the level and degree of cooperation on the part of the school is a question that should be addressed and one that may need some action or confrontation on the part of the worker. We're trying to build a partnership between mother and the school, and I'm not sure yet what kind of cooperation we have. If the teacher, in effect, says "Listen, you have a problem, I don't have a problem. You deal with it, and fix it," I think that's going to produce difficulties for the treatment process.

Stein: I can see it both ways. Because they encouraged the mother to seek treatment, they may be willing to cooperate.

Interviewer: What worker characteristics might you recommend here?

Shore: I think one would need a therapist who is strong enough to stay out of the parenting role and yet offer support. The other quality I would want is a therapist who is very experienced at dealing with these types of issues, who feels comfortable with very intense, affective feelings, and can work with them in a successful way.

Interviewer: Are you looking for a family therapist?

Shore: Yes, I would definitely see this as a family case, but family therapists include those who go in and do structural family therapy, inserting behavioral controls. In this case I would want someone who is very skilled at working with the family around affective issues in a supportive manner and in a manner that helps them to bring out these issues amiably so that they're dealt with, but with enough restrictions so that they don't become overwhelmed by the intensity of the field.

Interviewer: Steve?

Stein: In terms of behavior management, I'd want someone who's pretty energetic and entertaining and who could get those basic concepts across to mother in an effective way. In terms of the children, especially David, I would want someone who could really work with younger kids like him.

Mandel: I think that the therapist better know something about child development and better know something about the reality of a single parent with two kids who are different in tone and quality, who are at two different developmental levels, and who may very well both present some difficulty. One of the worst things I've seen is a family therapy scene where management is being focused on as an issue and the therapist is 25 years old and has no sense of kids whatsoever, and is thus using the principles of management without having some feel for the developmental quality of the interaction that goes on with kids and parents. Somebody who comes in thoroughly naive, in terms of quality of contact with kids of that age, I think would be a disaster.

Shore: I think the other problem with a 25-year-old is that a beginning therapist often rushes in to save the kids against ineffective or evil parents and that kind of message would be terribly destructive in this situation. I think that's another problem with inexperienced therapists. The more families you see, the less likely you are to say there are good kids, bad kids, good parents, bad parents. More accurately, this is a system situation. If this parent with these kids still works, that's the extent of the situation.

Interviewer: What goals or outcomes would you strive toward? What would indicate successful treatment for you? Harvey?

Mandel: I'm assuming that David's aggressive behavior is one of the major problems, and for me a measure of positive outcome would be some measurable, acknowledged decrease in aggressive behavior. I also hear this behavior as occurring both in school and at home, and therefore I would want to see a change both at school and at home. And I don't mean that I would want him to go from being David to being Billy, but some toning down of the aggressive behavior, so that he is no longer viewed as a problem. Another measure for me would be (I'm making some assumptions here) mother's beginning to sense that she is more on top of what's happening, in other words, that somehow she is more in control, she is leading as opposed to following, she is acting more than reacting to the things that are going on. Ideally, I would also be looking for some sense of Billy moving out a little bit more and opening up a little bit more in the world, and feeling less responsible for the scene. So those are some of the measures.

Stein: I agree. Billy and David, especially Billy, would have at least two close friends that they're relating to at this point in time. I would want to see mother involved in some community activities, without the kids, on her own. Singles group, parent group, Dancercise, whatever she can find.

Interviewer: Margie?

Shore: Well, I can't disagree with anything that's being said. I would term it a very successful treatment, given that we're dealing with 9- and 12-year-old boys, if mother were coming in with lots of problems and telling me how she handled them. There will be lots of problems, but she would handle them. If the mother were coming in and saying that they are not having any more problems, I'd be worried. I'd be worried that we had regressed.

Interviewer: What's the prognosis?

Mandel: The fact that the school made a referral, the fact that these boys are still young, makes me feel relatively positive. Again, that's based on the assumption that there will be some cooperation. I guess I would have to know more through the assessment process before I would make a prediction about outcome.

Stein: I'd have a hard time with it as well, especially with a 10-year-old aggressive child. When they start getting aggressive at a young age like that, I have a hard time predicting.

Mandel: For me the issue of a child being aggressive at the age of 10 is not the critical issue. I don't automatically think that we're in trouble because for me, a kid who's aggressive at the age of 10 may very well be healthier than a kid who's withdrawn at the age of 10. Somehow the energy is there and there is some expression of pain or of difficulty. The question for me is what personality structure we are dealing with in the boy. Are we dealing with a boy who's so out of control, from a superego point of view, that the aggressive behavior will have to be externally controlled for a long period of time, or are we dealing with a boy who is really in pain and expressing it through physical energy and who, if provided with some kind of support, will tone down internally?

Interviewer: Margie?

Shore: Well, I'm probably more optimistic about this case than you are and that's based on two things. One, it talks about a very caring, involved mother whose fears are out of control and who has admitted that. That's the first step. The second thing that I would mention is that David, on a one-to-one basis, did use external controls and was able to settle down and do a task. Given these two factors, I would suggest that the outcome doesn't look too bad.

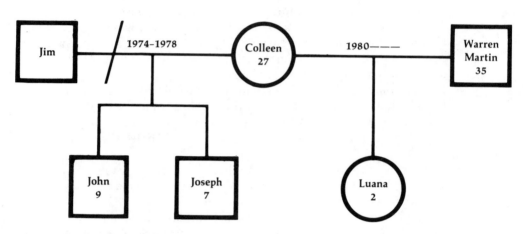

THE THOMAS FAMILY

Identifying information

The Thomas family comes from Jamaica and consists of Colleen Thomas, age 27, and her three children, John, age 9, Joseph, age 7, and Luana, age 2. Mrs. Thomas' common-law husband and father of Luana, Warren Martin, age 35, is often present in the home. Mrs. Thomas is seeking help for John at the urging of his school. She is concerned about his frequent running away from home for days at a time during which no one knows where he goes or how he survives.

History of problem

John's running away began about two years ago, shortly after the arrival of Luana. Lately he has been running more frequently (once or twice a month), and last week he stayed away from home for six days. Mother is at a total loss to understand the reason for John's behavior. She has tried to lecture him about it to no avail. She is particularly concerned that John's actions will have a negative impact on his younger brother. She is also disturbed because the school has reported that John is usually late and sometimes absent. Otherwise, mother claims, John does not cause problems in the home, although he has been increasingly "moody." Warren Martin sees John as a disobedient and unappreciative kid who should be turned out to learn the realities of life. John's only previous contact with community agencies was a court visit for a shoplifting incident two years ago.

Marital and family history

Mrs. Thomas comes from a family of seven children, of whom she was the second youngest. Her childhood was difficult. She had little contact with her father but always respected her mother, with whom she still communicates. Her two eldest children were born in Jamaica and left two years after their mother, when John was 5. During those two years the children lived with their grandmother. The boys' father, Jim Thomas, apparently still resides in Jamaica, and there is no contact with him. Mrs. Thomas has been involved with Warren Martin for the past three years. He provides some financial support for the family and is especially fond of his daughter Luana. His presence in the home, however, is unpredictable. He also comes from Jamaica and works odd hours as a roofer. The couple was introduced through common acquaintances.

Characteristics of family members

Mrs. Thomas is an anxious woman who appears constantly disorganized. She is very superstitious, attributing behavior to changes in the moon and other omens. She interacts very little with John and expects him to look after the other children and take care of household chores such as cleaning and dishwashing. These expectations are generally realistic, although they sometimes interfere with school attendance. Instructions tend to be delivered in an aloof, uncaring manner. John comes across as tense and withdrawn and spends his free time in the home in his room. Joseph is more outgoing and gets perhaps a little more attention from mother. Luana is the only child to whom the mother gives much physical or verbal affection. John and Joseph spend time together and appear to get along without too much rancor. Joseph, however, has his own set of friends. Recently Joseph stayed away overnight with John on one of his running escapades. Basically, mother experiences John as a nuisance, a fact that she expresses openly to him and to the intake worker. Both boys are responsible for looking after their younger sister and play a parental role with her.

Mother seems to appreciate Mr. Martin's presence in the home and is influenced by his opinions and authoritative stance. At the same time she acknowledges some resentment that he is not around enough in the home. Apparently he is rarely there on weekends. When present, he tends to relate to mother or watch television and only rarely attends to the boys. Both parents place total responsibility on John for the difficulties they are experiencing with him and claim that he knows what to do and can do it. They view Joseph as more cooperative and express warm feelings for Luana. The parents tend to relate to the boys through verbal warnings and criticisms. The tone and implication of rejection is constantly present.

The home itself is modest and relatively clean, although it is located in a run-down, high-crime area. The two boys share a small, shabby room which is much more sparsely decorated than the rest of the house. Household routines seem not to exist. The children generally fend for themselves and are responsible for waking up, getting breakfast, and getting off to school. Since mother works swing shift, she is not home when the children return from school. A babysitter or neighbor generally comes and stays with Luana.

School and community

John attends public school in the third grade. Academically, he completes his work and is not a problem. The school complains primarily about John's chronic lateness, which is seen as attention-seeking behavior that has a disruptive effect on the classroom. The teacher has seated John on a special chair for being late, but this strategy has not been effective. Recently, the school has been considering suspending the boy to teach him he cannot be late. The parents are pleased that John is a good student but are disturbed by the school's threats and wonder why they can't handle the problem. In the classroom John is a sensitive boy who frequently seeks teacher attention by volunteering to help.

John appears to have a few friends in his neighborhood, but the family views them as bad influences and they are not allowed in the home.

Special assessments

Intelligence testing reveals that John functions in the low-average range. Initially shy with strangers, he warms to them quickly and strives to gain their attention and support.

Case discussion

Consultants: Dr. Barbara Dydyk, Mr. William Carty, Dr. Peter Marton

Interviewer: Once again I will ask whether there are gaps in the information that you would want the worker to fill.

Marton: I would want to know what this boy does while he's running away. I think that's an important issue. Are there drugs involved, for example?

Interviewer: How would you attempt to find out?

Marton: Preferably by talking to the boy. If that didn't work, then I think I would have to start nosing around the neighborhood.

Interviewer: Okay. Are any special assessments indicated?

Marton: One suggestion is that the running is in response to the arrival of the younger sister and differential treatment of her in comparison with this older boy. I would suggest that the worker make some home visits and note any differences in parenting styles, how the mother relates to the sister versus the two boys.

Interviewer: What about treatment methods?

Carty: I'd see the whole family.

Dydyk: I'd second that.

Marton: I'll be different. I think it would be a disaster. I think this family is never going to show up. This man, especially, is never going to come. I don't think it would get off the ground.

Interviewer: What would you recommend, Peter?

Marton: It would be good if someone could form a relationship with the mother in order to try to get some changes directly in how she does things in the home. My reasoning is that a number of things have happened in this child's life. There was a separation when mother left for two years. At that time the boy was 3 and he stayed with grandmother. Two years later he separated from grandmother and came to live here. The other big change was the arrival of this girl. I would focus on the mother-son relationship. The mother needs to become a bit more organized. It appears that there are no household routines, just a lot of verbal criticism.

Interviewer: Are you talking about parent counseling?

Marton: Yes, except that I don't think you can come into this family and say "I think you should do this, I don't think you should do that." You would have to form a relationship with this lady and be of some help to her in organizing things. With that kind of entree you could begin to make some suggestions.

Interviewer: Do I understand that you would be working with her individually?

Marton: Yes, but I would do it in her house. Together, we would have to set up some rules and contingencies regarding the child's behavior. I'd structure in some positives because all there seems to be are negatives for doing inappropriate things. Since the boy's room sounds like a depression area within the house, I'd also try to modify the physical ecology.

Interviewer: Let's give the family therapists a turn and hear how they would start off.

Dydyk: To me this sounds very much like a "slum" family. The structural approach might work very nicely with this disengaged mother. It's a disengaged family in which boundaries are very loose. My idea would be to tighten things up, to make this more of a family, with the kids and mother and possibly this other guy, although I'm not sure how much he's involved. I would approach the mother and kids as a unit. My concern is that mother doesn't care about this kid, and it was the school that suggested that she come. She doesn't sound like she was concerned at all about his being away for six days. She didn't push for the agency involvement, so I think one has to look hard for some caring from this mother and reinforce it in terms of establishing boundaries around the family.

Carty: Mother has two families, one with her boys and one with Warren and the daughter and it's very tearing on her. It looks disengaged with everyone all over the map, but the presenting problem is John's leaving the family for days on end. I would want to start by defining how the family operates. Are there one or two families? Where is Warren in this, is he in or out? I would think, if he's in, he's not allowed in with the boys. I think he's the father of the girl and the boyfriend or husband or whatever to mother, and that's it. So maybe it looks a little bit disengaged, but I think there's just two families operating under one roof. Sometimes John looks confused. Sometimes he acts like a spouse to his mother and sometimes he's the number-one son. I'd start with whoever showed up and then I would learn about Warren's position, because I think mother would bring her three kids. I think she's a single parent at the same time she's a married parent. John is the one who is now experiencing the confusion. Running for six days is different from 24 hours, and it looks like it's getting worse. The fact that he's taking his brother with him suggests that his brother is also feeling uncomfortable in the family.

Interviewer: Let's say that your formulation is accurate and there are, in a sense, two families functioning here. What would you work on?

Carty: Well, if I had the family in, I would address Warren, his role with the boys, and his father role. The first session or two would be a fact-finding mission: who runs what, who does what, who decides what. The boys are on their own, they get up, they make breakfast, they go to school, everything is by themselves, Warren is by himself and I think the daughter is provided for by her mother through her kids, or by Warren, or by a neighbor. She's the center, but she's got a huge job. Can she get Warren to father the children? Is Warren allowed in? Is he interested?

Marton: I'm speculating now. Could another way of looking at this boy's behavior be that he's not so much a kid running away from the family as emulating Warren, who is sometimes there during the week, never there on weekends, and not there when he doesn't want to be?

Carty: I'd be curious to know what the boy does when he splits, too. It could be drugs or selling himself. Making some money, being a man, and bringing some home, as well as being hooked into invitations constantly. But again, I think Warren isn't allowed to parent the boys. All he says is that we should put the boy out in the street and see how he does. Pretty crazy.

Dydyk: I think mother also isn't committed to mothering these two kids. She can probably mother little kids, but I question what she does for John. It doesn't sound like two families, it doesn't even sound like one. There's no commitment from her to either of these two kids in terms of the basic instrumental necessities. The major focus would have to be joining with her and also getting around some of the cultural differences about seeking help.

Carty: Both parents agree that John knows what to do and can do it. It's a real test for John, as the problem, to see if he can bring Warren and his mother together. If you're bad enough maybe these two adults will come together to make some sort of decision or rant and rave at you, or do something.

Interviewer: How would you suggest that the worker help this family to be more of a family?

Dydyk: Getting them to do things within the therapy room together, play a game, play with the puppets, organize an activity, something concrete to define that group of people as having some interest in common. I'd also work with them in the home.

Interviewer: What kinds of things might a worker do at the home?

Dydyk: Look for something positive that mother does and reinforce it in terms of her management of the kids.

Carty: She has to be doing something right. He's 9 years old, he does his work at school, and he's not a baby.

Marton: If I couldn't work with the family, I'd be prepared to work with the school, because they sound concerned. There are some concrete things that a worker could suggest. For example, they say that he is late because he is attention-seeking, yet their solution is to put him in a chair in front of the class. That only seems to focus more attention on the boy and could be part of the reason why it's ineffective. Also, they're upset about the fact that he's coming late and is absent and yet their solution is to suspend him. Knowing that this kid has been running away on his own, that does not seem like a good solution, especially because we seem to be worried about what he may be doing in the community. There are a number of indications of good potential for this boy. In school, he seems to be doing well, he seems to be responding, he's sensitive and volunteers. If a teacher were willing to coordinate a treatment plan, a school program could be successful. It may be possible to set up some expectations for John that would allow him to become more responsible in a socially appropriate way. Such a program should build in clear-cut reinforcers so that he could realize that some good things were coming his way. I would also try to get this boy a significant male figure who would be available to him. I would look for a big brother.

Dydyk: There's another issue that has to be addressed, and that is that this kid was displaced from Jamaica and his grandmother at age 5. Is he still dealing with adjustment to a new culture? That should be looked at.

Interviewer: With this particular family, if something were to go wrong, what would you predict it would be?

Dydyk: They would drop out of treatment quickly if they weren't connected.

Carty: John would immediately test any change in the system. For example, if Warren should step closer to mother as the father of the children, John might go for another little run to see if it's different this time from the last time, and that might lead to the parents' discouragement. If you can predict a family problem before it happens, sometimes it doesn't happen, and the kid knows you're on top of things. I think this kid would test any changes very quickly. You'll know soon enough by John's behavior, probably by the same symptom of running away, whether the mother is in need of more help.

Marton: I would worry that Warren is not going to like what therapy has to offer. It's not in his interests. I see him as a potential nemesis in that respect.

Carty: I think if you have him, you make use of him. You might question whether he's going to get involved and support mother by asking him the same question.

Dydyk: There may be something else missing. The notion that a kid acting-out is sitting on somebody else's shoulders. I don't know who this kid is aligned with to allow him to act-out. Is there a grandmother in the picture, or is the biological father maintaining contact?

Carty: John is worried about his mom. His mom's been the only person. She had him and she took care of him, and she gave him to grandmother for a while. She has been the one who started with him and is still with him.

Dydyk: We don't know that. It could have been grandmother who took care of him for the first five years.

Carty: But she and John go back to day one. I think that is important for a kid. He has no one else when his grandmother's not there and his real father's not there.

Dydyk: That's what I'm saying. I'm not sure what his contact is with other relatives. For instance, does dad come and visit? Or is there some relative he's running to or who is available to him?

Marton: Could it not be that he's trying to tap mom on the shoulder and say "Hey, I'm here, I need you"? Especially if we go along with the notion that the new child has displaced him even further.

Interviewer: Are there other major problems that might come up with this family?

Marton: I think there is potential danger for this boy, and I think that that would be the worrisome thing for the worker.

Carty: He might be in need of protection.

Interviewer: What would you do if that's established?

Carty: I think you'd have to tell the mother that you're notifying the Children's Aid Society or the authorities and why you're doing it, and work with her while that's going on.

Interviewer: What things would tell you that this child was in need of protection?

Dydyk: Continued running.

Carty: Or if he came home with bruises all over him, or if he came home with $100 in his pocket, or if he came home high and was out of it, or if he had needle tracks. I think within the family you would ask him to explain to his mother where he goes, what he does, and why he does it. The mother would let you know, too. She sounds aware enough to know what's going on, if he's being beaten or if he's being taken away, or running with some real wild kids.

Interviewer: Are there particular things that any of you would advise the family to do about a run, either during or after?

Carty: I would tell mother to phone the police right away. Tell them that he has a history of running and that she's very concerned. What they do with it is another matter, but she needs to have some action, so she should phone the police and phone the school. She should get Warren, she could start doing something when it happens. I would imagine she probably waits and feels terrible, guilty, and worried when he's gone for six days.

Dydyk: I would want her to lay out something that's going to happen when this kid runs, so that he can get a sense that the mother cares. I don't get a feeling that she really gives a damn.

Interviewer: Could you give an example of what mother might lay out as a result of running?

Dydyk: That she will call the authorities and this might happen to him, or that when he does come home he'll lose a privilege or that there will be other concrete consequences. That may be what he's pushing for.

Marton: I would look for some incentives for staying home, because this lady is very punitive and there's very little that is given to these kids. So I'd worry about just increasing punitiveness. I would build in positive consequences for letting people know where he is. You only go away for such and such a period of time. If you follow these rules, then this happens. If you don't, then something else happens, reporting to authority, etc.

Interviewer: What kind of worker would be recommended?

Carty: A female worker, preferably. I wouldn't want any competition for Warren.

Dydyk: Somebody who is able to join well and work with people who are probably going to be fairly difficult to connect with. So a fairly warm person.

Carty: Patient and nonjudgmental. This mother's going to look very critical and rejecting of her kids.

Dydyk: I would reinforce the patience because of the major disorganization in the family. Somebody who will not be impatient to produce major changes. It may be a crisis-oriented family.

Marton: For John, a young, Black male could be very important as a role model, but wouldn't work as well for the family.

Carty: Mother has a Black male, she either uses him, or she should be looking for a male figure for her boys. I think the therapist's skill is more important than being a father figure.

Interviewer: Let's talk about goals. What should be the major focus?

Marton: That he not run. It can be very concrete.

Carty: To have mother and Warren be the parents of the three children, or mother be the single parent of the three children. Some sort of definition of who's running the show. Warren can be a visiting boyfriend, as long as it's clear, and mother can look after her boys by getting in a man who would do the job, or another male figure.

Interviewer: So the primary outcome that you would be after would be a clear definition of parental responsibility.

Dydyk: I would go with a short-term and a long-term goal. My short-term goal would be to get them to come to therapy three times in succession because I think they're the kind of family who might not make a commitment to treatment. My long-term goal would be to make this woman feel competent as a mother and as a woman. It may be that she's hanging onto this guy because she doesn't have any connection any place else.

Interviewer: What is the prognosis?

Marton: For this boy I think it's not bad. I think he has a lot of positive things going for him. For the mother, I don't know.

Carty: I'd agree. I think mother could make some changes for her boys, but I think it's going to come to a head very quickly. Six days out is a long time. Whether we like it or not, Children's Aid might be phoned by the next-door neighbor who's sick and tired of the yelling matches when John comes home.

Interviewer: Barbara, prognosis?

Dydyk: I'm not sure. I agree with all you say. We don't know what kind of trouble this kid is in, but he hasn't come to the attention of the law yet and he's a good kid in school. This suggests some reason to hope in the family.

Carty: I think John is going to another family. Is he in need of care, or is he, in fact, going somewhere and coming back better fed, bathed, and stuff? If that's the case, then the prospect is much, much higher because mother's got an ally somewhere out there whether she knows it or not.

Marton: It would also show some real integrity and strength in this boy, that he knows what he needs and he gets it.

Interviewer: Any final words?

Carty: I think if this were just a dyadic process between mother and son, John would be sleeping with his mom or tucking her in at night. I don't think he would be out in the community, I think he would be in the house. I think a third person adds something that is intolerable so he has to get out for whatever reason. I've never seen such extreme behavior between a child and one parent. It's extreme for a child of 9 to stay away for six days unless there was someone else for him or he was caught in conflict between two adults.

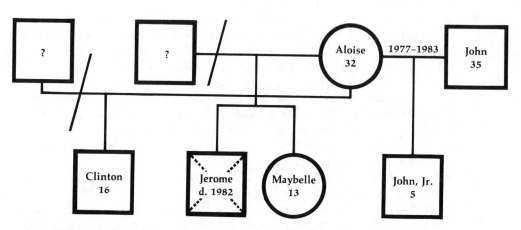

THE JONES FAMILY

Identifying information

The Jones family was referred by a physician at a local community out-patient clinic. The children in the family are Clinton, age 16, Maybelle, age 13, and John Jr., age 5. A fourth child, Jerome, drowned in an accident a year ago at the age of 14. The children are currently living with their aunt, Lucinda Hopkins, who is the sister of John Jr.'s father. The precipitating event for the referral was the discovery that Maybelle has contracted gonorrhea. Clinton had previously been in trouble for vandalism, and John Jr. is regarded as a behavior problem who is unable to adapt to kindergarten. Jerome had also been in some trouble together with his older brother.

History of problem

The Jones family has a long history of disruption and contact with public agencies. Clinton was first picked up by the police at age 12 for curfew violation and has subsequently been to juvenile court on charges of vandal-ism and destruction of public property. During the past year he seems to have settled down somewhat since he began a work-study program through high school.

Maybelle was regarded as the least problematic member of the family but is now the gravest concern. Last week it was determined that she had contracted a venereal disease from having sexual relations with several boys in the neighborhood. At issue also is a lack of adequate supervision of her.

John Jr., according to his mother, Aloise Jones, has always been "hyper" and difficult to control. He was dismissed from kindergarten three months ago for bullying the other children and being a nuisance. He has been taking Ritalin for about nine months without any noticeable change in behavior, but there is some question whether he is taking his medication regularly. The school believes that he is too immature to begin kindergarten this year and recommends that he try again next year. According to Mrs. Jones, the school problem with John Jr. was the last straw, and she sent all three children to live with Mrs. Hopkins, who has a 1-year-old baby of her own. Mrs. Hopkins claims that John Jr. is basically a good kid and just needs a lot of love.

Previous intervention efforts with the Jones family have not been successful. They have had some contact with a child care worker in the past but frequently canceled appointments while continually promising to do better. Both Mrs. Jones and Mrs. Hopkins receive financial aid from the government.

Marital and family history

Aloise Jones, age 32, mother of the children, grew up in a poor, Black inner city neighborhood. Her mother worked in a laundromat, and she never knew her father, who left when she was a baby. Her three oldest children were born out of wedlock, apparently to two different men. Six years ago she married John Jones when she was pregnant with John Jr. They are currently separated. John Sr. works part-time as a house painter, is an alcoholic, and was abusive to the children. He does not contribute aid to the family, and his whereabouts are unknown. Aloise last saw him four months ago. He used to drop by at unpredictable times to see his son, usually while on a drinking spree, but has not lived regularly in the household for two years.

Aloise works in the packing department of a large department store, a job she has held for two years. The children have alternately been looked after by neighbors, by Clinton, and by John's sister. Aloise is currently dating several men but has no steady relationship. Lucinda Hopkins, age 29, is unmarried and does not work outside the home. She receives family allowance benefits and some money from Aloise for looking after the children.

Characteristics of family members

Aloise Jones appears to be an overworked, anxious Black woman who dresses provocatively and seems disorganized. She may have a drinking problem of her own. She alternates between talking about how much she loves and misses her children, how troublesome they are, and how relieved she is to be rid of them. She speaks very angrily about her husband John and regards men in general as untrustworthy. She hopes that Clinton will soon be working full-time so that he can help out with the family finances, and she blames the neighborhood boys for defiling her daughter. She rarely speaks about Jerome but apparently harbors grief over his death. She regards John Jr. as a brat, "just like his no-good father." She resolutely refuses to consider giving up her children for placement or adoption and plans to get them back from Mrs. Hopkins as soon as she gets her life together. Currently, she works days and goes out nights with friends to parties and bars.

Lucinda Hopkins has very little formal education but has good common sense, and the children like her. She has broken relations with her brother John and feels sorry for the kids, especially John Jr. She assigns Clinton a lot of responsibility for taking care of Maybelle and thinks that Maybelle would not be in trouble if he were more reliable. She views her parenting role with the Jones children as temporary and hopes that Aloise "grows up" and becomes a competent mother. She used to look after the children whenever Aloise was unavailable or the parents were fighting. With the demands of caring for her own baby she is reluctant to take on permanent responsibility for all the Jones children. Lucinda has never been married.

Clinton appears tough and sullen and resents the intrusion of authorities into his life. He is learning to become a carpenter and plans to quit school after one more year and move out. He says he hates his father and seems both protective of, and angry at, his mother. He acts very much the man of the house and takes an authority position toward Maybelle and John Jr. He thinks Maybelle is okay but regards John Jr. as a pest.

Maybelle seems wide-eyed and innocent in her outward appearance but is probably very street-wise. Her acquaintances in the neighborhood tend to be involved in delinquent acts. She does not seem very upset about her sexual experiences nor the physical problems they have caused her. She appears to hunger for affection from Lucinda and other adults, says she misses her mother and looks forward to talking to her on the phone a couple of times a week and visiting her on weekends. She also misses Jerome, to whom she was particularly close.

John Jr. is into everything and needs to be watched constantly. He obeys Lucinda, but when her back is turned, he goes right back to misbehaving. Other children stay away from him because of his uncooperative style of play. He talks frequently about his father and says he is going to live with him soon. He thinks Maybelle is all right but is afraid of Clinton, who has been known to hit him.

School and community

Clinton is in the tenth grade. Since he began the work-study program, his grades have been passing, and he has not had trouble other than occasional truancy. Maybelle is in the seventh grade, is very cooperative in school, spends a lot of time with the teacher, but doesn't attend to her lessons very well and hence gets barely passing grades. Her IQ has been assessed as in the below-average range. The school regards the Jones family as unstable and difficult. Mr. Jones has never had contact with the school, and Mrs. Jones has been defensive and uncooperative when she has been called in about problems with the children.

Case discussion

Consultants: Dr. Rudolph Philipp, Ms. Elizabeth Ridgley, Mr. Bruce Stam

Interviewer: With regard to the Jones family, Bruce, are there any additional areas of information or assessment that you would require?

Stam: It is one of these multiproblem situations where one could come up with a whole list of other information but I do not believe it would help.

Interviewer: Rudy?

Philipp: I have only two questions. One is to review the Ritalin this child is taking or may not be taking regularly. That's not a major issue as far as I am concerned. I have to assume that the gonorrhea that Maybelle has is being treated. If it isn't, that's simply a matter of getting medical help.

Interviewer: Libby?

Ridgley: I think the biggest problem with this case will be the worker's belief or lack of it in the mother's competence. The worker's first job will be to find the mother's competence and strength and join her at that level. It is clear from the information that she cares enormously for these children despite deprivation and unstable conditions, she has never given them up for very long. The second thing you know is that she can hold a job. The third thing you know is that she has agreed to end a marriage that wasn't working. At the same time you know that she is overwhelmed and that the children are hard to manage and that she works and has lost a job. So this lady appears incompetent, but against considerable odds, she has kept the family going. This is a crisis, I think, as a result of the drowning accident. All the children have strengths. Clinton is at school learning a trade. He is enormously responsible for his mother and specifically for his two siblings. Maybelle is in the seventh grade, is cooperative at school, and relates well with the teacher. John Jr. responds to immediate direction and is basically a good kid who needs his mother. The school sees the mother as incompetent and the family as unstable, and it is important that the therapist not make the same mistake. I would start right away by saying to this lady how impressed I am at how she has struggled to keep this family together. It is no easy job to raise a family on your own, to be short of money, to be Black in a White-dominated city, to work long hard hours, and she has my admiration. I would get her to tell me about her job, how she got it, when she got it, how she manages to do it and come home and do the laundry, cleaning, and check homework, always with the idea that she *does* these things. She is a hard worker and a concerned mother.

Then I would ask her what her major concerns are right now about the children, how she views the problem, what she thinks needs to be done, and what her plans are. How does she want her children to be? What is her first step? What is her second step? I would begin softly to challenge how she can get her act together without her children because it must make her feel that she has lost. She has fought to keep this family together, and to lose one child by drowning is a terrible thing. I guess she is thinking that if she has lost one, she has lost them all.

She needs to be reminded that these kids need her, she is all they have, she is all they can count on, she is the only parent they know with any reliability, and she has stopped fighting before the job is finished. She is a survivor, she is tough, and her children need to learn how to survive. Whatever mother came in with I would reinforce and strengthen because right now she has nothing to believe in.

Interviewer: In terms of structuring the sessions, would you see her alone or with the children?

Ridgley: Always with the children.

Interviewer: Why?

Ridgley: Because I think that is where you have the best chance of joining her. Her major energy has been in keeping her family together. She cares enormously for them and I think that she regards herself first of all as a mother.

Interviewer: Would you work with the children's aunt?

Ridgley: No.

Interviewer: Would you make any attempt to reach the last husband?

Ridgley: No. I would go with the mother. After she has her children back again and has looked at John's Ritalin problem with the pediatrician and has looked at the school and dealt with him at home so he has more structure, if she then comes and says that John talks a lot about her "rotten" husband and she thinks of doing something about it, I would go with her, but I wouldn't introduce the topic.

Interviewer: Bruce, what approach would you take in this case?

Stam: Supporting the mother is the key to it. She needs to see that she has some control over the family and her kids. I would spend more time with her alone first. I have a feeling that with her family there surrounding her, she would be overwhelmed with guilt and immediate problems. I think she needs some building up before she can face that situation, before the rest of the family starts getting involved. It looks like we're going to have to deal with the relationship between mother and aunt whether we like it or not, because the aunt is a key figure. She'll have to be part of those sessions. Whether it is just a bit at the beginning or long-term support for mother, I don't know.

Ridgley: I would be very worried about that and offering long-term support for mother, assuming that she needs it, although I don't think she will need it. By bringing in the aunt you demonstrate to the children and to mother that mother is incompetent. I think the job is for mother to plan when she will take her children out, and I assume she will be able to manage that.

Stam: I agree that is a real danger, but I think that realistically, at the beginning, this aunt is there, whether we like it or not. The other aspect I would like to see worked on here is the community—to get mother to work on resources in the community like teachers, sports clubs, and so on, who can take over some of the support of the family rather than dumping them on somebody else such as the aunt.

Philipp: As tragic as the drowning is, I cannot assume that it was a pure accident. In the back of my mind a question popped up that the death may have been due to poor supervision. This child may not have known how to swim, and the mother may not have been around when he took out a canoe and tipped it over. That would simply underline the risks that these children have in being cared for by this mother as she is now and has been over the years. I think that even if you could get mother through the door for your first session, you may not be successful in getting her back. She has a long history of involvement with a lot of agencies. It would take someone with extensive experience to work with this woman. According to the information, the mother isn't willing to take the children back yet, and it may take six months or a year until she gets her act together. In the meantime, I think you have to support Lucinda because she is probably struggling with this responsibility herself. In the interest of the children's safety, sooner or later you may have to involve a child welfare agency because these children are at risk and you are a long way from being out of the woods with this family.

Interviewer: And so you would consider, or would you definitely recommend, involvement with a child welfare agency?

Philipp: I wouldn't jump into it. I would agree with Libby that if you go in saying this is another welfare case with another irresponsible mother who doesn't care about her kids, you are going to fail.

Interviewer: Would the primary intervention be working with mother in a family therapy format?

Philipp: I would make an attempt. You owe it to this mother, and you owe it to the family to make that attempt.

Interviewer: What about the children? Would any of you work with any of them individually, either therapeutically or connecting them to other groups or resources in the community?

Stam: Maybelle and John Jr. could both do with a big brother and big sister.

Ridgley: That would be terrific. (Sarcastic tone) It demonstrates mother's incompetence.

Stam: I couldn't agree more. It will have to be somebody who is culturally connected with the family. But I have a feeling that it will be a long time before the mother is going to give Maybelle and John Jr. what they need.

Philipp: I think that if we are counting on this mother being able to assume full responsibility for the family in six months or a year, we have to provide something for Lucinda. It may be some kind of preschool program for John Jr. that can handle him until the mother is able to take over. I think you have to convince mother that you are trying to help her children until she is ready to take over the responsibility.

Ridgley: The longer she doesn't have her children, the more difficult it will be to get her act together, and the more remorse, guilt, and inadequacy she will feel. I think if you worked with her, she would respond to the business of being a "survivor." She will take the children back, and I don't think this is a long-term case.

Philipp: I think it will be long-term because this mother has a long history of contacts with agencies. Therefore, I don't believe that you are going to work all this through in a matter of months.

Ridgley: I don't know about working through, but she never had any structural family therapy!

Philipp: What happens if she doesn't keep her appointments?

Ridgley: You are assuming she won't keep her appointments. There is nothing in the information that indicates that she will not keep her appointments. The only people she doesn't like to see specifically are at the school. If she doesn't keep appointments I would certainly be on the phone and ask "Are you doing this job or not? I thought we made a deal. I thought you said that you are up to this job, so get the kids in here." I may have to be after her, but I don't think it will be all that necessary.

Interviewer: Could we talk about what, if anything, you would do in relating to these kids? We have talked a lot about the mother and how to cope with her.

Philipp: Well, one issue that will have to be dealt with sooner or later is the sudden death of their brother.

Interviewer: So that's an issue you would raise?

Philipp: Not at first, but down the road, yes.

Ridgley: I would raise it in the first session. Because she has lost one child, she's acting as if she had lost them all. The children's experience in therapy is just as important as mother's. Because of all the stresses on the family, there hasn't been much individuating of the children, defining of differences and similarities, defining what one child needs but the other one doesn't need. Part of the therapy would be to enhance the children's competence as well as what they need.

Interviewer: Bruce, are there any special things that you would encourage a worker to do with these children?

Stam: The one who concerns me most is Maybelle at this point. She has to sort out her needs for affection and closeness. I don't know where she is going to get those needs met. We may have to teach her to get what she can from mother and learn to live in a more suitable manner without expecting too much from mother. I would use very practical ways of hooking into the community as an alternative to her present pattern of provoking the boys in the neighborhood.

Philipp: She may be street-wise but in need of some basic sex education.

Interviewer: Do you mean birth control information?

Philipp: Yes, birth control, V.D. prevention, the whole thing. She is 13 years old, and we can't assume that she knows the basics. Secondly, I think one could make the case that mother is very immature, hasn't grown up, and can't as yet assume the parenting role.

Interviewer: Is there anything that you would want to warn the worker to look out for in terms of how the therapy is going?

Ridgley: If they miss appointments, that would be a very specific danger sign that somehow the worker is not reaching the family.

Interviewer: You also said that a danger sign from your point of view would be a lack of confidence in the family on the worker's part.

Ridgley: That is the biggest danger. The worker must be convinced that this mother is competent.

Interviewer: Would you suggest that the case be transferred if that does not happen?

Ridgley: It depends on how cases are assigned. I would hope that it would come out in the assignment, as the worker starts to talk about what she or he would do. If I couldn't turn the worker around in that case discussion, I would reassign the case. If I had no opportunity to reassign, I would make sure that this case was supervised very clearly. I would give one directive to the worker— namely, no matter what this mother says, reframe it into something posi- tive. For example, if the mother says "I don't want these kids," and the worker feels terrible about it, the worker could say to the mother "I guess you want to make sure you can provide a good home for these kids."

Interviewer: Rudy, are there danger signals to which you would alert the worker that might merit a change in strategy?

Philipp: You are either going to reach this lady in one or two sessions or she is not going to return because she has had many negative experiences with agen- cies. If you don't succeed, then you have to make completely different contingency plans for the sake of the chldren.

Interviewer: Bruce?

Stam: Basically the same thing. Mother has to start immediately making some very specific decisions about what she is going to do with these children. If she cannot do that, it is not going to work.

Interviewer: Bruce, what kind of worker characteristics would you like to see with this case?

Stam: Optimistic, culturally oriented to this mother in a very affirmative sense. Somebody who can get very excited about the challenges of the subculture in which she lives.

Interviewer: Any special sex or age or experience characteristics for the worker?

Stam: Female, experienced, and very secure so as not to get caught up in over- protecting the children and telling mother what to do.

Ridgley: I think it would be very hard for a worker who has not had a child to understand this family's loss. It would be very helpful to have a worker who had a family.

Interviewer: Okay, let's talk about goals and outcomes.

Philipp: The first goal is to try to get mother to help herself by capitalizing on her strengths and making her feel that she is competent. The second goal is to help Lucinda look after the children in the interim. The third goal, if all else fails, would be to involve a child welfare agency to make sure that these children are not at risk in the community.

Interviewer: What degree of progress would you expect in this case?

Philipp: If you hook this mother into a therapeutic contract, you could be working with her for six months. It could take a lot longer than that.

Interviewer: Do you think that the goals you talked about could be reached in that time?

Philipp: If you are successful, you would be making significant progress in that direction, but you might not reach the goal in six months.

Interviewer: What would you say about general prognosis in this case?

Philipp: General prognosis? Not good.

Interviewer: Libby . . . prognosis and goals?

Ridgley: Prognosis is excellent, because she is a survivor and she has kept the family together. She is reacting to the crisis. The goals would be essentially to have the children's symptoms disappear. Maybelle would be at home watching television or reading, not on a street corner looking for affection and getting V.D. John would be at school and behaving like a 5-year-old. Clinton would continue his school and carpentry training and assume less responsibility at home. The primary goals would be to have this family function as a viable single family.

Interviewer: So the goal is for this family to be reunited as a functional unit.

Ridgley: Functional . . . and you would know that by the disappearing symptoms.

Interviewer: Bruce, goals and prognosis?

Stam: Simple goals of just putting the family back together and functioning. Everybody going to school and work, having meals and clothes. Secondarily, the kids getting their emotional needs met in the community and the home. Prognosis? Very guarded, 50/50.

Interviewer: Any last words on this case?

Philipp: The problem, as I see it, is that you have very little time to connect with this woman and then you have a long time to work on things.

Stam: I don't think Jerome's death is the cause of this problem; it is a result, one of a multitude of background factors.

Philipp: I was reflecting on something Libby said earlier about introducing the death of Jerome right in the first session. I think that would be a "heavy" for this family and they would have a hard time dealing with it.

Ridgley: Do you remember how I said I would do it?

Philipp: You would first build her up.

Ridgley: Yes, and the context would be important. I would not ask them about it, just acknowledge in the first session with this lady that she has lost one child, and although no one can ever make it up to her, she is acting as if she had lost them all. I think his death has to be acknowledged. Then you are treating her mother-to-mother, woman-to-woman with a lot of compassion.

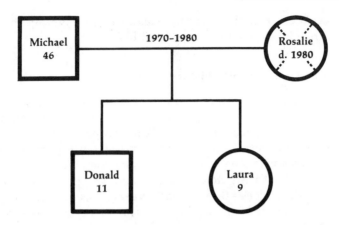

THE BARNES FAMILY

Identifying information

Donald is the "identified patient." Donald was originally referred by the family's G.P. to an outpatient clinic in a general hospital. This clinic's assessment recommended residential treatment, resulting in a referral of the family to the children's mental health center. The family consists of Mr. Barnes and his children, Donald (11) and Laura (9). Mrs. Barnes died three years ago of cancer. Presenting problems with Donald include disobedience, violent and defiant behavior, lack of communication and friends, frequent retreats into fantasy, and chronic school problems.

History of the problem

Parents had sought help from a child guidance clinic when Donald was 6 years old—whiney, immature, enuretic, and highly dependent on his mother. The clinic provided parental counseling, emphasized basic child management skills with Mr. and Mrs. Barnes, and terminated after approximately four months. Parents reported some improvement at that time, but the clinic termination report expressed concern about the father being a peripheral figure in the family and suggested that Mrs. Barnes was seeking emotional compensation in an overclose relationship with her son. Two years later, Mrs. Barnes developed cancer and died within six months of the initial diagnosis.

In school, Donald has been a marginal student, silly and giggly, lacking in confidence, and bullying younger children. Mr. Barnes complains that Donald has become progressively more difficult and defiant at home and has been the cause of two babysitters quitting the family. In the past six months, Donald has engaged both his sister and father in bitter arguments, has thrown things at them, and after one angry scene with Mr. Barnes, broke a window. He also kicked one of the babysitters. Mr. Barnes expresses great frustration with Donald and has beaten him with a strap on at least one occasion. Father admits the idea of "giving him up" has crossed his mind while he struggles to cope with his son.

Marital and family history

Michael Barnes's family of origin includes two sisters and his parents. His father is dead, and his mother lives in an apartment about a 30-minute drive from the Barnes's home. Mr. Barnes reports that he has always been close to his mother and that his relationship with his father was "satisfactory." Both his sisters have tried to boss and dominate him, and they "never got on too well." Each sister is married and living in a different city.

Mr. Barnes's father died 18 years ago, and Mr. Barnes continued living at home with his mother until his marriage 13 years ago. He met his wife at work and they were married after a very brief courtship. Mr. Barnes assesses their relationship as "average," acknowledges that there were some frictions, but "no different from any normal couple." It is difficult to elicit details or elaborations about the marriage from Mr. Barnes.

Following his wife's death, Mr. Barnes's mother moved into the home for eight months, but then resumed living alone. Mr. Barnes has been dating for more than a year and is now seeing one woman steadily. She often stays with the family on weekends and joins them for outings.

Characteristics of family members

The family presents as a disengaged trio—that is, as three isolated individuals. They find it difficult to identify common interests other than eating at restaurants. They spend little time together and are involved in separate life pursuits. There is little sense of emotional connectedness among them, although father and daughter do show some warmth toward each other. Father seems like a mild, quiet man who is feeling overwhelmed by his role as a parent. Laura is clearly identified as the "good" child in the family. She is outgoing, gregarious, and active in clubs and sports at school; her father also describes her as highly responsible and helpful at home. Both Laura and her father acknowledge that, at times, Donald can be fun and that he has a good sense of humor. On the other hand, he presents as surly and distrustful of adults. At home, he spends most of his time in his room, listening to records, sometimes just staring into space. Donald and his father appear distant and uncomfortable with each other.

School and community

Though Donald does poorly with his academic work, he has passed each year and is now in the sixth grade. Aside from sporadic silly behavior and a reluctance to try new work, he is not a management problem in the classroom. During lunch periods or recess, he has frequently been reported for teasing or hurting smaller children. Donald has no friends or hobbies and spends his spare time at home.

Special assessments

The hospital outpatient clinic had an intake interview with Donald and his father before referring the case for residential treatment. No other recent assessments have been done.

Case discussion

Consultants: Dr. Gerald Beckerle, Dr. Gregor Finlayson

Interviewer: I'd like to talk about what information or formal assessments, if any, you would recommend to a caseworker who is beginning to tackle this case.

Finlayson: When I look at the problems described in the family history, it would seem very clear why the boy is having some of the problems he is having. Yet, what I've realized from my own difficulty in treating some cases like this, is that there may be other problems that don't figure within the family's emotional problems. For that reason I would suggest taking a closer look at whether this boy has academic difficulties and specifically whether he may have a formalized learning problem. He is apparently doing fairly well in school, but the kinds of problems that he shows—disobedience, violence, defiance, lack of communication, and poor peer relationships—also go along with learning problems. I think that it's too easy to overlook this possibility, but it's also easy enough to rule it out, and that should be done. That doesn't negate the other difficulties in the family, which are pretty compelling.

Beckerle: I wondered about that a bit too, but the notes state that he is not a management problem in the classroom. Because they have passed him each year, I am assuming that he probably has not had learning difficulties, but it would be worth a phone call to get further impressions from the school.

Finlayson: And it would be relatively easy, depending on the availability of someone appropriate, to do a few tests to see whether there's a significant gap between his achievement level and what he seems capable of doing.

Beckerle: I'd like more information about Mr. Barnes's relationship with the new woman he's been seeing. If his general outlook on life is improving as he is forming this new relationship, I would expect that to have a positive carry-over with the children, unless there are many unresolved issues around their mother's death. Since Donald has been getting progressively worse, I would want to know how much Barnes talks to the children about issues around his wife's death.

Interviewer: So it's both the extent to which they've been able to talk and work through feelings about mother's death and also their feelings about the new lady?

Beckerle: Both those areas.

Finlayson: In this case previous treatment was attempted a number of years earlier. It's not clear who terminated that contact, and I think it would be important to understand how the family members felt about it. Laura is perhaps not that much involved because five years ago she would have been 4. But I think it would be important to tap Donald's and his father's memories of that contact. A good way generally to begin treatment is to understand what happened in previous treatment attempts because it yields clues about the kinds of pitfalls to avoid.

Beckerle: Definitely. Are they, for example, going to terminate abruptly because the therapist is too confronting?

Finlayson: Especially since the clinic expressed concerns about the family's functioning after termination. It sounds as though the termination may have been prompted by the family and that the clinic wasn't totally satisfied with what had taken place.

Interviewer: What kinds of treatment modalities would you recommend to a worker in approaching this family?

Finlayson: For me the modality follows from identifying the problems we're going to be working on. I think you would have to sit down with the family and clearly identify their concerns. When the areas that need change have been identified, I think you're in a better position to determine whom you're going to work with, whether with Mr. Barnes alone, or with Mr. Barnes and his son, the three of them together, or involve Mr. Barnes's mother as well. Generally I would suggest starting with the whole family and then seeing individuals or different groupings or systems of individuals depending on the treatment focus at the time.

Beckerle: For me, one of the issues is trying to assess how seriously disturbed Donald is and was, even before his mother's death. I wouldn't see anything of a residential nature for this case, but maybe Donald is more seriously disturbed than he has been portrayed at this point. If it's a fairly chronic, serious disturbance, then I might consider that. If I have the impression that there is a problem primarily around father's difficulty with feelings, his not allowing people in the family to talk, his not having worked through the grieving process, I would stick with a family approach and do some modeling and relearning for the children by teaching father how to listen and how to talk to the kids. If Donald's more seriously disturbed, then I'd see him, and maybe father, individually.

Finlayson: I'd like to add something about the residential placement. At this point I certainly wouldn't recommend it because this is a disengaged family in the sense that these members are depicted as isolates. To remove this boy and fulfill his fear about leaving the family, or his father's threat that he's going to have to leave the family, would not be helpful.

Beckerle: Yes. If father ends up marrying this new woman, this would be a tremendously important transition period in the family's adjustment. It would be very difficult for the boy to get back in afterward.

Finlayson: You have a family which, at this point, has probably not resolved their grief over the break-up of the original family and who, at the same time, are perhaps moving toward setting up a new family. I thought it might be helpful to involve Mr. Barnes and, perhaps, his friend in a parent group.

Even if it's Mr. Barnes alone, he might benefit from that kind of support, because this man is essentially a new parent. He has had these children, but he has been peripheral to the family. Suddenly he has these new children and he also has the loss of his spouse. He's swimming over his head.

Interviewer: Would either of you want to involve any other community agencies in this case?

Finlayson: For a father and a son who are uncomfortable and isolated from each other, I would like to see the boy become engaged in something that has to do with peers outside the home. For that reason I would want to sound them out about his joining, say, a scout group or something like that. Depending on the father's skills and willingness, it should be something that he and his son could do together. I'd certainly try to get the boy engaged in some kind of community activity with the necessary support so that he begins to have more contacts with his father.

Beckerle: I don't think that just the big brother aspects of scouts or sports is going to do it for this boy. The father would have to be involved. I also don't see bringing outside people like a child care worker or public health nurse into the case for home visits. Father is likely to be working during the day, and the chances of getting a person in are minimal. I think also that relationships are pretty strained and that that kind of thing might produce more strain in the home.

Interviewer: Do either of you think there's any kind of child protection issue here because of the one reported strap incident?

Finlayson: It would be worth spending some time exploring Mr. Barnes's frustration. One of the things that has to be established is how serious he is about giving his son up. In exploring that issue, you might learn whether the strapping incident was isolated and unique or whether this man is reaching the end of his rope.

Beckerle: And has he verbalized the thought of giving up his son? Or is that just something that he's felt in his own mind? I'd also like to know whether the strapping antedated his wife's death. If it postdated the death, I would be a little less concerned and see it in terms of the added stress.

Interviewer: Let me draw this out a bit more for the guidance of the hypothetical worker who's taking on this case. What criteria would the worker use to decide whether to involve a children's protection agency or child welfare agency?

Finlayson: Well, one criterion for me would be evidence of a possible repeat performance. Even before that, if Mr. Barnes could discuss his frustration with the worker and felt that there was a danger that he was getting to a point where this might happen again. I'd certainly try to do it that way. Ideally Mr. Barnes could involve the protection agency himself. That way it would be done with his knowledge, so that some semblance of a trusting relationship with the worker could be retained.

Beckerle: Yes, I'd go along with the notion of repeated incidents. Other than that, I think it's a subjective sense of his level of control.

Interviewer: Let's talk about more specific techniques and strategies that you could use with this family.

Beckerle: I would focus very much on family issues initially to try to decide how much unresolved grieving is present. I would want to have Mr. Barnes talk about his relationship with his father and his feelings about parenting, so that the son found out more about him and that might be a joining point between the two of them.

Finlayson: We have a parallel between the generations, where Mr. Barnes felt closer to his mother. Although he said his relationship with his father was satisfactory, one wonders whether that simply covers over some feelings of distance from his own father. And now we have Donald, who was closest to his mother in this generation, and he's lost that contact. One wonders how difficult it is for Mr. Barnes to parent his son when he may not have had a very close relationship to his own father. I think it could be helpful for him to explore how it was for him and how it must be for his son. Because it's a disengaged, isolated family, I'm pretty sure that things don't get aired and talked about. They probably didn't deal very well with the death of this woman. I think one way to help them look at the issue is to get them to bring in some pictures of her. What do they say about her? What did they talk about at the time she died? How much did they talk about it before it happened? Focus the discussion around some photographs. It can be an emotional session or two, but if it's done sensitively it can help the family along their grief process.

Beckerle: There's a lot of evidence to suggest that there may be precipitating stresses that bring on cancer, 6 to 24 months prior to the illness. Was there anything going on with Mrs. Barnes in their marital relationship? Does the father have any guilt about his wife's death?

Interviewer: What would you do if the family responded to any inquiries about mother and her death with a lot of denial of feelings and attempts to refocus on other things?

Finlayson: First of all, I think it's doubtful that all family members would deny it. I wouldn't be surprised if Laura showed a little emotion about it, and so you might have a bit of an "in" there. Maybe the other family members can respond to her, or whoever shows some feeling about it. I'd be inclined to pursue it gently, by talking about the good times they had together and suggesting that it's important to go back and to remember what it was like, and bring in the family photo album.

Beckerle: That sounds like a good suggestion. Pictures sometimes cut through the words and guardedness. I'd start out with a gentle approach, but use the words *death* and *dying* a lot: "What was it like when your wife was dying? It must be hard for you now that she's dead." I would stress those kinds of words. People frequently use fancy words like *expired* or *passed away,* while I would tend to hammer it home more effectively.

Finlayson: If they absolutely denied any interest in discussing the topic and I couldn't get anywhere by pursuing it, I would pull back, at least for the time being, and go in another direction. If you don't, you're going to lose them.

Interviewer: What if you got good response in terms of a lot of affect? What do you do with the family to help them mourn? You've given some concrete examples of bringing in pictures and talking about recollections of mother. Are there other things?

Finlayson: It might be helpful to explore whether any of them had things they wished they had said to her before she died. They could talk about those things or even use an empty chair technique, imagining that she was there and reliving that period. Although I think this family would have a hard time doing it.

Beckerle: If they were a very responsive family, they might buy it.

Finlayson: From what we know of them at this point, I would question their capacity to do this. If it were possible, I would try to foster their helping each other with their feelings of grief by encouraging them to speak to each other keeping me as the person they're talking to.

Beckerle: And I might do some modeling in terms of touching and supporting them, with the goal of eventually getting them to do that with one another. I definitely have no taboos about touching clients. There are times when a touch is worth ten thousand words.

Finlayson: If we're doing grief work, it would just be these three family members, rather than the father's friend, because at this point we're trying to resolve the original family's grief.

Beckerle: Right. There might even be some anger expressed at her as a potential spouse, and it wouldn't necessarily benefit her to hear it. It would be a reaction or a finishing off of their feelings for their mother.

Interviewer: O.K. Meanwhile, there is Donald, who was identified as the problem. Many families, when family work begins, persist in identifying that child as the problem and wanting you to attend to him. What would you do about that?

Finlayson: Well, you can't forget what they think is important. In the process of identifying their concerns, you can get into this work around grief. But this is a boy who has problems with friends and defiance at home. I think it would be important to explore those defiant incidents, find out what happens between father and son, and determine whether there's a pattern. It may be that the father could handle it differently. It could be that Laura becomes involved and is drawn into something between her father and brother. She needs to be encouraged to stay out of something that isn't her business. That's one possibility.

Beckerle: Sometimes I will isolate family members individually and ask them how they view the problem. Sometimes the kids will surprise you in how free they are to talk about things. I remember one 5-year-old who said very clearly that mommy yells at daddy and daddy doesn't fight back, and bingo, that was right on. When you bring those problems back into the whole family discussion, it reframes it quite a bit. It's not just Donald who's the identified patient.

Interviewer: Gerry, you did say that if you had some indicators that Donald was more seriously disturbed, you would be inclined to do some individual work with him. Could you talk a bit more about what you'd attempt to do with him individually?

Beckerle: My style is to use play therapy pretty nondirectively, allowing him to

Finlayson: explore, and bring up areas of conflict and issues that are concerns for him. I wouldn't try to force him to talk about certain areas or guide him into certain areas.

Finlayson: I might use some projective technique.

Interviewer: For instance?

Finlayson: Well, I might want to use a Children's Apperception Test with him to get some idea of how he perceives his environment and the people in it. It's a way of drawing him out to talk a little more than he might otherwise be drawn out. Ideally, I would want to do that as part of my relationship in working with him.

With regard to the discipline issue at home, I think it is important to go back to Mr. Barnes's mother because she seems to have had such a strong relationship with her son, who's now the father, and find out what power she has in the extended family system. Is this man raising his children as his mother thinks he should? How much contact does she have? Does he, for example, talk with her every day on the phone? I think the worker has to clarify the disciplinary hierarchy in the family system. If we find that this woman has the power in this extended family system, we are doomed to fail unless we get her working on our side.

Interviewer: Would you have Mr. Barnes's mother in?

Finlayson: I would have the nuclear family in, first, and I would leave it to the father whether he wants to invite his friend. I'd certainly want to have Laura there, I wouldn't have only father and son, because I noticed that the father and son did go for one assessment appointment. That wasn't enough. I wouldn't exclude Laura. And then I might suggest that we have the grandmother come in if Mr. Barnes were agreeable.

Beckerle: I think that's a good point, because for all the warmth and closeness that supposedly exists between Mr. Barnes and his mother, he was not able to form much of a relationship with his wife. Why didn't that good relationship carry over? Is he still overly attached to her and overly dependent? Were they repeating that pattern?

Finlayson: I noticed she moved into the house for a while. Why did she do that, and then why did she move out again? Did she move out because she wasn't getting along with Donald? Perhaps she moved out because Donald was such a pain, and therefore Mr. Barnes is resentful of Donald because of that.

Interviewer: More comments about treatment strategies?

Finlayson: I'm trying to think about Donald's strengths. He has a good sense of humor apparently. I think the therapist could explore when Donald's fun to be with in the family. This is a family that needs to have some fun together. It strikes me that they're isolated and maybe a little depressed. I think if they experience some fun with one another, that will help to take some of the edge off Donald.

Interviewer: Let's go from fun to danger signals. Are there any particular things that might start to go wrong for which the worker should be alert, to bring the case back to conference or reconsider the strategy?

Beckerle: Early withdrawal from treatment. I don't know where you would get a handle to get them back into the clinic, unless part of that early withdrawal seemed to involve father's beating Donald. Then you might have sufficient evidence to involve a child welfare or some other agency to pressure them back into treatment.

Interviewer: Anything else that could go wrong with this family?

Finlayson: I think, in general, pushing them too hard would be a danger. I think that's why treatment would fail. Pushing in the direction of trying to develop their relationship skills faster than they are able to. When we see an isolated family, it makes our mouths water because we pride ourselves on being able to get people communicating. Yet families and people who aren't used to doing that can be pushed too hard. I think they'll begin to tell us in subtle ways, perhaps by missing appointments or canceling them. If that happens, I'd look back at recent sessions and explore whether there was something they might have been uncomfortable about.

I think another danger signal might be that we've lost sight of Donald's problems. Mr. Barnes saying to us "This is all well and good, but Donald's still a pain, and we're still having discipline problems at home and he's still giggly and inappropriate at school." We've been making the assumption that Donald's behavior is, in part at least, an expression of grief, and that if we address that, his behavior is going to change. If his behavior doesn't change, then we have to back up and consider that we've misunderstood his problems. I think the worker has to have contact with the school. We have to be able to monitor whether he's changing at school, whether his behavior is getting worse or better. Perhaps interpreting his behavior to the school will help them respond more constructively to him. This is a boy who's caught up a lot in fantasy. I think you have to keep a watch on whether that's increasing and whether he withdraws more into himself. That would be a danger signal and would concern me about his psychological stability.

Beckerle: That's one of the nice things about working with a child as the identified patient. Often we have more sources of information—for example, from the school regarding ongoing adjustment progress, or lack thereof—than we have with adults. Often we don't have good informants in the community, and we have to go more by their word of how they're coming along. Here we have not only the family but objective sources outside the family as well.

Finlayson: One point I wanted to make about treatment strategy is that here we have an unusual family constellation. Usually if there's a single parent, it's a mother, and so it's somebody who is generally used to dealing with household routines. Here we have a father who is new in that role. I would be interested in how they organize their family life together. Who looks after the meals? You may well be able to work at a redistribution of duties and responsibilities in the family. Maybe Donald doesn't do anything, maybe Laura does, and maybe Laura's resentful. She may have been thrust into the role of a pseudospouse. That would be a danger in this family, Laura as a parental child, even though she's younger than Donald; and Donald, I gather, acts a lot younger than he is. I think that you may be able to create better contact in this family by looking at such instrumental issues as preparation and cleanup of meals.

Interviewer: What kind of worker do you think is best suited to this kind of case?

Beckerle: The first thought that flashed through my mind would be a warm and supportive male who's comfortable as serving as a role model for father. Other than that I don't have any special characteristics.

Interviewer: It sounds like the connection with father and the focus on father and what he needs to do is critical.

Beckerle: As we've been talking, I'm realizing that if we have an identified patient in the family, it's father, not Donald.

Finlayson: I would agree with a male, and somebody who didn't come in like a bull in a china shop. It has to be someone who is sensitive to the fact that this family's in pain. They need a therapist who's not going to try to push them together too forcefully.

Interviewer: Okay, let's talk about the kinds of goals on which the worker should focus.

Finlayson: Well, I think you have to pay attention to what they're complaining about; so if you're successful, they're going to report an increase of appropriate behavior at school, an increase in positive interactions at home, and less defiance from Donald. Those are the guideposts I consider to be very important.

Beckerle: If in one of the early assessment sessions they acknowledge isolation as a problem, then I'd see more warmth and affection with each other as a central goal.

Interviewer: Okay, any other major goals?

Finlayson: I would hope that Donald would come out of his room more and make some contacts with other children. Later on in the treatment process he might be able to use a therapeutic group experience, and out of that, work on relationship skills. I would hope to see him investing his energy more appropriately outside the home.

Interviewer: What about prognosis in working with this family?

Finlayson: I'm generally hopeful, and I think it's important to convey that sense of hope to the family. I think that as long as we keep realistic goals, we will be able to help them and build on their strength.

Beckerle: Yes. This man obviously has some strengths. He's made it as an assistant bank manager, he's functioning out in the world, he probably has a lot of solidity. And the fact that he was able to set up a new relationship within a reasonable period of time says that he's not tremendously schizoid or withdrawn. So I'm moderately hopeful that if they hang in with treatment they can move a fair distance and become more solid as a family.

Finlayson: He's also been able to keep this family together for three very difficult years. That speaks well for him and the family.

SUMMARY

The families in this section are having difficulty functioning as cohesive, organized units. Both in terms of emotional bonds and behavior, there are significant questions about the extent of mutual consideration and cooperation in family functioning. The therapeutic task in each case is to strengthen the family structure and to discern some semblance of predictability in the children.

The first family introduced in this chapter, the Allen family, consists of a single parent and her two sons. Mr. Allen is dead, and Mrs. Allen is struggling to be the sole financial support, as well as the leader, of the family. While emotional bonds between mother and sons are apparent, the family remains disorganized and displays little cohesion or cooperation in the face of substantial family tasks. The boys, David and Billy, frequently fight at home and in school, and Mrs. Allen is feeling overwhelmed.

The consultants believe it is important to identify the relative priority of the many problems in this family, including David's aggressive behavior and Billy's withdrawn behavior. They suggest assessing the impact of Mr. Allen's death on all family members and that, in fact, the children's acting-out may be keeping mother from acting depressed. It is also important to consider the effect of Billy's hearing impairment on his emotional functioning. The consultants suggest that the therapist function as an intermediary to create a working partnership between the mother and the school. In addition, mother needs more confidence as a parent and could be taught specific behavior management skills such as contingency contracting and time-out.

The Thomas family is a West Indian family consisting of Mrs. Thomas, her common-law husband, and her three children. The 9-year-old son in the family is running away from home frequently, disappearing for days at a time. The adults in the family appear to be fully accepting of their 2-year-old daughter only. Both boys get scant attention and are often expected to fend for themselves. The common-law husband seems like a peripheral member of the family, and Mrs. Thomas is anxious and disorganized. The school is also concerned about John, the runner, because of his chronic tardiness.

The consultants emphasize the fragmented nature of this family. It is even suggested that two parallel families—one involving the common-law husband and the other involving Mrs. Thomas as a single parent—are coexisting. Fragmentation is also reflected in the family history—years of separation between the mother and her sons, different biological fathers. The consultants recommend interventions that could clarify and strengthen family roles and bonds. Because the mother's role is so central in this family, many of the recommendations have to do with supporting her and teaching her to be a more effective and positive manager of the children and of household routines.

In the Jones family, Mrs. Jones is unable to parent her three children at all and has placed them instead with her sister-in-law. All the children have behavior problems, and the 13-year-old daughter has contracted a venereal disease. Mrs. Jones is a tired, overworked woman who is separated from her husband and who may have a drinking problem.

Involving the mother and maintaining a relationship with her the consultants identify as a crucial first task for the therapist. Underlining Mrs. Jones's strengths and supporting her caring and concern for her children is essential. The consultants speculate that the accidental death of a fourth child may be significant in the mother's current difficulty in assuming a parental role. If so, feelings about this tragedy must be explored and resolved. Beyond forming an alliance with mother, it is pointed out that the children have immediate needs for adult support and relationships and help in finding community alternatives to delinquent behavior. It is agreed that the ultimate goal of treatment is to reunite the family.

Finally, in the Barnes family, the mother has died and Mr. Barnes is trying to care for his son and daughter. Donald, the 11-year-old, is disobedient, destructive, and prone to violent outbursts. His sister is defined as the "good child," and father is physically punishing Donald and threatening to place him out of the home. Donald is aggressive and defiant at school as well. Family members are generally seen as isolated from one another and as sharing few common interests.

The consultants emphasize that treatment must strengthen the father-son relationship, facilitate the family's mourning process for mother, and help the family to develop a more cohesive family life. It is suggested that father and son be helped to find activities in which they can participate together and that Mr. Barnes be helped to explore his feelings, both negative and positive, about parenting this boy. Further, the consultants recommend specific "grief work" exercises (for example, the use of photographs and/or role-playing) to help all family members resolve their feelings about mother's death from cancer. The consultants think the family should be assisted to find ways of organizing themselves to tackle household routines cooperatively and ways of having fun together.

STUDY/DISCUSSION QUESTIONS

1. What antecedent conditions and environmental events can contribute to family fragmentation?
2. What is the relationship between family fragmentation and emotional disturbance in children? Why do some children cope and develop well in a fragmented family?
3. How does the therapist prioritize the various unmet needs of fragmented families? Which needs should be addressed in therapy and with what urgency?
4. How can a therapist help estranged and isolated individuals to become closer? What techniques can be used to unify a family?
5. Is it likely that a child's problems will disappear once a family is more cohesive? If not, is effort to unite the family justified?

3

Children and
Marital Conflict

The parental relationship is a powerful force acting on the development and behavior of children. When parents are in conflict, children can be sought as allies, confidants, distractions from the problem, scapegoats, agonized and terrified spectators, spies, informers, or hopelessly torn loyalists. The one thing they cannot be is uninvolved. Thus many children will present problems in reaction to the stress they experience when their parents are in conflict. In addition, when parental strife is dominant, the parents have difficulty presenting their child with common and consistent expectations, limits, rewards, and/or punishments. Too often, one parent will overcompensate for the perceived punitiveness, rejection, or strictness of a resented spouse with over-permissive, placating parenting and vice versa. Both parents become locked in a seesaw battle with the unfortunate child becoming the fulcrum.

Treatment often begins with helping parents to acknowledge or even to recognize the role of marital tension in their child's difficulties. In many cases, parents adamantly refuse to see any problems except their child's inadequacies, no matter how obvious the marital problem is to an observer. In other cases, the fighting between spouses is so open and bitter that the child and his/her needs are utterly ignored during therapy sessions. This chapter offers case examples of three families in which marital conflict is a significant factor. In considering the web of family interdependencies confronting the mental health worker, it should be remembered that the child's problems may stress a marriage as critically as the marriage problems stress the child.

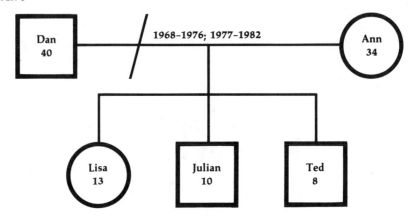

THE HARPER FAMILY

Identifying information

There are three children in the Harper family: Lisa, age 13, Julian, age 10, and Ted, age 8. The boys live with their father, Dan, age 40, and Lisa lives with her mother, Ann, age 34. The school made the referral of both boys. They are concerned about Julian's effeminate behavior and efforts to dress up in girls' clothing and about Ted's high anxiety level and excessive need to succeed academically.

History of problem

Julian's voice, walk, and mannerisms have been decidedly effeminate since the age of 5 or 6. The school was not unduly worried until this year, however, when two incidents heightened their concern. On Halloween, when few other students his age wore costumes of any sort, Julian came to school wearing a complete set of girls' clothes. Second, in trying out for the school play, Julian very much wanted to play a female role and frequently tried on girls' clothes in the wardrobe department.

   Ted's teachers have been reluctant to define Ted's behavior as a problem because he has consistently received very high grades and is clearly intelligent. However, he becomes unusually upset if he receives anything but an "A" on a paper or test, and he responds by challenging the teacher, asking what he can do to improve the grade, trembling, and staring into space. He also volunteers answers to questions *more* frequently than the teacher would like because he doesn't give other students a chance to respond.

   Dan Harper defends the boys' behaviors and is reluctant to see them as problems. On the other hand, his ex-wife Ann is eager to view the boys as having problems and attributes the problems to Dan's personality and lack of child-rearing skills. Dan is concerned, however, about his daughter Lisa. Lisa is difficult for Ann to control and runs around with a wild group of friends who are using drugs (mostly marijuana) and are perhaps involved in sexual experimentation. Lisa doesn't always come home nights, and on two occasions Ann has called the police to have her picked up for curfew violation and brought home. Dan attributes Lisa's behavior to Ann's irresponsible lifestyle and offers Lisa a haven for support. He maintains that Ann's active social life prevents her from adequately supervising the girl. Ann blames Dan for trying to "seduce" Lisa into leaving home and indirectly for her obstreperous behavior.

Marital and family history

Ann comes from a middle-class background and has two younger sisters. She adored her father, who was a salesman, and fought constantly with her mother. Her father died of a heart attack seven years ago, and Ann blames her mother's terrorizing and withholding behavior for literally breaking his heart. Ann attended college for two years and dropped out to marry Dan at the age of 19. She has minimal contact with her mother.

Dan's father is an accountant and his mother an artist. He is very close to his mother, whom he describes as sensitive and dynamic, and he has a cordial but distant relationship with his father. Dan's younger brother died in Vietnam. Dan graduated from university and completed training as a pharmacist. He met Ann at a party. They regard their early relationship as romantic, and she was impressed to be going out with an older man. With the arrival of children came difficulties in their marriage. Ann sees Dan as dour and unexciting; Dan accuses Ann of being irresponsible and unfaithful. The couple initially divorced seven years ago and remarried a year later. They divorced again a year ago after numerous separations. At this time Dan and Ann both claim their divorce is final, yet they live only about a mile apart and have frequent telephone contact regarding the children. Visitation rights are open and flexible.

After their first divorce, Ann took custody of the children, felt overwhelmed by the responsibility, and worked for a reconciliation. After the second divorce they decided to split the child-rearing responsibilities. Dan did not want to lose his children and also feared that Ann's "wanton" lifestyle would be a bad influence on them. At the time, all parties agreed about custody issues. Now Lisa wants to live with her father, although Ann insists on retaining custody of her, and Ted isn't sure where he wants to live.

Characteristics of family members

Dan Harper is a serious, soft-spoken, introspective man who works as a pharmacist in a large drugstore. He is small in build, lisps slightly, and appears polite and thoughtful. He seems very concerned that others realize how hard he is working to raise his two sons and empathizes with the instability they have experienced in their lives because of his and Ann's marital troubles. He sets aside some time for the boys every evening, for example. He is pleased that they do well academically and is especially proud of Ted's achievements. He hopes Ted will go on to university and a professional career. He realizes that Ted is high-strung and says that he was also sensitive as a child. He is not very concerned about Julian's dress preferences, regarding them as passing curiosities. He admires Julian's sensitivity and artistic talents and maintains that not all children have to be "macho athlete types." Dan appears to be bottling up considerable anger at Ann, who he says is going through a second adolescence.

Ann Harper is an average-looking woman who dresses and makes herself up to look flashy and attractive. She is dramatic in voice and gesture. Ann works as a legal secretary and says that raising a teenage girl is not easy. She worries that Julian and Ted will turn out to be as joyless as their father and admits that she has difficulty controlling Lisa. She says that Lisa idolizes her father and that he has turned Lisa against her. She also blames the friends Lisa chooses for introducing her to drugs and being a bad influence on her. She wants to raise her daughter and be available to her but does not intend to allow Lisa to destroy her social life. Apparently Ann dates frequently, has men sleep over, and takes weekend trips while she makes arrangements for Lisa to stay with girlfriends.

Lisa presents as a reasonably attractive, surly, adolescent girl who wants more freedom, less interference in her life, and regards her mother as "bitchy" and her mother's boyfriends as "losers." She says she wants to live with her father but that he maintains this isn't possible. Lisa feels no particular closeness to her brothers.

Julian is a very slight 10-year-old who speaks in a high-pitched voice and appears effeminate. His interests are largely artistic; he plays the piano and draws and paints. He has few friends but seems fairly happy. He admits that he likes to clown around with women's clothing and silky materials but doesn't see the harm in it.

Ted is more serious and tense. Very concerned about pleasing others and being evaluated by them, he spends his time reading and works hard at school. Ted says he doesn't mind living with his dad but misses his mother. He frequently visits her but complains that she is usually busy or not at home. He says his best friend is his brother, and he has some other friends at school.

School and community

Julian, in the fifth grade, and Ted, in the third, are both of concern to the school. Ted is near the top of his class in grades, and Julian receives "B" grades while being acclaimed as excellent in art. Lisa is in the eighth grade, and her grades are poor. She is regarded as sassy by her teachers and not working up to her potential. There is concern about the quality of her friends and the lack of supervision of her by her mother.

Case discussion

Consultants: Dr. Richard Berry, Dr. Gerald Casey, Dr. Howard Irving

Interviewer: Let us turn to my familiar question. What additional information would you recommend that the worker get in this case?

Berry: What struck me is the school's concern that one of the boys is asking too many questions and seems to be exhibiting a high anxiety level. There is also concern about the other boy's feminine behavior. The school is seeing it as a problem, but I am not sure how often these incidents have been happening. There is some suggestion that his "gay" mannerisms have been present for a long time, but I don't know whether the problem is in terms of how he relates with other children or how he relates with his teachers or his parents. The parents don't seem to recognize it as a problem. I don't perceive a willingness on the part of the family to recognize that they are encountering difficulties, other than that the spouses are blaming each other. What is the likelihood of the family engaging earnestly in any kind of therapeutic endeavor? That would be the first thing that I would want to check out with the parents.

Interviewer: How would you assess that?

Berry: In a more in-depth interview. I want to know what they define as the problem as opposed to what the school is presenting as a problem. Whether you can get the two parents together is questionable. There are indications that they have frequent contact around the children. I would also want more information on Lisa's behaviors. It sounds as if she is a child who is getting into more serious problems with drug use, perhaps promiscuity, and general defiance of her mother. I don't need specific testing or assessments beyond answers to these questions. I would try to get the school records, but that would be the extent of it at this point.

Interviewer: Howard?

Irving: I find that in most postdivorce situations, the parents are the architects of the family system. I would start by wanting to know more about the parents in relation to how they see one another's role in this unusual family situation and what the wife says about the husband as a parent and what the husband says about the wife as a parent and what the kids say about each parent. We don't have a very clear picture of what is going on, so I would like more assessment material from the parents and from the children, maybe in a family group meeting.

Interviewer: Okay, Gerry?

Casey: I think that the assessment would be incomplete without individual meetings with the children, as well as a family meeting, as well as a meeting with the couple, and even meeting with the adults individually.

Irving: I agree. I would see each parent individually, because you get blaming rather than honesty when you bring them together. I agree with Gerry that I would also see the kids individually, the parents together, and the whole family. I would do all combinations of the family unit to get a complete picture.

Casey: There is one further assessment I would consider, and that is a possible referral to a gender identity clinic. I have some mixed feelings about that, but there is a sufficient concern at the diagnostic level to suggest that, without active intervention, Julian stands a good likelihood of heading toward transsexuality, homosexuality. There are arguments toward intervening and not intervening. There's the values argument . . . but I think the parents need to know that there is some concern.

Interviewer: What kind of special assessment are you talking about?

Casey: I guess it would be an in-depth look at his psychosexual development.

Interviewer: Okay, let us move on to talk about modalities of treatment. Gerry, would you like to say something?

Casey: I think that one of the first things that would happen would be mediation work with mother and father since they have recently split up, and when they split up the first time corresponds with the boys' difficulty. I would want to move them toward a parental role rather than a fighting spouses role, get them to be more responsible as parents. It is likely that visitation guidelines are not very clear. Certainly the undermining of each other is quite prominent, so I would want to cool them out to get some order.

Interviewer: Would you do that through couples therapy?

Casey: It would not be couples therapy. . . . I would be flexible and probably introduce the children, but I would feel quite free to kick them out because ultimately the parents have to deal with each other.

Interviewer: Howard?

Irving: I agree with Gerry. I would work with the remnants of the emotional ties between the spouses. I would like to bring them together as a couple and help them disengage properly. I would bring the kids in periodically to set up the family structure properly and work out issues of authority, responsibility, and support.

Berry: I would want the parents to come to some agreement and use a consistent approach in dealing with the children. Right now they have a rescue system going on whereby father is reinforcing Lisa's acting-out. She wants to cut up, and he provides a refuge for her.

Interviewer: Would any of you want to involve any community resources or a social agency in this case?

Casey: One might consider a separation group experience, depending on what you find with regard to the parents' adjustment to singlehood. One of the issues that would likely be brought up would be the boy's effeminacy. This is quite a classic presentation. If the parents were to agree that they would like the boy to avoid social stigma and conflicts in later life, that would be a whole other arm of treatment and might well include individual treatment for him.

Interviewer: There is agreement that one of the early major tasks is to shift the parents away from fighting and assume more cooperative parenting roles. How would you advise a worker to do that?

Casey: I guess you give a fair amount of straight information that this is damaging to the children and that they are being irresponsible. Then work with them and give them lots of strokes.

Irving: I would use a little paradoxical intervention. I would first assure them that they are stuck with each other and that isn't going to change, so they need to set aside their mutual disappointment in the best interests of the children. Then I would assert that it's an extremely difficult thing to do and not too many people can handle it, and I would inquire about what they think they can do about this awesome task.

Interviewer: So you would do some challenging and paradoxing?

Irving: Right. I would give them permission to dislike each other, but they have to rise above that for the sake of their kids. If they can't do that, then I would introduce the idea of having legal representation for their children, because if the kids' rights are not going to be upheld by the parents, they should be upheld by somebody. It is a bit of a threat, but it sometimes clarifies issues when parents get so caught up in their own legal struggles that they forget the rights of children. In this case, Lisa is asking for a change in custody, so you might say "If you are not going to resolve it, we may have to get her a lawyer." That throws the reality on the situation that it isn't only their problem but that the kids have a problem too. That usually helps.

Interviewer: Did you have some thoughts on how to get these adults to agree on parenting?

Berry: I was thinking of contracting. It would be helpful if they could come to an agreement on how they are going to work with each other. The paradoxical approach should be very effective to give them a challenge. They sound like fairly well-educated people who should be able to grasp the realities that confront them.

Interviewer: Beyond that, what concrete suggestions would you have for the worker?

Irving: One of the problems concerns the openness and flexibility of the custody and access business, and I think that they are having difficulty handling the responsibility. We need to contract, or build an agreement, that spells out the nature of visiting, who has custody, when, how, and so forth. That kind of commitment can't be left flexible with these people. I think they would screw around with it. Everything needs to be put in concrete, very specific terms so that they know what the expectations are.

Berry: I would also look at involving an outside, community-oriented group such as Boy Scouts to give the kids some role models.

Casey: There are some curious findings in the literature on feminine boys. They prefer girls as playmates, they avoid rough and tumble games, they like to wear dresses, they really do like the frills, they easily take on the opposite sex role. Their parents are inclined to be quite theatrical, so the treatment they recommend is to push them toward appropriate sexual behavior. This is quite a lengthy process, and I do think there is a value issue involved. . . . Father is saying he is not concerned about it and he is described as being a little eccentric. That is probably a touchy issue in the treatment planning.

Interviewer: Okay, what about the other children? Do you have specific recommendations with respect to any of them?

Irving: I think the daughter has much too much power in this family. She seems to be controlling both parents. I think she needs some individual work and eventually some work with the parents to help her realize that she is not omnipotent. She has them running from one to the other and I think that is probably scary for her, and I think that is why she is acting-out the way she is. She is asking for the controls that these parents are afraid to give her in the fear that they will lose her. I think somebody has to move in quickly to stop her playing one off against the other.

Berry: The material that we have suggests that the girl is asking to live with her father. It sounds as though mother needs a lot of freedom and may not be in a position to be a good parenting model for her daughter. I think we need to look at whether she wants to be in a mother role.

Interviewer: So perhaps before trying to get these people to work together as parents, there would need to be some clarification of parental roles individually. Are there any specific recommendations with respect to Ted, the high achiever?

Casey: I think a good part of that is a reaction to the chaotic situation. I would want to monitor it and be sure that it is not more complicated.

Berry: Father likes to see the child achieving and has high expectations for him. He may need to be made aware of the boy's anxiety with regard to not meeting father's expectations.

Irving: The school might be able to help the father understand his problem and also to work with the kid around his high anxiety level in terms of getting "A"s. I think he is a "B" student as it is. But I would think the school could come in and work with him.

Berry: It may be that father is a perfectionist who, in the boy's perception, always does things perfectly. Ted needs to see father fail a few times or make mistakes, and that everything is still okay. Father needs to be able to communicate that to the boy.

Interviewer: The recommendations you are all making are focused on individual children and their individual needs. Would any of you recommend or consider some kind of sibling group work?

Berry: I think it would be very helpful. I think that these children, in part, are reacting to the anxiety and chaos expressed between the parents. They are probably not feeling a lot of support. If they can be given permission to express their feelings and give support to each other that would strengthen the kids. Ted and Lisa would benefit a lot from that, and it might help to reduce Julian's anxiety.

Interviewer: Howard, what is your reaction to that?

Irving: I would see that intervention coming a little later in the treatment program. I think it would be very difficult for these kids to improve as long as the parents are the way they are, no matter what kind of group you put them in. These kids don't even know where they are going to be living. I think their behavior, other than Julian's feminine behavior, is an appropriate response to a very chaotic situation.

Interviewer: Gerry, do you have any comments on the sibling approach?

Casey: I would conceptualize treatment as a flexible family therapy approach. I would think the kids would have some difficulty if they were held in a position of siblings on an ongoing basis because of the suggestion of betrayal and ganging up on their parents.

Interviewer: Let us talk about special problems that you would want to warn the worker about in this kind of a case. Howard?

Irving: I don't know about special problems, but I would worry if the conflict between the parents continues. I would then worry about more acting-out behavior by the kids in any form. It looks like the next thing for Lisa would be heavier drug taking; for Julian, more acting-out in terms of his sexual identity problem; and for Ted, more anxiety about not achieving. The parents can easily continue to undermine the whole bloody thing. You have to be careful not to be fooled by the parents because they are articulate, they are bright, and they know what to say. So I would like to see somebody have close contact with the whole family, just in case what the parents are saying and what they are doing might differ.

Interviewer: If you saw an increase in the seriousness of the acting-out behaviors and an intensification of the conflict between parents, what would you recommend that the worker do?

Irving: I think I would recommend a referral for neglect to an appropriate child welfare agency. I take that as a last resort. If the parents can't handle the responsibility of parenting, no matter how intelligent and articulate they are, then you have to act in the best interest of the children and bring in a court order.

Interviewer: Are there other potential problems for the worker to consider?

Berry: I see two issues, deciding where these kids are going to live and how the parents are going to work together. If they can't resolve these issues, the problems will intensify. If I saw that coming, I would recommend that Lisa try living outside the family. I think that she is at an age where she is highly vulnerable to more serious acting-out behavior if she were left in that chaotic situation. I am not sure if Julian's behavior, on the other hand, is related to the family situation.

Casey: There is one other possibility and that is to go for a larger unit. We still have two grandparents on his side and the mother on her side, so one might call a pow-wow with them.

Interviewer: Would you consider a network approach?

Casey: I personally would not, although I could easily consider seeing the grandparents.

Interviewer: Involving the extended family. Okay, Gerry, would you comment on the characteristics of a worker you would like to see take on this kind of case?

Casey: I read it as a mixed prognosis of some duration that could involve various crises, so I would want somebody pretty steady and someone older.

Interviewer: Dick?

Berry: I would want a skilled family therapist working with the two parents. They have been married twice, and on both occasions it has fallen apart. Whether you can get them to make any kind of lasting resolutions, even to the point of separating their own needs from those of the children, is highly debatable. I think this will require a very skilled therapist.

Interviewer: Howard?

Irving: I would see three phases with three different therapists. The initial one would be somebody who could help them separate properly. I don't think that has ever been done at an emotional level. Then I would see bringing in somebody to help mediate the legal aspects of custody and access. Then I would use an ongoing family therapist to help this family to work out something better than what they have. The same therapist might do individual therapy with any one of the kids who might need it at any particular point and time.

Interviewer: Can you roll those three therapists into one?

Irving: I don't think so because they conflict. If you are working on the separation, that will get in the way of mediation issues because there are confidential things that will come out of phase one. That kind of a thing.

Interviewer: What goals and outcomes would you want the worker to focus on?

Casey: I would like to see the parents parenting. I would like to see them "decoupled." I would like the children to be without symptoms or nearly without symptoms. Those are the major ingredients.

Interviewer: Howard?

Irving: I would agree. Getting them to separate properly, having an amicable mediation, and making sure that the kids are not acting-out the way they are acting-out now.

Interviewer: Dick?

Berry: I couldn't ask for more than that.

Interviewer: Would you also comment about your expectations for success in this case?

Berry: I have a pessimistic feeling regarding this family. The parents are twice married and divorced and haven't yet been able to resolve their differences.

Casey: Yes, one would have to get in and see whether it is like that. I suspect that they have difficulty getting together and being apart.

Interviewer: Howard?

Irving: I am more optimistic because I think that these people haven't been dealt with properly. I don't think a highly structured, tough approach has been taken with these people. To deescalate their conflict, you may have to create a conflict for them, so that the two of them have to rally together. So far it has been the two of them fighting between themselves "for the sake of their kids." "Now you are going to fight us for the sake of your children, and you either shape up or we are going to move in and do something about it." I think that might do it because these people have the capability, if one can break their emotional pattern.

Casey: I would be somewhere in the middle, less optimistic than Howard, and less pessimistic than Dick.

Irving: I think a lot of cases fail when the therapist tries to get parents to be friendly and helpful to each other. As soon as you give them permission to hate each other and instruct them that the only reason they are going to have any contact is for the sake of the children, you tend to see a different kind of thing happen. Once they understand that they don't have to like each other, then they can get on with doing a good job of parenting.

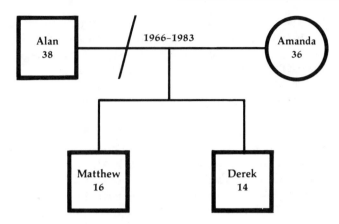

THE RIPLEY FAMILY

Identifying information

The Ripley family consists of Alan Ripley, his wife, Amanda, and their two sons. The Ripleys have recently separated, and the boys live with their mother. Mrs. Ripley is concerned about Derek's depressed state and his potential for suicide. The incident that precipitated contact with the agency was Derek's ingesting about a dozen aspirin and being taken to the hospital.

History of problem

Mrs. Ripley claims that Derek has always been a relatively quiet and isolated boy and moodier than his brother Matthew. When the Ripleys announced their intention to divorce two months ago, Derek became very upset. Since that time he has been belligerent toward his mother, difficult for her to control, and has threatened to kill himself. Derek wants his father, who moved out a month ago, to return home. Several suicidal threats culminated in his taking the aspirin from mother's medicine cabinet and swallowing them when she was out. On her return, Derek volunteered that he had taken the pills, and she rushed him to the hospital. His stomach was pumped, and the doctor recommended that she seek treatment for Derek. At this time Mrs. Ripley is feeling anxious and helpless. Mr. Ripley minimizes the suicide risk and believes that with patience and a firm hand Derek will be all right.

Marital and family history

An only child, Mrs. Ripley was indulged and overprotected by her parents. She met Alan Ripley when she was 12 years old, and they grew up in the same neighborhood. She always considered Alan's family her second family and spent a lot of time in their home. On graduating from high school, Amanda took a secretarial job and married Alan two years later. The marriage was satisfactory at the beginning, in part, according to Amanda, because she felt so comfortable with Alan's parents with whom they spent a lot of time. Alan and Amanda's relationship has been deteriorating during the past few years, however. During this time they have not been communicating well. Alan has been staying away from home, and Amanda suspects he has been seeing other women. After many years of tolerating this unhappy marriage, Amanda finally announced that she was filing for divorce. Alan reluctantly agreed and moved out one month ago. One reason Amanda resisted initiating divorce proceedings earlier is that her parents were pressuring her to remain with Alan and maintain the family for the children's sake. She returned to work as a secretary six months ago and plans to continue to work and raise the boys.

Mr. Ripley was the middle child in a family of three boys. His family was close until his father was killed in a hunting accident seven years ago. He now has less contact with his mother and brothers, lives by himself in an apartment, and is seeing another woman. He sees his sons on alternate weekends.

Characteristics of family members

Amanda Ripley presents as a woman who is struggling to assert her independence and prove to herself that she can competently care for her family. She now feels very helpless and overwhelmed about how to handle Derek. Vulnerable to criticism, she finds it difficult to cope with him when he yells at her or has angry outbursts. She also feels that Alan is not supporting her by responding appropriately to Derek's depression and suicide threats. Amanda has a number of women friends. She can also call on her own parents but resists doing so because they criticize and dominate her.

Alan Ripley, who works as a tool and die maker, was interviewed separately. He is articulate and presents as controlled and serious. He believes that there is no serious suicide risk with Derek and that he will come to accept the divorce. He thinks that Amanda is being melodramatic and overprotective of Derek. Alan appears to be angry at her but determined to reconstruct his own life without her. He conveys a sense of responsibility for his sons but little apparent warmth.

Derek is a blond, blue-eyed 14-year-old who is a little smaller than average for his age. When spoken to, he looks at the floor and appears depressed. He is alternately tearful and angry and is clearly upset by his parents' divorce plans. Both boys have always been especially close to their mother. Mr. Ripley has not been a particularly devoted or available father, although he has taken his sons on outings and played ball with them. Now Derek is very upset with his mother and blames her for the marital problems, saying that she had always criticized his father. Derek is afraid that he will not see his father again. Although Alan has reassured him that this is not so, father probably does reinforce the fact that the divorce is Amanda's idea. Derek says that he was not serious when he took the aspirin and that when he really wants to kill himself, he'll do it right.

Derek and Matthew do not get along very well. They are very different in appearance and personality. Matthew is tall, dark, and personable. Derek resents the fact that Matthew studies so much and does well in school. Matthew has more friends than Derek and is more outgoing. He thinks Derek is immature and not seriously suicidal. He is handling his parents' separation much better than Derek is and supports his mother in her decision. Matthew appears to be the favored child with both parents; at least, they do not worry about him.

School and community

Derek is in the ninth grade and has generally been an average or somewhat less than average student academically. Lately he has been falling behind in his schoolwork and becoming more disruptive in the classroom. His teacher does not regard him as a behavior problem, however. He is seen as fearful and somewhat of a loner. The school is aware that the parents have been having problems and regard these problems as affecting Derek's performance at school.

Case discussion

Consultants: Ms. Sandra Birenbaum, Dr. Joseph Kluger

Interviewer: This is the Ripley family.

Kluger: When I read Ripley, I said this is the "Ripley's Believe It or Not." This is definitely "believe it" because it's understandable.

Birenbaum: That's right.

Kluger: Well, I don't think that any of them are presenting with serious psychopathology. In general, they continue to be fairly active in whatever work they do. I am using the term *work* very loosely. They function reasonably well with the exception of the identified patient, who has dropped off as part of his depressive reaction to his parents' separation. I think whenever there is depression and a suicide attempt in an adolescent, it's serious, in the sense that one can't ignore it; but I think it's a mild case in the sense that it's reactive and the functioning all along has been reasonably good. There is no model for suicide or self-destructive behavior in the family. There are no major difficulties in the relationships. I say major difficulties in the sense of extremely needy folks, so I would say we are dealing with a fairly promising case in that response to treatment will be quick and positive.

Interviewer: So you are seeing a lot of strength in this family.

Birenbaum: I'd agree with Jerry. I think it's probably reactive to the situation. There is nothing to suggest otherwise. The only thing that makes me a little suspicious is the death of father's father in a hunting accident. That may have been some kind of bad judgment. I'm not sure, but apart from that everything seems fairly intact, and we have no reason to suspect that there is any deep pathology.

Interviewer: O.K. Is there anything else that you would want to know?

Birenbaum: I would want some previous history about Derek. What kind of a kid was he prior to the separation? I would want to discount any possibility of him having been a depressed child with lots of difficulties that we haven't heard about. The other thing that I like to do in working with a suicidal adolescent, even though it was only 12 aspirins, is to seek a second opinion with a psychiatric assessment.

Interviewer: What would you be asking in this individual assessment of Derek?

Birenbaum: I'd be checking whether there is a suicide risk at this point in time. And I think we have to look at it in depth during the assessment.

Kluger: The alternative is a personality assessment done by a psychologist. In either case, we're talking about the degree of depression and the nature of the child's functioning beforehand. We have some indication that he tends to deal with things by withdrawal, which makes him a little more vulnerable to loss such as occurred when his father moved out. But I suspect this child is not seriously disturbed, that his difficulties need to be taken seriously, but that he is not an immediate suicide risk again.

Interviewer: Let's talk about types of treatment interventions.

Birenbaum: This is always a trick when I am dealing with separated families and I fluctuate from time to time depending on the family. My preference would be to bring them in, all of them, even though mother and father are separated, and work with the parents and the boys around the separation. That would be my first thing. If that was too tricky, and many times separations are very touchy, I might have to work with the parents until I felt they were ready to come into a family session. I would not ultimately stay with the intact family except to deal with the separation and some kind of structuring for the future. Then, if need be, I would deal with mother and the two boys and then probably move to individual therapy for Derek.

Interviewer: You're implying that the separation has not been adequately dealt with in the family, and I'd like to come back to that when we talk about strategies. In terms of an overall approach, I hear you moving from some family assessment meetings to some subsystem meetings with the boys and the mother, and then perhaps some individual therapy. Jerry, how about you?

Kluger: I would suggest individual counseling for the child, probably a combination of supportive and interpretive counseling, bearing in mind that he is a teenager, so the amount of interpretation one does has to be judicious and limited. One of the central themes, I agree, is separation and the reality that there are issues that continue to be unresolved but one can live with. I would have some kind of parent counseling and/or family counseling and, again, it would depend on how well the parents could cooperate and come together around that. If they found it very difficult to be cooperative, if they were destructive, abusive, or unsupportive, if they were undercutting each other, if they were embroiled in their own difficulties, then it wouldn't be helpful to see them together.

Interviewer: What would you do instead?

Kluger: I'd meet with them separately at least once, and perhaps in some combination with the kids. One of the things that needs to be done is for both parents to say to the child that this is the way it has to be. Father left reluctantly. One gets the impression that he clearly pointed out that he didn't want to leave and that it's all mom's fault, which reinforces the child's wanting to vent his resentment and hostility onto mother. It makes it very difficult, and I think it's one of the crucial issues in the separation process that needs to be looked into.

Interviewer: You're both identifying some ambiguity and some hanging issues in the separation that need to be worked out. Let's talk concretely about that. What would you envisage that would help this family deal with the ambiguous issues in the separation?

Kluger: There are a number of ways to go. Let's assume the parents were reasonable and they were prepared to come together for the kids.

Birenbaum: There is nothing in this file to indicate that they are so angry at each other that they are not going to come together.

Kluger: I'd get them to articulate how they dealt with, or tried to deal with, their parting. Did they talk to each other? Who heard what? What were their expectations? When did they first feel that things weren't right in the family context? I think that would do it.

Birenbaum: When you bring them in as a family, I think you immediately have to state that although you are bringing them in together, you understand there has been a separation and that people are living in different places. Although this separation has occurred, however, they share a purpose in coming together as parents. I think it speaks to their strength that they are able to come together and try to sort out this boy's problems. I'd begin on that basis. Then move toward helping them to talk about the changes and how they are going to deal with those. The reality is that at this point this family is living apart and maybe they'll get back together, but right now this is the way it is. And although they are separated, they are still parents and that part will never change; the rest is negotiable.

Kluger: If there is any room for the parents to minimize the blame in the child's eyes, they ought to make every effort to do so and at the same time reassure the kids that they still care for them actively through what they do and what they say.

Birenbaum: Precisely. I'd also want to work with the guilt the children would have about the separation. Kids don't cause their parents' separation, but they think they do. And clearly this little boy must have some of those feelings.

Interviewer: How long would you work on this?

Kluger: I think it'd be fairly short-term, within six months. I think the prognosis is very good. I think we're talking about 95% positive outcome. This is the kind of child who can really go places when he feels support and can feel safe expressing some of his resentment. In terms of individual counseling with the child, I suppose I would take three avenues of approach. One is supportive, two is interpretive, and three is cognitive. A very cognitive, problem-solving approach.

Interviewer: Sandy, you had a reaction to Jerry's short-term, six-month plan.

Birenbaum: I would agree with everything Jerry said except the six months. I wouldn't see it as desirable or appropriate to work with this family as an intact family for more than six to eight sessions. I think that's putting a quality of unreality in it. I think that there are things that we have to sort out in terms of roles, because it's important for this boy, particularly, to have some kind of predictability around visiting with father and getting support from the parents. Then I would move to the family if the need is for the family— mother and boys or father and boys.

Kluger: When I say six months, I mean within six months. That would be an absolute outside in terms of any kind of contact, and I'd probably taper off and meet the child every week, once a week, and then after three months, every second week, and certainly by six months it may be once a month. As part of the termination process, I would leave it up to the child to decide whether he needs or wants to come back.

Birenbaum: How about the initiation process? My concern is that if you are going to initiate it and suggest that the child have individual therapy, there is a message implicit in that. Would you leave it up to the child to say that he needs more, or would you suggest it?

Kluger: I'd vary it. It depends on the child and the family. With some families, I say that their child has to come in. The child comes in and doesn't want to talk and I say "That's up to you." But if I talk, they listen and respond occasionally to what I say. I might point out initially "I understand you don't want to come, but the reasons for your coming are. . . . So since we're together I'm going to share some ideas with you. You can let me know if I'm on or off."

Birenbaum: I think it's quite possible that this child and family will be able to make enough gains so that we wouldn't have to go to individual therapy at this time. It's a difficult age to work with. We'll know very quickly whether there's more to be worked on, but I'd leave it to him.

Kluger: I suspect that his tendency to withdraw affects his social relationships and reflects his overall adjustment, not simply his adjustment to the current crisis. I think there needs to be some input over and above the issues of the current crisis to see where this kid stands and what concerns he has. So that's why I'd want the opportunity of talking with him as an individual.

Birenbaum: In any family assessment, I would do an individual assessment with this kind of a situation, but had we not had this crisis with the pills, I don't think this is a child who would have had any individual therapy.

Kluger: Yeah. Then you have to ask yourself how come he reacted in this way. There were several warnings. First he threatened a number of times, then he did it, then he told his mother. This kid is dependent and the mother has been overprotective; the father, despite his best intentions, has been a little uninvolved and unavailable.

Birenbaum: If we're really good family therapists, we'll try to understand this child's behavior in the context of what the father and mother do. It would be fascinating if this child's behavior would bring the father and the mother back together to deal around him.

Kluger: Well, that's the intention.

Birenbaum: That's right. So, he may not be so sick. He may be clever, as children are. I don't know. But, you're right. There certainly are other clues and his feeling of being less than the chosen child with his family, but I wouldn't rush to give him family therapy.

Kluger: I would want to check out some of the typical tasks that he will be facing in the future and try to predict how he will cope with change, given the event and sense of loss he has experienced around the separation. What I am saying is that I would want to look at his adjustment over a longer period of time.

Interviewer: Derek is described as a loner and somewhat fearful in school. Are you concerned about his social skills? Is that an area that you would want to follow up in some way?

Birenbaum: Yeah. I guess the thing that we didn't check out and probably should have if we had been very thorough is how this child has functioned in school until now both in the classroom and with respect to peers.

Kluger: When the early adolescent is depressed, he usually has difficulty in concentration, lack of or reduction in motivation, so the barometer of school performance is important.

Interviewer: How would you gauge how he is doing in school?

Birenbaum: I think previous report cards will tell you, and I think you ask the teacher how this child gets along with his friends and what he does during recess. Does he have lunch with the girls? It's amazing what a wealth of information teachers have when specifically asked.

Interviewer: So you would be in direct touch with his teachers or teacher?

Kluger: I would certainly be in touch with them once, and I would want to cover four areas. I typically do this—I'd like to know about the child's functioning in academic, social, emotional, and behavioral areas, and I list them that way. If it seems that these are not major difficulties, then I'd go on the straight term report card. I would want a copy of each of those for at least the remainder of the school year and probably the first term of the next year.

Interviewer: Let's look at the potential for special problems in this case. What might go wrong? What should the worker who is dealing with this family be on the lookout for?

Kluger: I think that the child may minimize concerns in the face of being embarrassed, in the face of being angry about being involved with any kind of professional person despite the underlying dependency, which I think is there. Along with that, what he has to say ought to be checked out by behavioral observation and other peoples' reports. It's not enough to rely on what the child says. I would also very clearly state concrete goals for individual counseling with the child. I would say "What do you think would be a good sign that you are on top of things?"

Interviewer: Why are you making a particular point of that?

Kluger: It is not enough to take his not threatening suicide as a sign that he is well-adjusted. He has a tendency to withdraw in the face of stress and I am concerned about that. Making the grade is pretty important from a social point of view, too.

Interviewer: So you are warning the worker not to get so focused on the suicide gesture as to lose track of this boy's general adjustment?

Kluger: And not just in the family context. In the social and academic context as well.

Birenbaum: My concern is with the parents' sabotaging each other. I think we've already had some indication they are going to do that. One is minimizing and one is maximizing, so I'd try to bring that into some kind of a balance. The other piece that I'd focus on is getting the family to deal with their own pain and stress, which I suspect they push down so that this child is expressing it on their behalf. I'd want to get them to be able to share more openly, and I think that will make it easier for the boy also to share some of the things he's inclined to push away.

Kluger: The mom is trying very, very hard to make it on her own. She's striving for independence both from her husband and from parents whom she finds dominating and controlling. I think it's very important that in the process the mother continue to share responsibility for parenting with the father. The typical finding is that two years after a separation the parent who lives apart has dropped off in his contact, so the initial working out is crucial in terms of what the long-term picture will be like. I think it's important that mom be rewarded for working hard to keep her family up and provide for them, but at the same time not to cut the father off from any parenting that he may be able to and want to provide.

Interviewer: Okay. If the parents start to undermine each other, what would you do?

Birenbaum: Make them stop. *(Laughter)*

Interviewer: How do you do this?

Birenbaum: I'd just say that what you're doing isn't good for your kids. It's all very well for you to be angry at each other, and you're mad because she threw you out and you're going to have to behave like responsible adults and I don't expect you to carry on in this way. Clear and simple. You don't dump on your kids if you don't get your alimony payments or whatever it might be. I am pretty rigid about that. I find it's a very tense time, and people get very silly in their way of dealing with each other.

Kluger: I agree with that. The other thing that I think I would add is to say to father that a suicide attempt at any time is serious. How Derek has dealt with it is not how the majority of kids deal with it, and the tendency to hurt himself in the process speaks in part to how he feels about himself.

Interviewer: Are you suggesting you would use that as leverage in terms of getting the parents more directly involved?

Kluger: Well, I would consider using it if the father were minimizing any concerns about his son. I would simply use my position as a professional and state clearly what I think.

Interviewer: What kind of worker would you like to see dealing with this family?

Birenbaum: A very directive worker. Someone who is comfortable with separation. Someone who can literally say to the adults "You're not behaving in an adult fashion." And someone who is not frightened by suicide. You need someone who is fairly solid to deal with this particular unit.

Kluger: I would probably encourage Derek to have a male as an individual therapist.

That's less important if the father's relationship with the boy is reasonably good and can be improved. It's more important for him to have a male therapist if his relationship with father continues to be strained.

Interviewer: Fine. Let's talk about goals. What should the worker be shooting for?

Birenbaum: Well, one thing you'd want to work out, of course, is the separation. The whole business of how it happened, the guilt, some kind of structural planning for the future. That is essential here.

Kluger: I would set as a goal this child's capacity for dealing more effectively with the disappointment in loss and I would also want to have him more involved with peers. I am not talking numbers here. I am talking quality of relationship. He may be the kind of child who makes one good friend. He may not be the kind of child who's a socialite or who goes to parties or becomes involved with groups, but I think he needs to have some kind of fairly solid relationship with peers to deal with the general issue of separation and individuation.

Interviewer: How would you measure his ability to cope with loss?

Kluger: There are a number of ways to measure that. One could look at the degree of withdrawal in the face of disappointment, literally, behavioral withdrawal. Does he leave situations in which he's uncomfortable? Does he withdraw into his own thoughts even though he doesn't leave the situation? Does he interact less? Is he able to articulate what's bugging him? Can he share those things with someone he feels close to, or does he keep it inside? I'd look for change in three areas—I'd look at behavior, I'd look at attitudes, I'd look at affect.

Birenbaum: In the same way that Jerry has set a goal of helping this boy to deal with the loss, I think there's a mourning process they have to go through. Hopefully, they'll have some comfort in talking about their pain and anger. I doubt if they have been able to deal with that as a group in any way. Also I guess you have to help mother deal with her overprotective feelings toward this boy.

Interviewer: You'd like to see her letting go more?

Birenbaum: Yeah, or at least starting to.

Kluger: It's the other side of the coin in the sense of encouraging this child to develop and enhance his peer relationships.

Interviewer: The general tone, I think, of our case discussion around this family has sounded pretty optimistic to me. Would you like to comment on prognosis?

Kluger: It's very good.

Birenbaum: One of the things that doesn't relate to prognosis necessarily is that these boys have become polarized with mother and I would want to reallocate that a little bit. Mother has kept father from these boys, and he's played a part as well. I'd like to reframe it in such a way that father feels he has something to give the boys.

Kluger: It's possible that the father would, in fact, develop a better relationship with them now than he has had previously.

Birenbaum: At least he'll have them on his own.

Interviewer: Do you have a prognosis?

Birenbaum: I think they're O.K. He'll do fine.

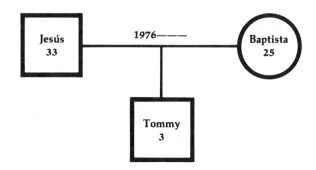

THE LOPEZ FAMILY

Identifying information

The Lopez family consists of Jesús and Baptista Lopez and their son, Tommy. The parents approached the mental health center because Tommy is aggressive, defiant, and has unpredictable tantrums. When frustrated and angry, he swears, screams, and throws household objects at his mother. Tommy hurts his peers and has no friends. Both parents agree that he is very attention-seeking.

History of problem

Tommy was born six weeks prematurely. He was conceived shortly after mother had had a miscarriage, and Mrs. Lopez reports that he was sickly as an infant, with frequent colds and cranky periods. Developmental milestones were reached within normal age ranges. Father claims Tommy is not a problem for him but that his wife indulges Tommy and can't control him. Following an intake interview, mother called the interviewer and reported that she is severely abused by her husband, that he threatens to beat or kill her, and that they have had no sexual relations for two years. Mother also acknowledged that Tommy sleeps in her bed and that her husband sleeps on a couch in the living room.

Marital and family history

The parents met and courted in Mexico before they emigrated. Both families of origin remain in Mexico, and Mrs. Lopez has not seen her family since she left Mexico in 1978. She claims her family pressured her to marry Mr. Lopez and that she was doubtful about the marriage from the start. Baptista has three younger brothers and an older sister. She feels she was very close to her mother, whom she now misses intensely. She describes her father as a kind, gentle man.

Mr. Lopez comes from a family with seven children. His father is dead and was described by Jesús as quiet, withdrawn, and a heavy drinker. When drunk, he would become loud and aggressive and often beat Jesús and his siblings. His mother is still alive and visited the Lopez family two years ago.

Jesús felt that Baptista was cold and rude to his mother during that visit and often reminds her of this.

Mr. and Mrs. Lopez, when seen together, acknowledge no marital problems. As noted above, however, Mrs. Lopez privately claimed extreme marital stress. She also felt that her husband had totally rejected Tommy and has nothing to do with him at home. Mother has frequently considered separation and divorce, but has not followed through. At one point, she sought counseling from a distress center for women and was put in touch with a lawyer. However, she felt her husband behaved better after that and took no legal action. After several months of individual counseling at the distress center, Baptista discontinued this.

Characteristics of family members

Mr. Lopez presents himself as polite and guarded. He works as a mechanic in an auto repair shop and sporadically moonlights as a carpenter. He often spends time out of the home with male friends and expects his wife to take care of their apartment and child. He feels his wife needs to learn how to handle Tommy more effectively but is dubious that the mental health center will help this. Mr. Lopez has been observed to play appropriately and warmly with Tommy and seems amused by some of his son's defiance of Baptista.

Mrs. Lopez, on the other hand, appears high-strung and emotional. She is easily moved to tears and reports that she often screams at her husband and becomes involved in physical fights with him. When not agitated, Mrs. Lopez wears an air of depression, looks glum, and sighs dramatically. Super-stitious, she wonders whether her husband may have placed a curse on Tommy. She speaks English haltingly and spends almost all her time at home. The family's home life is described as chaotic and tense, with fre-quent angry eruptions between husband and wife. That both parents are using Tommy and his behavior as a weapon with which to attack each other is obvious. Tommy shows an obvious attachment to his mother but also goes easily to his father and does not appear intimidated or apprehensive with him.

At an individual interview, Tommy flits quickly from one activity to another and seems to lack persistence at tasks. He deliberately tests limits and explores adult reactions to destructive activity and to running out of the room. However, he does accept firm limits and was able to react playfully to the interviewer. All in all, he seems to be a friendly, active, and restless boy of average intelligence.

School and community

Tommy has not attended nursery school or any day care program. He will be entering junior kindergarten next year. As noted, he does not get along well with other children and usually winds up hitting them. Peers in the apart-ment building avoid him, and, in fact, Tommy spends little time out of the apartment. Mother occasionally takes him to the play area behind their building but complains that he always gets into trouble there. He has run into the street at times and once narrowly avoided being run over by a truck.

Special assessments

No formal assessments have been conducted with Tommy. His pediatrician reports no current abnormalities.

Case discussion

Consultants: Dr. Gerald Beckerle, Dr. Gregor Finlayson

Interviewer: Let's talk first about missing or additional information. What else would you like to know?

Finlayson: Well, I'd like to know a little more about Tommy's prenatal and birth history and developmental history. I'd like to be able to rule out what we might call minimal brain dysfunction which may contribute to this boy's attentional problems, his overactivity, and his aggressiveness. That's not to say that there aren't emotional problems in the family, but he was premature and sickly as an infant. I would also be interested in food allergies for this boy because we know that behavioral problems often mask these.

Interviewer: Would you use other assessments in addition to a developmental history to rule out the minimal brain dysfunction?

Finlayson: If there were somebody available who could do developmental testing for a 3½-year-old child. The parents' report of milestones is always retrospective, so it might be worthwhile to have somebody determine whether he's where he should be.

Interviewer: And would you have him see an allergist?

Finlayson: I would have him seen by an allergist and/or a pediatrician at the outset.

Interviewer: Gerry?

Beckerle: I very strongly agree with what Greg's saying. Very often we clinicians jump in when there are "obvious" emotional factors and say that's the whole picture. I wouldn't put too much faith in developmental milestones in a 3½-year-old and the testing you can do on that. I would observe him in a playroom situation and at home. How hyperactive is he? How much can he set limits on himself or can he respond to limits set by other people? I think it's very important not to jump to the conclusion that this is all emotional without further testing.

Finlayson: One other thing I might be inclined to consider during the course of treatment is investigating Mrs. Lopez for manic-depressive difficulties. We understand that she is very tantrumy and emotionally upset at some points and then depressed at others. That may be very strongly related to what's happening in the family relationships. If her symptoms didn't change while the family relationships were changing, then I might consider a psychiatric assessment for her in that regard. I think that's a long shot, however, based on the little information that there is here.

Beckerle: That's an interesting notion. I hadn't even thought of it, but I've played with the notion that some forms of learning disability in children seem to me to show up more often in parents who have been labeled manic-depressive.

Finlayson: I think also that hyperactivity tends to go along with alcoholism in a father. Jesús is not described as alcoholic but his father is described as having a drinking problem, so that's a question for me about Jesús as well.

Interviewer: Okay, let's talk about treatment strategies and modalities. What would you recommend that the worker do with this family?

Finlayson: Well, it's an interesting one because of the collusive information. What I mean by that is the message that this woman has given to the therapist in the absence of the husband. I would be inclined to see these people as a threesome and then split off into whatever arrangements seem indicated by the treatment focus. I would encourage the therapist to look for what the parents can jointly identify as a concern, and they have identified a concern with his attention-seeking behavior. I'd want them to explore that with Tommy present. What do you mean by attention-seeking? How is that a problem for you? Encourage them to work on attention-seeking and disciplinary issues that come up right in the context of the interview situation.

Beckerle: See if you can get some agreement between them as a way of joining them.

Finlayson: That's right, because Jesús has said that he doubts whether a clinic can be of any help. I think it's a particular challenge to the therapist to show that he has something to offer the family by way of working with his boy. I think that the therapist's going to have to be active and jump in and help them do something right in the session.

Beckerle: I think one of the key issues again is going to be hooking Jesús and getting some contact with him. I'm not sure you'll get it quickly enough by following the kind of approach that you were talking about, Greg, of identifying the central problem that they both agree on. Even if they do agree to work with you, that might be three or four sessions and that might be one or two sessions too many for the father in this family. I wonder about being very sensitive to his strengths, playing to his ego, and trying to hook him in that way. I'd also be very concerned about the cultural issues in this family and getting a therapist from the same culture or somebody who clearly feels comfortable in working with people from this culture.

Finlayson: You might even ask them if they think that you understand the uniqueness of their family. "I'm not from Mexico, I'm not sure whether I'm going to be able to understand exactly your point of view. I know that things are a little different, so please explain to me."

Interviewer: Would you use any other modalities or recommend that the worker involve any other services in the community?

Finlayson: Well, there's one thing I wouldn't do right now and that is see Mrs. Lopez alone. I think that by calling the therapist and giving this alarming message, which is really very inviting to us as therapists to respond to, she is attempting to align us with her against her husband, much as I think Tommy has become aligned in the family. I would be inclined to say to her that I'm concerned about what she's saying and that I would like her to bring it up in the family session. So the responsibility is put back on her either to use the information there or to drop it.

Beckerle: This woman seems to raise a lot of issues. One other thing I was thinking of in that same vein was her saying that her husband had placed a curse on Tommy and seeing that as a meta-communication of her feeling cut off or isolated at Tommy's identifying with his father and becoming like his father. Maybe what she's trying to tell us is that she has to play this masochistic, one-down role with men, and that's what the placing of the curse on Tommy might be.

Finlayson: You can carry it back a generation too, to the father's father, and the "bad genes" that are passed down. You might get a sense of how she uses the "uproar" game and creates a sense of distress by understanding why she terminated her contact at the distress center. I get a sense of a woman who alarms people and then "calls off the dogs" when her husband comes more into line. So it's easy for the therapist to come in like a white knight to rescue this woman, but that spells death to the therapy.

Beckerle: One bit of information is that Mr. Lopez has been observed to play appropriately and warmly with his son. He doesn't sound as if he's that frightening a figure, so you have even to question her truthfulness.

Finlayson: It could be that this father and son do enjoy some very positive times together and that Tommy really isn't aligned with his mother as much as she would have us believe.

Beckerle: She had an extremely close relationship with her mother and it makes one wonder if she's threatened by father and son having some closeness. Perhaps she needs to place him in the "bad guy" role so that she can have the son to herself.

Finlayson: There really seems to me to be a boundary confusion in the family. We've got Tommy in bed with his mother and the father off by himself, and it should be the other way around.

Interviewer: How do you work on it?

Finlayson: Well, I think that you have to try to understand why they've got it that way, first of all. Kids sleeping with their mother is something we get concerned about, and I think we have to be careful not to come charging in because we don't know what we're upsetting. We might get Tommy out of mother's bed, but is she afraid that her husband will take Tommy's place? Maybe we want to understand their sexual relationship to the point where they could let us talk about it, but you don't want to take Tommy out of the bed unless you understand what it means when he climbs into it. It may be as instrumental in the family as whether Tommy's got a bed and a bedroom. If the only other sleeping place is the couch, then maybe that's not appropriate for the boy. How does he come to be in his mother's bed? Because he cries at night? Or is it because he doesn't have a place to sleep? The therapist has to become involved in a very instrumental way in providing appropriate boundaries in the physical setting of the family.

Interviewer: Would you seek to involve any other services in the community around the issue of the physical conflict between the parents?

Beckerle: I wouldn't deal with that until I got it clarified with both husband and wife present. I think this is the kind of woman who is liable to make several phone calls in between sessions and needs to be constantly referred back to the sessions. Unless it got into child abuse, which I don't get a feel for so far, I don't think that I would involve outside agencies. If it came out he was beating his wife and the kid, I'd be confrontive about that being inappropriate behavior, that has to stop. I would use myself as an authority, because a lot of treatment programs dealing with abusive husbands try to take a nice understanding approach and go down the drain.

Finlayson: You obviously can't jump into the marital issues right off the bat because they're presenting their son and because she's not prepared initially to bring it up in the session. I think that you might very soon get into marital issues if you're trying to focus on the disciplinary issues with Tommy. I think the marital issues—sexual and abusive—will come up through getting them talking to each other and gradually drawing the conversation away from Tommy. Then I would ask them whether they're comfortable talking about these things with Tommy there. I think the choice is theirs, so I might be inclined to move into marital sessions with them if they didn't want Tommy present. On the one hand, you don't want to make the mother more anxious by excluding Tommy, but on the other hand, you want to get him gradually out of his parents' relationship. Right now he's in the middle of it. It's a question of timing and of being sensitive to how much they can tolerate of Tommy being removed from between the two of them.

Interviewer: Gerry, you spoke earlier about doing some work on the father-son bond. What specifically would you do to promote that?

Beckerle: I'd suggest that father and son try more activities together. I see that as a structural readjustment to eventually get Tommy out of mom's bed so that the father and son can bond more closely, again being supportive of mother. I think I'd tend to do it mostly outside the sessions. I don't think I'd have too many sessions between the two of them, or she's going to become terribly threatened.

Finlayson: I think the therapist might be able to use the father's work as a mechanic and a carpenter, building things with Tommy, making things out of wood. Has Tommy ever been to where his father works? Kids of that age are usually interested in that kind of thing. The father may need some building up in the son's eyes to believe that he has something to offer his son.

Beckerle: I think we have to be sensitive to what are culturally appropriate things for this man to do with his son.

Finlayson: I think that's a good point; we could very quickly impose our own values on what he should be doing.

Interviewer: Any other specific treatment strategies?

Finlayson: I'd be inclined to hold back on "insight" because I don't have a sense that they can use a lot of insight. I think that they can use some action and concrete suggestions. The therapist has to be prepared to get up physically from his chair and do something with them in the session.

Interviewer: Any characteristics that you would recommend in a therapist for this family?

Beckerle: I'm worried about hooking Mr. Lopez. I think Mrs. Lopez is going to be very easy to hook. I might tend to go with a male therapist, although if the issue becomes child abuse and wife abuse, many male therapists do not work well with males who abuse. But I think I would involve a male with Mr. Lopez, somebody who could be sensitive to cultural issues.

Finlayson: I agree. I think this is a family in which the therapist steps right into the marital fray and has to be particularly sensitive to the pull of the family system and their marital problems. I think the therapist has to be skilled in being able to shift alliances in the family—alternately aligning more with her and then with him. Or the therapist has to adopt a definitely neutral position and stick to it.

Beckerle: I'm not certain how any therapist can stay completely neutral.

Finlayson: Yes. Well, it's very difficult to do. The therapist has to be able to say "Maybe I made a mistake the last time." We haven't really talked about Tommy's problems, and maybe that's a sign of how easily we can become drawn into the marital difficulties. I think that this boy has real problems with the other children and with tantrums and, while we can work on discipline within the family, I think we need to explore whether we can get him into a situation where he's around other children, for example, a nursery.

Interviewer: One of the potential problems that I'm hearing is that the therapist may become identified with one or another of the spouses and then lose the other one. Are there other potential problems working with this particular family?

Finlayson: If the therapist is going too fast into the marital relationship, the parents may become anxious and say that they came about Tommy. Losing sight of Tommy and the parents' concern for him is a very real danger.

Beckerle: That's right.

Finlayson: They have to feel confident that the problems with Tommy are being addressed. Then they're going to have to be convinced that their marriage plays some role in Tommy's difficulties, and that's going to be a challenge to the therapist. If they were given to insight, you could draw the generational parallel, but I don't think that's going to hold much water with them.

Beckerle: Although I'd rather try a genogram-oriented, insight approach rather than a straight verbal one.

Finlayson: Like in drawing the family tree and asking questions such as "Who else was like this?" We don't know how much they believe that behavior is inherited, and we may have to reeducate them about the fact that people can change how they behave.

Interviewer: What should the therapist be aiming for in terms of outcomes?

Finlayson: I think first and foremost he should be looking for a reduction in Tommy's problematic behavior with other children, Tommy's beginning to form some friendships, learning some peer skills and more cooperative behavior at home. In other words, some shift in the disciplinary relationships at home if it is culturally appropriate for Mr. Lopez to become more involved in that area. Another goal to work toward is giving Tommy his own bed. I think it's conceivable that Mr. and Mrs. Lopez would end up staying in separate beds, however. A decision may have to be made about the future of the marriage down the road and whether they're going to remain together. At this point, I think, they've decided they're together.

Beckerle: We would hope that they would change their relationship. They would start talking more honestly and she would stop the hairsplitting, he would stop denying. That's our hope, but that's not necessarily what they're going to present.

Finlayson: And they should begin to feel that Tommy is less attention-seeking in the ways that are troublesome for them. However, it may be that Tommy is asking for attention that he properly needs to have and isn't getting. It may be that the attention-seeking is at an appropriate level.

Beckerle: Maybe father is able to set more appropriate limits with Tommy, and maybe that's why he feels more comfortable with father, even though father's ferocious at times.

Finlayson: At least the boy knows where he stands with him.

Interviewer: So the area of attention-seeking would involve a consideration of age-appropriate expectations.

Finlayson: We may be drawing on comparisons with other families that they know. This family is open and socially active, I believe.

Beckerle: At least Mr. Lopez. I wonder about Mrs. Lopez. Her English is poor. Has she become assimilated? She seems to be concerned about a lack of support. Maybe she needs to become more involved in community activities outside the home.

Finlayson: Yes. So we might hope in this way to see some change in her high-strung, emotional behavior and depressed feelings.

Interviewer: How do you think this family will respond to treatment?

Finlayson: I'm optimistic about working with them because I think a lot of things can be tried. The prognosis is hard to determine ahead of time, but there is strength, activity, and zest in the family. There's a sense of relationship in the family. They're not isolated, and I think all those things are strengths. However, there's also a previous treatment attempt and a sense of unhelpful equilibrium around the abuse which weigh against the positive aspects of the family. It's not as though this is a sudden crisis. There's a chronic aspect to it.

Interviewer: Gerry?

Beckerle: Greg's comment about the zest brought to mind that we as therapists would rather work with the prostitute than the nun. I and many therapists enjoy their liveliness. I would feel a lot more optimistic after about four sessions than I would at the beginning. If you can hook them for four sessions, I think then you have some kind of a relationship.

Finlayson: Something we didn't talk about is what happens if we lose Jesús. I think that we can still work with them, but it's going to be a lot harder. I would continue to work with whatever part of the family I had available. I don't know whether Baptista would stay involved if we lost Jesús, but I would certainly want to encourage that because of Tommy's behavior and how difficult a time he's going to have if he doesn't get on the rails fairly soon.

SUMMARY

In the preceding cases the most striking characteristic is the extent of conflict between the parents. While marital conflict does not necessarily generate behavior problems among children, the children in these three families are suffering, and their needs are often obscured by the intensity of the parents' conflicts.

The Harper family is divided physically and emotionally into two camps. Mr. and Mrs. Harper, who have married and divorced each other twice, remain angry and accusatory. The two sons are living with father, and their school is concerned about the 10-year-old's effeminate mannerisms and interests in cross-dressing, as well as his brother's perfectionistic attitude toward school achievement. Mrs. Harper is caring for their 13-year-old daughter, who is staying out all night and may be experimenting with drugs and precocious sexual behavior. Each parent seems rigidly fixated on the inadequacies of the other.

The consultants suggest placing primary emphasis on helping the Harpers to focus on their common parental responsibilities and not on their own tangled relationship. In fact, it is advised to give the parents permission to hate each other if they wish, as long as they rise above this emotion for the good of their children. It is felt that, in this context, the parents will be helped to formulate a clear separation agreement that addresses vital custody, access, and related parental issues. If successful, this type of mediation can then assist the family to focus on the specific needs of each of the three children. The consultants emphasize that the parents are bright, articulate people who can probably provide effective parenting if properly mobilized.

In the Ripley family, a 14-year-old boy is reacting to the recent separation of his parents by making a suicidal gesture and showing continuing signs of depression and upset. Mrs. Ripley is seeking to develop a new self-sufficient identity and to cope with parenting two teenage boys at the same time. Mr. Ripley cares about his sons but demonstrates little warmth or intensity in his relationships with them. The depressed son is a loner at school and is falling behind in his work.

The consultants suggest that this is a reactive problem and that the boy is probably not seriously suicidal. They suspect that some of his behavior is designed to pressure the parents to reunite. It is felt that both parents need to clarify their individual parental responsibilities with the boys and that the family needs to be helped to talk through their feelings about, and reactions to, the separation. This will provide an opportunity for both parents to reaffirm their attachment to their sons. The consultants predict that this family will require only short-term treatment and think that the prognosis is good.

The Lopez family is an ostensibly intact family, although Mrs. Lopez has consulted a lawyer and has considered leaving. Both parents are concerned that their 3½-year-old son is attention-seeking. Mrs. Lopez is especially at a loss about how to deal with his tantrums, swearing, and aggressiveness with peers. After an intake interview with the family, mother privately informs the therapist that she has been chronically abused by her husband, that he has "cursed" their son, and that she and her husband are sexually estranged. Mrs. Lopez herself appears high-strung, emotional, and volatile.

The consultants suggest that the possibilities of minimal brain damage or an allergic reaction be ruled out before addressing the problems evident in the family dynamics. They emphasize that the worker has a challenging job in engaging a skeptical father in treatment and that seeking to "rescue" mother would doom the therapeutic effort. Instead, they suggest that the worker must win the parents over by effectively managing their son and helping them to manage him. Therapy should be concrete and action-oriented (many specific suggestions on parenting for both mother and father). Ultimately, the parents must be helped to stop using their son as a vehicle for their disputes. If a therapeutic alliance is formed, the consultants suggest that the couple will voluntarily bring their marital dispute into the discussion at an appropriate time and place.

STUDY/DISCUSSION QUESTIONS

1. What feeling and behavioral reactions might children display when a family experiences marital conflict?
2. What indications are there for directly addressing the marital conflict versus directing the therapy to other areas?
3. What techniques are helpful in getting angry and bitter ex-spouses to cooperate on parental tasks?
4. How does a therapist evaluate the seriousness of a suicide attempt and the risk of further attempts?
5. How do cultural patterns influence marital behavior in general and marital conflicts in particular? Give examples.

4

Transgenerational Psychopathology

When one or both parents experience serious and prolonged emotional disturbance, their children tend to be at greater risk for mental health problems. The multiple demands of the parenting roles, both affective and instrumental, are not easily met, even by the healthiest of parents. Mental illness in a parent can significantly compound this difficulty and impact on the child's mental health in several critical ways. First, the parent may not be physically or emotionally available to the child because of preoccupation with his/her own problems or even hospitalization. Second, the parents' problems may well disrupt their marital relationship and the relationships they have with other important persons in the child's life. This will vastly complicate the child's own efforts to maintain positive, conflict-free bonds with significant others. Third, emotionally troubled parents may seek to meet their own needs using the child as a vehicle. The child may consequently be subjected to distorted perceptions, inappropriate expectations, and mistreatment. Clinical experience suggests that regardless of the child's degree of suffering in these circumstances, he or she usually feels intense guilt, anxiety, and responsibility for the parents' problems.

The mental health worker again faces a complex challenge in treating such families. The therapist either takes on multiple clients or clarifies which therapeutic roles he/she can or cannot play. The need for multiple therapists creates its own complications. For example, from the perspective of individual therapy with a parent, often conducted independently from the child's treatment setting, the pressure to change and improve parenting may appear to be a distraction and an untimely burden. At best, simultaneous treatment of parents and children requires excellent and time-consuming communication among therapists. Alternatively, a family therapy approach to such multiple problems may overwhelm the skills, time, and energy of the therapist and still insufficiently meet the family's individual needs. The three case examples presented in this chapter provide a sample of the problems and potentials of such families.

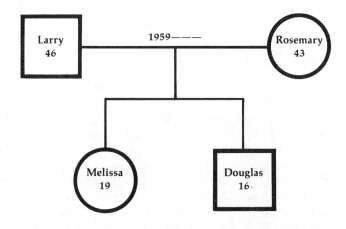

THE BELL FAMILY

Identifying information

The Bell family consists of Larry and Rosemary Bell, their daughter Melissa, and their adopted son Douglas. They sought help from the mental health center following a meeting with the guidance counselor at Doug's high school. Doug claimed at that meeting that he had tried to kill himself by walking in front of a moving truck but that the truck had avoided him. He also claimed that he had wanted to jump off a subway platform six weeks ago but had been unable to make himself do it. At this point, Doug denies having any suicidal wishes. Parents complain that he is withdrawn and evasive at home and that his grades at school are poor.

History of problem

Douglas was adopted at age 4 months and is described as having been a "wonderful baby" by both parents. Parents also saw him as a bright, sensitive, articulate child who preferred to be by himself but still formed significant friendships in elementary school. Doug's behavior changed the year he entered junior high school. He became sloppy and neglectful at home though not openly defiant, spent increasing amounts of time alone in his room, and was difficult for his parents to engage in conversation. His grades have dropped substantially, and he has been barely passing at school. These problems have intensified over the past two and a half years. Mr. and Mrs. Bell have attempted to talk with him and uncover problems. Mrs. Bell, who appears to have done more of this, seems especially frustrated and angry that Doug has not responded. A year ago, they consulted their family doctor, who found Doug in good health and, after talking with him, advised the parents to "ease up." Because of his poor grades and isolated behavior at school, the guidance counselor recently sought to engage him and came away feeling that Doug was seriously depressed. During a follow-up meeting with both parents, Doug disclosed suicidal ideation. Referral to the mental health center was made at that time.

Marital and family history

The Bells have been married for 24 years. During the first years of marriage, mother had three miscarriages, two before Melissa's birth and one thereafter. following the third miscarriage the Bells decided to adopt Douglas. Two of the miscarriages were near full term, but both parents deny any lasting feelings about them. Douglas is actually the natural son of Mrs. Bell's younger sister and was born out of wedlock. Douglas was told about this five years ago, and parents feel that all his questions have been satisfactorily answered. He continues to call his natural mother "aunt" and sees her at family outings. Mrs. Bell remains close to her family of origin and speaks with her mother almost daily. She also keeps in touch with her sister and younger brother and describes her family as a happy one. Mr. Bell is more distant from his family and describes both his parents as cold, reserved, and very strict. He is an only child. This is the first and only marriage for both parents, and they feel their relationship is free of any problems.

Characteristics of family members

Mr. Bell is an accountant in a large firm. He spends long hours at work, but both he and his wife agree that this is necessary and accepted. He appears to be a quiet, contained man who is genuinely concerned about his family and is somewhat more objective in talking about them than his wife. He is accepting of the mental health center, wants to help in any way indicated, and seems as worried about his wife's welfare as about his son's. He does not appear well-connected with Douglas and is stiff and ill-at-ease when relating to him. In contrast, his warmth and comfort are apparent in his interactions with his daughter and his wife. Mr. Bell has problems with ulcers but otherwise appears to be in good health.

On the other hand, Mrs. Bell suffers from chronic hypertension, is on medication, and often feels weak and tired. The rest of the family is under an injunction not to upset her, and she regards Doug's behavior as an indication of his lack of caring for her. Mrs. Bell is clearly and intensely angry at her son and can find little positive to say about him. She even complains about the way he pronounces words and sits in a chair and views these items as indications of Doug's insensitivity. Mrs. Bell displays little warmth in her dealings with her husband and daughter but verbally expresses satisfaction and pleasure with both relationships. She reacts in a highly defensive way to any questions about herself and is quick to assume she is being blamed for Doug's problems. Mrs. Bell vehemently denies having any problems or concerns in her life other than Doug. She has not worked since her marriage and states that she is content in the role of housewife.

Melissa seems to be a peripheral member of the household. She has recently entered university locally and is very active in her studies, her social life, and extracurricular activities. She is athletic and enjoys swimming and racquet sports. She appears to spend very little time at home and to enjoy the admiration of both her parents and Doug. She presents as warm and friendly and poised in interviews. Melissa seems more frightened about her brother's suicidal ideas than her parents and to take them more seriously. She seems sympathetic to both Doug and her mother, but also avoids taking sides with either of them.

Doug has clearly been labeled as the family problem. He appears to have accepted the role and presents himself in a "beaten," sometimes sullen manner. In addition, he accepts all his parents' criticisms of him as valid and has no complaint about the way he is treated at home. He finds school boring and apparently spends a good deal of his time there lost in daydreams. Douglas looks and acts less mature than his chronological age. Eager to gain family approval, he is totally unable to elicit it. Any element of anger at his situation has been directed at himself, and he sees himself as an incompetent. As noted, Douglas is bright, can be articulate, and likes to read. He has a dry, sarcastic wit but displays it only rarely. He appears mildly to moderately depressed.

School and community

Doug's work in school is uniformly poor, although grades in math and science are higher than those for other subjects. This performance seems to be mainly the result of effort, though he turns in many reports and projects late or half-done. He does not participate well in classroom discussions but can give adequate responses if pressed. Some of his teachers note that he is prone to "fooling around" with other boys, but he is not a behavior problem in school. Doug was a top student in elementary school and a winner in science fair and writing contests.

He spends some time in the community, usually alone and often at the library. Sometimes he is away from home for several hours and will not account for his time. He is not dating, nor does he seem to have a consistent set of friends. He is not involved in organized sports or clubs.

Special assessments

No special assessments have been done. The family doctor reports Doug in good health. Group intelligence tests done in grade school identify Doug as having above average intellectual ability.

Case discussion

Consultants: Dr. Julian Rubinstein, Ms. Mary Pat Tillman, Mr. William Wetzel

Interviewer: What additional information or assessments, if any, are needed before you treat this case?

Wetzel: I would want more information about how Larry and Rosemary adopted Douglas. Douglas was a natural son of Rosemary's younger sister, and I would like to know each of the adopting parent's feelings about adopting Doug. I wonder whether they did it out of some sense of obligation.

Tillman: I would want to get a better history from both parents, do a better genogram. Are there any blocks in their families of origin? Members of the family that either one doesn't speak to? I would look for repetitive patterns. Do Larry and Rosemary know other couples who have adopted, or is that something that also goes back into their history? Horror stories that they have heard, their expectations, etc. And also further down the road I would want to know about Rosemary's relationship with her sister. Also Doug's sense of his natural mother and his relationship with her. Since Doug is 16 I would give him the opportunity of being seen alone initially and see what kind of information we could get from him without the family being there.

Interviewer: Could you describe what you mean by a genogram?

Tillman: Okay. Primarily an intergenerational history. In other words, having the parents in and finding out a bit more in terms of their own families. Who the brothers and sisters are, where they are, where their parents are, who is involved in the family, who isn't involved. There is a good article on doing a genogram in a book by Guerin.* I think that it is also a nice idea because it is a nonthreatening intervention in the initial session.

Wetzel: I would do the genogram with the parents and Doug and Melissa present and look specifically at alliances within the families. I wonder how much of Larry's reserve with Doug could be reflective of his parents, who are described as cold and very strict.

Interviewer: Any formal assessments that either of you would recommend?

Tillman: I was particularly interested in Doug's functioning at school. I would be curious whether there are any learning problems at this point. But from the report there don't seem to be.

Interviewer: His school performance is poor but his intelligence seems to be at least average.

Wetzel: I wonder about using a depression index. Just in terms of how serious a suicide risk he may be.

Interviewer: What do you mean by a depression index?

Wetzel: A formal depression scale to help determine how high a suicide risk someone is.

Interviewer: Julian, do you want to add anything in terms of additional information or assessments that you would recommend?

Rubinstein: Yes, I think Douglas needs a formal psychiatric assessment with a mental status exam. I think that should be done fairly urgently.

---

*Guerin, P. J. *Family Therapy: Theory and Practice.* New York: Gardiner Press, 1976.

Interviewer: Specific information from that assessment?

Rubinstein: Well, I think a judgment would need to be made about this boy's suicidal risk, a clinical assessment to determine the presence of, the nature, and degree of his depression. A pretty comprehensive life history is needed. I would also like to know more about the functioning of the family.

Tillman: Certainly to some degree the sister is a figure in this family for the son and possibly for mother and father. I would like to know what kind of relationship this family has with mother's brothers and sisters.

Wetzel: Douglas is in fact the son of her younger sister, and Mrs. Bell speaks with her mother almost daily. This indicates to me that an extended family system is very much emotionally involved. Not that I would want to involve them in sessions, but I would certainly want to know more about their emotional involvement.

Rubinstein: From Mr. and Mrs. Bell?

Wetzel: Yes. I would focus the family assessment on affective expression, affective involvement, and on roles. Like Mr. Bell's long hours at work. I get some sense that that has been that way for a while. I'd like to know more about Doug's role, whether he has assumed some of the husband's functions in this family. Father certainly seems peripheral. He is contained in terms of affective expression, so my formulation would be that Douglas' emerging adolescence is upsetting the system in terms of his possible role as replacing father in some way. He may also represent mother's protectiveness of her younger sister, so his emerging adolescence, I think, is a real threat. It may also be a threat in terms of the parents' own sexuality, concerns around guilt, and feelings about the miscarriages. His emerging adolescence may certainly restimulate concerns around sexuality and the marital relationship.

Interviewer: Where would that point in terms of interventions?

Wetzel: Well, in terms of interventions I would think marital therapy would be indicated, but the timing would be important. If we went to that initially, we would probably lose this family. I would focus around the concerns the family is presenting and move into marital therapy as the issues emerge.

Rubinstein: I didn't quite understand what you meant by Doug's function in terms of Mrs. Bell's relationship with her sister. Protector?

Wetzel: Well, I wonder how much she, as a child or as an adolescent, had to function in her own family of origin as a parent to her younger siblings. I wonder about Mrs. Bell's relationship with this younger sister who had Doug out of wedlock. Was she more of a parent and protector to her? And does Doug represent that for her? Does she need to be overly protective of Doug? Is that something that has been transferred from the family of origin?

Rubinstein: The description of Mrs. Bell and Doug's relationship seems to be contrary to that formulation. At least superficially, she is intensely angry and noncaring. If anything, Doug represents the part of her that the family wants to get rid of. I wonder about the history of Mrs. Bell's relationship with Doug. Has it always been this way? My hunch is that it has probably been a long-standing pattern. I would like to know what father thinks about it. Has he just been a passive observer or has he tried to help mother or Doug deal with it?

Interviewer: How would you address those issues with the family?

Rubinstein: I would start with the family as a whole. I think there may be a need for marital therapy, but I would see that as quite a long way down the road. I would want to begin addressing those issues. I would want to understand their origins and what they are willing and capable of doing about them.

Wetzel: I think that is a good point in terms of finding out from the family if these are long-standing issues, finding out what means they have used to problem-solve in the past.

Tillman: Even though there is a rejecting quality, there is still an overinvolved quality to the mother-son relationship. That is something to keep in mind with the family. The other thing that just came to mind is to look at distance and closeness in the family. I wonder whether there is an overintrusiveness in the mother-son relationship and what the space is like between father and son.

Interviewer: I have heard the suggestion of moving to family therapy and I have heard the suggestion of some marital counseling. Are there any other modalities you would consider using?

Tillman: With adolescents, it always gives me more information to see them at least once or twice on their own and to establish some sort of formulation.

Wetzel: I would have a different worker see Doug individually from the one who is seeing the family because I have been caught in that bind and I think it can be very difficult to balance.

Tillman: I know that for many family therapists there is a great resistance to seeing anybody alone, that right in the beginning one has everybody come in, otherwise you are labeling the IP. But I would like to get a handle on what Doug is like apart from the family.

Interviewer: Let us move to some treatment strategies. What are some of the concrete things that you would want to suggest that a worker do with this family?

Tillman: One concrete thing I would advise her to do is join well enough with this family. Mother definitely needs some sort of support. She is going to be very difficult to work with. She has all kinds of somatic symptoms. The therapist can be in a position of power but also has to confirm each member of the family. I think if she alienates mother, she has lost the ball game to some degree.

Wetzel: I would do the same thing with father. I would specifically ask him about his job, his working hours, how long he has been working such hours, and give him a lot of support around being the breadwinner.

Rubinstein: I would try and help the family articulate what they would like to see changed, individually and as a group. Then I would work toward a therapeutic contract with them around the issues that they have defined.

Interviewer: What if they can't agree?

Wetzel: One thing I tend to do is to ask each family member to give two or three wishes of something that he or she would like to be different, that would make this family happier together. I have never had the experience of not finding at least some commonality.

Rubinstein: I would want them to declare that there are differences. If they don't recognize them, then one of my tasks would be to point them out and see if they can negotiate them. If the differences are between Mr. and Mrs., I would attempt to get them to work together to resolve the disagreements. If they are between the two parents and Doug, that might be more problematic. If, as is suggested, they are determined to have him out, the situation may be quite difficult to resolve. He is 16. How I would handle it would depend on my assessment of where Doug is in terms of his developmental stage, his suicidal potential, his level of depression, and so on.

Wetzel: One aspect could be to work with Melissa. She is concerned about Doug's suicidal ideas, and there seems to be some bonding between Melissa and Doug that could be strengthened.

Interviewer: Okay, let us assume that there has been some joining and there has been some contracting and some agreement. Could you talk a bit more about other things that you might wind up doing with the family?

Rubinstein: One of the things I meant to mention is that I would want to advise the worker to contact the family physician as well. We need more information about mother's blood pressure and the various hypochondriacal complaints. For example, this business about not upsetting mother. I would like to get some confirmation from a medical standpoint as to whether this woman is ill, or whether they have her blood pressure under reasonable control. I suspect her illness is a family myth and is used as a method of control. If that is the case, I would want to deal with it in the family sessions.

Tillman: It puts her in a position of power with her husband, too.

Rubinstein: For sure.

Wetzel: Father also has ulcers. I might spend a session talking almost metaphorically with the family about some of these physical complaints and utilize that as a way of getting more affect. I think that their various physical illnesses are reflective of their means of affective expression.

Interviewer: Any other treatment strategies that the worker might use?

Tillman: There may be tension between the husband and wife. You could test that out. You might want to bring the parents closer together and negotiate around how they are going to handle Doug in certain situations. See if they could agree and support each other. One of the things that may be happening is that they cancel each other out in parenting Doug. You could help them to be more effective parents. I would want to test out the nature of the relationship between father and son. See what happens when they talk to each other, who interrupts, if mother gets into the middle. I would look at the sequences of behavior in the family when dad is talking to son, when mother is talking to son. If mother does intrude on that, develop some ways of keeping her out and improving the dyadic relationship between father and son.

Interviewer: What are some ways of improving that kind of relationship?

Wetzel: I might give a task to father and son. Perhaps ask father to talk to Doug about his own parents, particularly his relationship with his own father.

Rubinstein: My initial focus would be more on the marital relationship than the relationship between mother and Doug or father and Doug. I suspect that a fairly distant relationship exists between a controlling, hypochondriacal mother and a distant, passive father. If we made some gains in that regard, changes in the relationship between the parents and children would follow more readily. That is the sequence I would use because I suspect that neither parent is having his or her own needs met, or at best, poorly met. This is probably a significant factor in this boy's depression.

Tillman: How do you handle it when parents say that they are not here to talk about their marriage but to fix up their son?

Rubinstein: I would give them a "mini-lecture" on systems, in language they could understand. If they can accept that all relationships in the family influence all the family members, I could establish an expectation for change.

Wetzel: I would let them know my belief that when a family member is having problems or hurting, the family itself can do more to help than a hundred professionals.

Rubinstein: I have a store of "tricks of the trade" that I can use according to particular circumstances and my judgment of what they will respond to. The use of metaphors is one example. The parents will have to acknowledge that all is not right and agree that something has to be done, if the family is going to be helped.

Interviewer: Let me press the possible problem facing the worker around focusing on the marriage. What if the parents deny that there is any difficulty with their marriage?

Tillman: If the kid's behavior can settle down, often that is when things start to get very rocky in the marriage and then they are asking for something more for themselves than for their child. By getting the parents at least to agree in certain situations so that they are not always detouring their conflict through the child, you can look into the marriage but not move into the marriage right away.

Rubinstein: How are you going to get the kid's behavior to settle down?

Tillman: Given that mother is overinvolved and dad is distant, if father can move closer to the son, then mother has to move farther away from him, either into conflict with the husband or closer in some sort of way. That would be the move into the marriage. The biggest first step is getting the kid out of the marital dyad.

Wetzel: If you worked toward strengthening the bond between dad and Doug, mom might sabotage it with the attitude that if she is not getting much of her husband, why should Doug get it? As you work on the problems that are presented, certain conflicts will emerge from the marital relationship. At that point, when you have evidence, you can clearly say to the parents that there are marital difficulties.

Tillman: I wonder if there is some way that you can help this boy and start to improve his social connectedness and relatedness outside the family. There is a part of him that is very much tied in with his family. Chronologically that is not exactly age appropriate for a 16-year-old. That is more the time to be getting out. I am wondering how Doug can move more outside the family, which also might put more stress on the marriage.

Interviewer: Could we talk about the kind of worker that you think would be most successful with this family?

Rubinstein: As far as characteristics are concerned, I don't have anything special in mind. I think this is going to be a difficult family, so to the extent possible, an experienced and skilled family therapist will be needed. I think mother could intimidate an inexperienced therapist who is not very self-confident. But I guess that is probably true for all complex family cases. I would advise the worker to monitor the mother most carefully. The likelihood is that at some point in time the therapist is going to have to stand up to the mother, since I suspect that she will try to take control of the whole therapeutic process.

Wetzel: I recommend someone who is able to conceptualize this family's difficulties in terms of systems theory. I also think a fair bit of sadness and anger is bound to come out, and I think the worker needs to be someone who could deal with that effectively.

Rubinstein: If the situation changes as I hope it would, there is a good possibility of mother becoming depressed. If it is a nonmedical family therapist, the therapist should have medical backup readily available, both for the boy and for mother.

Interviewer: What should the therapist be looking out for in terms of danger signals in addition to Doug's level of depression and mother's potential depression?

Rubinstein: I am more concerned about children who jump in front of cars or think about jumping off a subway than I am about children who take overdoses. The level of his depression needs to be carefully watched.

Tillman: If Doug starts to act-out again, that gives some indication that this family is having difficulty.

Interviewer: By acting out, you mean————?

Tillman: I mean in terms of suicidal threats. I agree with you that whatever worker is involved in this is going to need a fairly effective consultation group that includes a medical person. If they try and change anything in this family, they are obviously going to produce some stress and crisis and in a sense that would be a signal of something good happening. Although as far as the worker is concerned it can be very frightening.

Wetzel: One last suggestion is that I would ask Doug's teacher to keep a log on his school performance and behavior as a way of monitoring his depression.

Interviewer: Let us move to objectives. What are the major goals and objectives that you would want the worker to be working toward for this family?

Tillman: One thing is increasing Doug's socialization skills, increasing his autonomy outside the family, and increasing the closeness of the parents.

Wetzel: I don't have much to add other than strengthening the bond between Melissa and Doug. I might even want to see if it were possible for dad to cut down on his working hours. Of course, I don't know what this would mean in terms of financial pressures. And for mom possibly to get some kind of volunteer job or part-time employment. I think there would be advantages financially and in terms of another outlet for her.

Interviewer: Julian, other outcomes?

Rubinstein: Doug doesn't kill himself. I agree with the increased socialization and working toward more autonomy and independence. As far as family goals are concerned, I would want to base that to a large extent on what comes out of the negotiation process. I would work toward a greater degree of affective involvement and responsiveness between the family members at all levels, but the specifics of that would depend on what they wanted.

Interviewer: Okay, how about prognosis?

Rubinstein: Guarded for the family. I don't think it is going to happen immediately, but if Doug is able to separate and get into some other form of therapy down the road, he should be okay. I don't think this family is going to change all that much in the immediate future.

Tillman: I agree with that. I said guarded, but hopeful in the sense that you elaborated.

Interviewer: Bill, prognosis?

Wetzel: My prognosis would depend upon how long-standing the difficulties are. If they are quite long-standing, my prognosis would be more guarded. If they have emerged in the last two to three years I feel more hopeful.

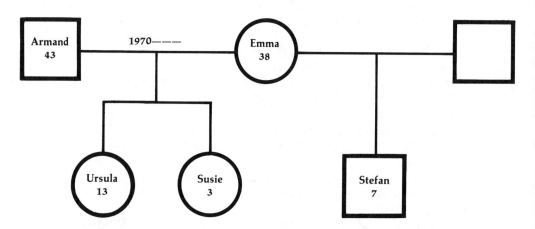

THE LOPAT FAMILY

Identifying information

The Lopat family consists of Armand Lopat, his wife, Emma, and their three children, Ursula, Stefan, and Susie. Stefan is the identified patient. The parents report that he has been setting small fires in the home and that he wets and soils himself several times a week.

History of problem

Stefan has been difficult for his parents to control from an early age. As an infant, he did not sleep well and demanded a lot of attention. Mr. Lopat's mother lived with the family until Stefan was 2 years old and is thought to have "spoiled" him by picking him up and caressing him almost constantly. He was toilet trained at age 3 but began soiling a year thereafter. Now that he is 7, the parents find it difficult to tolerate. When upset or angry, Stefan will make a mess in the house by urinating or defecating and wiping his dirty hands on the wall or furniture. He is able to bribe his parents into giving him things by promising not to do this.

The parents are most worried about several small fires that Stefan has recently set in the house. Mrs. Lopat has talked to him about the danger of playing with matches and has slapped his hands for doing so, but her warnings have not worked. Stefan seems unaware of the danger involved in several things he does, the outstanding incident being a fire he started in his bedroom, which burned a hole in his bed cover. He also steals cigarettes from his parents and smokes them when they are not around. When confronted with his behavior, Stefan laughs or gets angry. When pushed, he screams in protest and becomes destructive.

A year ago, the Lopats went to a private psychiatrist who felt that Stefan was too young to make use of his services. He did put Stefan on Ritalin, however, which he continues to take daily. This has slowed his pace somewhat, although the problem behaviors have not diminished.

Marital and family history

Emma Lopat grew up in a poor area of Toronto as the youngest of four children. Her parents owned and ran a small grocery store. Primarily raised by her oldest sisters, Emma was courted by Armand Lopat for six years, married him at age 25, and conceived a daughter shortly thereafter. Stefan is the product of a liaison Mrs. Lopat had with a married man. On learning about the affair and pregnancy, Mr. Lopat temporarily left his wife and moved out on his own. Armand's mother moved in with Emma to help take care of the children. A year later Armand moved back and has since accepted Stefan as his own son. Susie, the youngest daughter, was an unplanned child.

Mr. Lopat's family emigrated from the Ukraine. His father, a cabinet-maker, died ten years ago. His mother now lives with Armand's younger brother Michael. Mr. Lopat runs a dry-cleaning establishment and works long hours.

Characteristics of family members

Stefan Lopat is a small, dark, attractive 7-year-old boy with a very active and boisterous manner and a loud voice. He can be well-behaved but all too frequently runs around freely getting into things. He appears to have considerable power over his parents. He refuses to talk about his fire setting and soiling behavior. His parents complain that living with Stefan is living from crisis to crisis, and they cannot understand the reason for his difficulties. In contrast, they cite the more appropriate behavior of his sisters, both of whom seem to have age-normal interests and emotional development. In general, Stefan's sisters keep out of his way.

Mrs. Lopat is a very anxious woman who has been hospitalized on two occasions for "nerves" and is currently taking tranquilizers. Mr. Lopat is rather passive and unavailable. He leaves the childrearing to his wife, and although he takes part in activities with Stefan, he seems awkward making physical contact with him. Stefan likes to go fishing with his dad, and they play ball together on the few occasions he is not working.

The Lopats find it difficult to look at their own dynamics and the role they may be playing in maintaining Stefan's difficulties. Their relationship with each other appears quite formal and distant. Mrs. Lopat seems to dominate the relationship through the use of her symptoms. Both parents are open to suggestions but come across as immature and dependent. They clearly indulge Stefan and have difficulty showing him true warmth. They are also afraid that Stefan will be taken from them by the authorities and placed in a residential setting.

School and community

Stefan is doing adequate work in the second grade. He has to be nagged to complete his schoolwork but is not causing problems there. The school sees him as bright and active and in need of adult direction to channel his energy.

Both in school and in the community Stefan has trouble making friends. He plays roughly with peers and gets angry when things don't go his way, but his parents are not concerned about this aspect of his behavior.

Case discussion

Consultants: Mr. Michael Blugerman, Ms. Catherine Jackel

Interviewer: Is there information or are there special assessments that you would like to see or would like to ask for about the case?

Jackel: You need a developmental history of the kid and we don't have a good one. We don't have a record of birth. All we know in terms of milestones is that his toilet training was accomplished and maintained for a year.

Interviewer: So you'd like a thorough and detailed developmental history.

Jackel: Most of what seems to be happening to him can be accounted for environmentally, but I would have to know about his birth history. Obviously he was an unplanned pregnancy.

Interviewer: Give some examples of what you would be looking for.

Jackel: I want to know what her emotional condition was when she was pregnant. I want to know what kind of a birth it was. I'd like to know at what point in her pregnancy the father left. I'd also like to know if Stefan was breast or bottle fed. I'd like to know how much of the maternal behavior she delivered. How much of the bonding was with her versus with the maternal mother-in-law?

Interviewer: Okay, are any other types of information or assessment needed?

Jackel: I'd like some clear information about the marital relationship and interaction. I think that's a bit vague. I'd like to know the reason for mother-in-law's departure to live with the uncle. Is there a particular kind of ethnic relation between the male child and father? What are the family's values?

Blugerman: I agree that it would be nice to know those things, but when I do consults I'm concerned mostly about the interaction between the worker and the work, so I'm assuming that this material was prepared by the person who is doing the work. So I don't know whether I have the luxury to go and get all that information and if I can get it, it's nice. I don't particularly track the kind of developmental milestones that Cathy's talking about. Let's see if I can give an example. Take the paragraph saying that Stefan was too young to make use of the service. So I would like to know what the psychiatrist thought the problem was, and since he prescribed the Ritalin, I hope that he did a work-up, in which case you would get the material you want to know. You mentioned "environmental." I think most of this could be cleared up with marital and behavioral control work. When I looked at the kind of symptoms that were there, well, those are scary kinds of symptoms and I thought that they would probably mystify these parents. There's not only a behavior disruption, but there's also a physical disturbance like the soiling. So you would think there's something clearly wrong with the kid, so the prescription of Ritalin may be a way the psychiatrist cooled the parents out. The worker states that Stefan has slowed his pace somewhat as a result, although the problems he has have not diminished. I would like to know if it is enough of a gain for either of the parents to feel better, because if it's only somewhat then I'm not crazy about the kid being on Ritalin. And even though it's a year I don't know there is regular contact on review. I've seen too many kids that have been on Ritalin for long periods of time.

Jackel: Yes, the myth of the hyperactive kid. It seems to me that the firesetting behavior has escalated. His school behavior has maintained, and the school sees him as simply a bright, active kid who needs adult direction, but the fire-setting behavior has escalated despite the medication.

Blugerman: So for me it is less in the category of hyperactivity and more an interactional thing with the family.

Interviewer: So you'd want a fuller picture of the psychiatric contact?

Blugerman: Yes, and I want to know if this is just a temporizing move by the psychiatrist, in effect, saying, "Okay, I'll supply the treatment, you guys can feel better and we'll see if we can change the thing around that way."

Interviewer: Or did he really think that the child is hyperkinetic?

Blugerman: Right. I don't really work scientifically, objectively with a case. I demand more interactional information between the person who is working and the people, based on the assumption that everybody has troubles. I want to know what kind of skills or strengths they have to change, and I would gauge that by the quality of interaction the workers have. Now I can extrapolate a few things. For example, the fact that he does okay in school but not with his peers suggests to me that when there's adequate parenting he'll respond. The school setting is mostly a replication of parenting for him.

He's not moving through that to peers so that my target is what goes on in the marriages in the respective families, as there are some in-laws involved here as well. Mostly I would start looking at this case from the perspective of parental control, executive function in the family.

Jackel: I was listening to what you had to say and I was also thinking about some of the detail that's still missing for me from the assessment of the writer. For example, what are the alliances of the parents with the kids? What's mother's relationship with Susie, her new baby, as opposed to Stefan? Because his toilet training problems started at her birth, I'd like to know some basic functions in the family. Can the family express negative emotions to each other directly or is he really the covert carrier for all of it? What's father's affect level with the other sibs?

Interviewer: Okay, Michael, you were beginning to move into talking about the kinds of treatment you might be using with the family. Could you expand on that in terms of what you most likely would be doing with them?

Blugerman: Okay. I use a structural map to organize the big picture and collect an overview. So I would look at who the in-laws are, the relationship between them and this couple. I would look at marital history, because there's a kind of casual enmeshment between the couple and the in-laws. At the point where the guy leaves, he's sort of injured by the fact that the wife has gotten pregnant with someone else. His mother moves in, so it's either extreme loyalty or a vote of nonconfidence or both. As I look at the marital thing, I'd like a little bit more continuity in the development in the marriage and the significance of the various things to these people. For example, the father and mother knew each other for six years. Shortly after, they conceived this child. Now I don't know if "shortly after" means shortly after term or she was pregnant before they got married, in which case I'd wonder what their motivation was to marry in the first place.

Interviewer: Who would you recommend that the worker see to get this material?

Blugerman: I think I would be directed by who's living together now, and I would like that family unit present, and, at a point where I'd like to do the marital stuff, I'd probably get the kids playing in another corner or ask them to leave for a little bit and collect that information. I like to take a model of elegance in the sense of not working harder than I have to. If I can get enough material or interaction demonstrated to me between the couple, then I may not need the mother-in-law because I don't know about her current interaction with them. I knew at one time it was problematic. I don't know if it still is. If I found that they didn't live up to the tasks that were presented or couldn't fill in gaps, then I would think about inviting her.

Interviewer: And would you, in terms of ongoing work, recommend that the worker see the couple and focus on marital things?

Blugerman: No, I'm mostly concerned with giving the kid an experience of being in control and having consistent limits. I would work or have the counselor work with the couple and kid in doing limit setting and boundary setting. Any marital work I would do would be experientially through causing both parents to deal with the child issue, because I'll presume limited intellectual and verbal ability and I'd rather create the experience and have them understand it.

Interviewer: Cathy, how about you in terms of treatment?

Jackel: I like very much the idea of using a vehicle of moving in with the parents or on the parenting role and doing it together, and using that as an opportunity to provide Stefan with the boundaries that he needs. I also would like to see some individual work with him. I'm left with an impression, because he's been out of control for a long time and he's been bouncing off walls for a while, that he's really quite desperate and his level of anger seems somewhat profound. He's desperately crying out with his behavior, and I'd like to see some work with him around ways of expressing his emotions, positive and negative, in much more productive ways. I'd also like to see him get into some socialization stuff with peers.

Interviewer: Are you talking about a therapeutic group?

Jackel: Yes, for sure, but I'm not sure at what point. I'm not sure if that should happen immediately or if it should happen after a bit of one-to-one.

Blugerman: My view about these things is that I like to work as minimally as possible. I would push the limit of what the parents can modify through their doing better limit setting, and if that wasn't enough or if I thought the kid was too slow to give them a sense of encouragement and success, then I'd go to your choices.

Jackel: I'd just "whomp it all on" to see how far we could get.

Blugerman: Technically, the risk for me in that approach is management, in that this is a kid who gets different messages from mother and father now; and just to check out the extent of that, I would like to minimize the number of significant caregivers and try to hold the field constant. Also, I don't know the agency setting and about the luxury of services, so again I'll go the economical route.

Interviewer: No frills.

Blugerman: The thing that I agree with Cathy about is that some of his behavior will alarm therapists, never mind parents, so there would be a great temptation to jump in and do something about that. However, I'd like to play this straight with the first intervention and then add the extras, because I also want to avoid any iatrogenic creation of problems.

Interviewer: What about other community resources in this case?

Blugerman: Well, there are two notices in the record, one is the school and the other one is the impression the parents have that Stefan will be taken away by authorities; so that suggests there has been some contact with authorities and I think it would be worthwhile to have a review meeting with those people and buy time to have the worker do his business and assure the parents that working with the therapist is in their best interest in connection with that anxiety.

Jackel: I really wasn't sure whether the authorities have been involved at all. I thought that if they had, that would have been referred to, and that's why I was more interested in taking a look at the value system and ethnicity of the family.

Interviewer: Could we talk more specifically about concrete strategies that one might use to "hook" this family? For example, we've got a father who is concerned about the problem but is also described as being fairly uninvolved in the family life. What would you do to "hook" him? What would you do to get this family moving?

Jackel: Try to double-bind father into presence of some nature.

Interviewer: What do you mean?

Jackel: Try to set up a double-bind situation where both his options are options of involvement and then help him make a choice of what kind of involvement.

Interviewer: For example?

Jackel: To really do a good one, I'd have to know a lot more about him. I think I'd take a look at his level of motivation and where he expressed interest. Maybe he expressed interest or joy or pleasure around his playing with Stefan. Fishing and playing baseball, for example. I think I'd try to hook him around that kind of involvement by letting him know the positive value of it for Stefan on a consistent basis. Then lay out some other options, all of which are positive and have to do with his involvement and let him choose the one that he thinks he can handle. Certainly they'd have to do with co-parenting roles. That's going to be difficult because his value system suggests that it's mother's role to parent. So we'd have to do this very softly and gently, in stages.

Interviewer: Any other strategic hints or suggestions to the worker while working with this family? Or with Stefan?

Blugerman: I think if we did a survey of different theoretical models, the common first stage is something like joining or rapport. The impression I get of these people is that they are awkward about contact and connectedness. The mother is described as anxious, has a case of nerves, so that's some anxiety about making contact interpersonally. The husband dealt with her affair by leaving, and he's reported as being passive and more related to work, so he also has a removed style in terms of making contact. The worker would somehow have to match that model. I wouldn't rush this father into heavy-duty parenting. You could do something consistent with his values by having her do the prime child-raising provided that he gave her support which would be consistent with that value. I'm not sure what kind of support he does give her. There's a statement here that they find it difficult to look at their own dynamics. I don't know if they have worked out what the affairs meant. It says that he's accepted Stefan as his own son. That may be, but I don't know if he's accepted her as his wife, because even though he came back and he has "accepted the kid," their last kid was unplanned. So I'm not sure if there has been a resolution between them at a significant level.

Jackel: And you really do have to wonder about the rebonding after separation. I assume that if father left, he left when he found out she was pregnant, and he was gone for a year only. Mother-in-law was there for the first two years of Stefan's life, which means that he had three people living in the house. It would seem difficult to move back with your wife after she's had a child while your own mother is living in the house. Again, we know nothing of his reasons for returning. I'm concerned very much about whether Stefan is the vehicle for expression of negative emotions in this family. I don't get much of a feel for the girls as being anything other than avoiders. They certainly avoid Stefan.

Blugerman: That's true. They could be coping as a way of avoiding being dependent on the inadequate mother. You say that the kid may be vocalizing the conflict between them. That's sort of the top-down approach. I look at it as a rescue operation, as a bid from the kid for consistent limits and to pull them together. I think you get more mileage out of the rescue operation approach than you do out of what the kid is expressing. You may be right, but I don't think we're going to get them to express much as a family. If you start with the presumption that the kid is expressing negative emotions, then you'd hypothesize that if you got the parents to express it directly, he'd quit. I wouldn't have much investment in using that as a strategy for action. If you take it as a rescue operation, it would be possible to direct them both around the parenting and the consequences and reach the same end within a less threatening framework.

Interviewer: Cathy, you talked about some individual work with Stefan. What would you want to give him?

Jackel: I'd want to work on his self-image. I think about his first two years of nurturance and the term that comes to mind from the assessment is *smother versus mother*. He has very few realistic boundaries at a time when he most needs those kinds of boundaries.

Interviewer: Would you play with him? Would you talk with him? What would you do with him?

Jackel: I'd use a modified play therapy approach. I wouldn't use a traditional play therapy approach, but I would allow him to bomb and bang within specific limits that I set. I would keep the limits simple. I would have very few of them, but they would be consistently enforced, and within those limits he could express what he wanted to. I'd do a lot of reflecting of both positive and negative emotions and I'd do modeling around expression of them. I'd also see that there was fun built into it. I think this kid needs some joy, and I don't think he's getting much of it.

Interviewer: Can you give me an idea of how long and intense a relationship you would be seeking to develop with him?

Jackel: Well, in terms of the model that I am thinking about, there would be at most two workers involved. I see it as perfectly appropriate that the worker who does the management with the parents also does the individual work with Stefan. It seems to me to be individual work to the point where his self-image is intact enough for him to approach his peers less defensively and more equally. Then I'd move him gradually into a group experience and move him slowly out of individual with the input to the family.

Blugerman: The first thing that strikes me in this case is the negativity, the pathological description of the fire-setting and so on. On the other hand, I have a very positive statement from the school. I agree with Cathy's goals. Again, I'd try to keep it closer at hand. I would say that with the father leaving, you have a withdrawal of support from the mother. Now both parents deal with conflict by withdrawal. How else could I explain the fact that early in the marriage she had an affair with another guy and had a child? Now the child may have been accidental, but going somewhere else for help is reminiscent of his going somewhere else to live, so I have as a model parents who withdraw when trouble comes. So if we look at the early development, acceptance of the kid's individuation plus closeness are missing. The mother is described as very anxious and Stefan's lack of individuation would be a reflection of the mother's anxiety. In a family session I would encourage the kid to play with me and to do all kinds of individuating, autonomous things in the presence of the family, and contain their anxiety and allow them to contribute in a positive way. This would help him understand that the mother's anxiety hasn't got anything to do with him and it can be contained. I think that would be the route to self-esteem and also a way of teaching the parents. It would be modeling for them.

Jackel: It's interesting that we didn't at any point suggest that we would like workups from the hospital where mother had her nervous breakdowns.

Blugerman: I don't think I need it for the way I'm working. I ground my interventions more on the results of what I do over time, so I would get the diagnostic material by intervening rather than take a very objective point of view, strategize, and then move in. It would be an ongoing hypothesis that would be reelaborated as data changed.

Interviewer: What do you think might go wrong?

Blugerman: The risk of the fire-setting would contribute to their anxiety generally, and stimulate their coping style of withdrawing. The fire-setting is a definite risk to management. The second area of concern would be that, as we brought the parents together to provide this consistent framework for the kid, they would become aware of any real differences that they had. A final fall-out area for me would be that if it's true the sisters also deal through avoidance, and everything starts pulling together, they'll be challenged to reformulate some of their style and we may get some misbehavior on their part. The parents may interpret that as a failure in terms of the therapy and opt out or withdraw.

Jackel: They would have to withdraw their attention from Stefan at any rate, because they've spent too much attention on him. That's what happened to the girls.

Blugerman: That's right, and then they might say "Well, they were fine and now everybody's in trouble," so somehow you'd have to bind that therapeutically and predict it.

Interviewer: What would you do if the fire-setting became extreme?

Blugerman: My approach, first of all, would be to get a contextual sequence of how the fire-setting emerged. If I saw a fairly clear interaction about the fire-setting, that would direct me one way, and I would work with it in the context of family. There's a famous case from the Philadelphia Child Guidance Clinic in which the parent is encouraged to teach the kid how to set fires appropriately in order to neutralize the family interaction over it. If, on the other hand, I went through a sequence and I found that this showed some more primitive developmental regression, then I would have to make a judgment about safety and work with the parents about what they wanted to do at that point. If, after I had my worker start working, the fire-setting got worse, then I'd look for some kind of misalliance or deepening of the problem and I'd have to question whether the family is a safe setting for the kid at this time.

Interviewer: If your answer to that was no, would you be looking at placement?

Blugerman: Then I might be looking at placement. If I could find out the nature of this misalliance or whether the family is going to fragment, then I would try to predict if we are looking to a permanent placement or a reintegration in the family. I'd look for strengths. Is it likely that one of them would be able to pick up the kid or kids? Is it likely they'd get back together or should we find an alternate plan?

Interviewer: Cathy, do you want to add anything?

Jackel: Yes, just two minor points. It might be interesting to focus on toilet-training as one of the parent-management activities. I was thinking of that not just from the point of view of mother, because she's successfully toilet-trained two other kids and knows how to do it. But I was also thinking it would focus Stefan on an area that he could act-out, and it would defocus the fire-setting because he really seems to be getting a lot of mileage out of that. It's catastrophizing behavior. He bribes his parents now with the toilet-training issues. He won't swear or he won't defecate or whatever if they give him what he wants. I would like to focus on that because I think there might be some payoffs in terms of his acting-out behavior being more directed toward them. The other point is that I want him off Ritalin as soon as possible if the psychiatric report indicates that he was just popped on it, as is often the case. I think that's going to increase the family's anxiety, and I think taking him off Ritalin has to be done as improvement begins and relationships are established even though my initial reaction would be, "Get him off, and get him off fast." I think it's going to create such anxiety within the parents that it's probably therapeutically valuable to go slowly even if it's not doing a damn thing for him.

Interviewer: If you could choose a worker for this family, what would the worker be like?

Blugerman: I would say that the person would have to have flexibility in his personal style because these would be relatively hard people to engage. So it would have to be somebody who could pick up little idiosyncratic things about each of them and join them. When you get families who want to deal with their problems, then you can get someone who doesn't have to reach out as far, but with these people I want someone who is quite fast on—I was going to say *his*, maybe I'm thinking male—his or her feet.

Jackel: I think father would get really uptight if a male moved into that family.

Blugerman: Well, maybe yes, maybe no. You see, his father died, his mother seems quite strong, and I don't think he knows how to deal with this woman. A male that could engage her as a model would be helpful.

Jackel: Yes, it would be very important for that male worker to be clear about mother's myths, which may be seductive, and know how to cope with them or how to make it clear to father that support moves for mother are not moves against him. That's a very difficult thing for a man to do, I think.

Blugerman: There is also a statement about father making awkward physical contact with the kid. That contrasts with the statement that he's accepted the kid as his son and suggests that maybe he hasn't, or he hasn't seen male engagement in a range of activities. If you had a male worker who had that kind of flexibility and could model it, I think the father could get a great deal of satisfaction from this case.

Interviewer: Any particular biases about age of worker if you had your choice?

Blugerman: There's nothing in the case that hits me. It has to be someone whom the parents can relate to, and someone whom this kid can engage with.

Interviewer: Which might be someone of any age?

Blugerman: Yes.

Interviewer: Are there any other worker characteristics that could be important?

Blugerman: Somebody who doesn't easily get anxious about these kinds of symptoms. Most people read these symptoms and they go bananas. For example, if this came across the desk of a child welfare authority for placement, most people would get panicky about the fire-setting and the potential danger and a lot of people wouldn't like the soiling.

Jackel: I'd like someone who had dealt with a tremendous range of behaviors in kids and could deal with his threats and his escalating behavior. I'd also like someone who would be able to play with Stefan and move up and down with him. That's a hard combination to find in a worker. Michael, would you try for a male-female team with the family if you couldn't find the kind of male worker you are looking for?

Blugerman: No, I'm really hot on the parental control and the fewer characters the better. For example, he sets fires at home, he doesn't set them away from home. I would be more worried about the kid if he set them away from home. So there are very clear messages about control. I'd like to limit the field of authority, and he obviously finds that he can split his parents. If I had a male-female or other co-team, I'd worry about splits between them. If I wanted extra help I would go to an outside consultant behind a mirror.

Jackel: So you're keeping it simple?

Blugerman: Yeah. It's boundary work.

Interviewer: Let's talk about what kind of outcome you'd be working toward with this family. At what point would you stop? What goals would you set for yourself with the family?

Blugerman: For me, the first thing is symptom reduction because these symptoms are alarming to the parents and to most people who would deal with the kid. Never mind reduction, but elimination, that would be the final outcome. How I would know where I was along that track would be the extent to which the kid could show individuation and differentiation in front of the parents and not be overwhelmed by their anxiety and to what extent the parents could model dealing with differences in front of him. He's dealing with differences with them and they're dealing with differences with each other, so as long as I saw progress in that area and a reduction of the coping by withdrawing, I would think I was on a fairly good track and then I would watch for reports of self-esteem approval from peers in school. Then I would know if the approach could hold right through the course of therapy or whether I'd have to add something.

Interviewer: Good, that's nice and clear in terms of criteria. How about you, Cathy?

Jackel: I think that the real key for me would be when they can begin to operate as a team and when they can handle minor crises as a team. I'm not sure that this couple is going to go much further than that unless they decide jointly at the end of that process that they actively want marital therapy and actively want to explore further. I wouldn't necessarily look for that. I would try to see how far they go with co-parenting in the face of crises and their ability to tolerate increased pressure from the kids and remain together as a parenting team.

Blugerman: I'd like to make one other comment. The description of Mr. Lopat's mother picking him up all the time and caressing him almost constantly. There we have a three-generation model of failure to deal with anxiety and failure to model containment, a constant attempt to avoid any risk of individual stress. So when his wife gets anxious, then he'd get anxious and they wouldn't know what to do with each other. So I would be tracking that kind of thing. It would fit with the increasing ability to deal with differences together.

Interviewer: What would exemplify an interaction that would suggest to you greater tolerance of individuation?

Blugerman: Let's say the kid does something that's upsetting, the mother becomes anxious, the father comes home, she tells him about it. He listens to the sound of her voice and looks at her face and feels the distress and then panics, so he can't contain his feeling about her feeling about the kid's feeling. If there was improvement, then I would encourage the kid to fuss, hold the mother while that happens—I mean hold "therapeutically"—and do the same as she reports her anxiety to father, side with him to support him to contain her. The more I saw of that kind of thing happening on their own initiative, the more I would think we're on a good track.

Jackel: So you're looking at strengthening ego boundaries in all three members?

Blugerman: That's right.

Jackel: I was just thinking back to mother's history. She was basically parented by her older sisters. That suggests again that there was not only an absence of a mother but also of a father figure. So you're probably right to choose a male if you're going to use one therapist.

Interviewer: Prognosis? How optimistic are you about reaching the kinds of goals that you've just talked about?

Jackel: They're coming for help. They have no pressure in coming for help because the school's handling the kid. I didn't look significantly at the outside authorities because a number of first-generation families who have middle

European backgrounds often regard authority in a particular way. They often fear that the authorities will somehow "find out." So I am looking at them in terms of what they have going for themselves in coming for help. The kid hasn't burned down the house yet. His biggest thing is the small hole in his bed. They are avoiders, and they could still be avoiding it. He's in trouble with his friends but the teachers aren't finding any major problems, no one's complaining, so they're coming on their own. They are back together again, and there does seem to be at least an expressed motivation by father to parent Stefan. The goal I set in terms of them beginning to parent jointly might be reached. I see it as taking one-and-a-half to two years. I see it as long-term involvement, and I see the last part of it as very gradual withdrawal with an open door because I think this family's going to need that kind of support.

Interviewer: Michael?

Blugerman: I'm more optimistic about the kid. I feel optimistic about the family, and I feel quite optimistic about the kid; so even if the couple fail to stay together, I think the kid would do all right with the kind of treatment that's available. Given the kid's age and the kind of factors Cathy's talking about, I think there's a good chance.

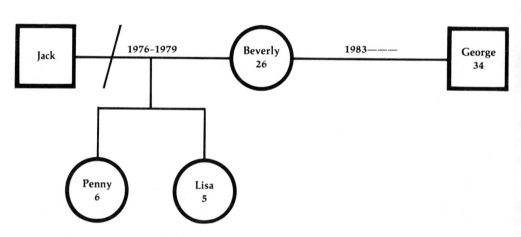

THE VENTER FAMILY

Identifying information

Beverly Venter and her common-law husband, George, have sought help for both of Beverly's daughters, Penny and Lisa, from the mental health center. Beverly complains that both daughters are "hyperactive," constantly attention-seeking, and insecure. Both children have been taking Ritalin, prescribed by the family doctor, but mother feels this has brought little improvement. Although Penny and Lisa are very strongly attached to each other, they fight frequently and also are both having peer problems in school.

History of problem

Beverly has a long history of psychiatric problems and has had several moderate to severe depressive episodes. One of these depressions, which required hospitalization, occurred shortly after Lisa's birth. At that time, both daughters were placed in foster care for approximately 19 months. Beverly's husband, Jack, who is Lisa's natural father, is an alcoholic and was unable to care for them. Beverly was released from the hospital following four months of treatment, including electroconvulsive therapy, and the marriage began to deteriorate rapidly. The couple separated, and Beverly went through a mild depression but managed to stay out of the hospital. Jack and Beverly were divorced in 1979, and neither she nor the girls have had any contact with him since then.

In 1980, Beverly reassumed custody of her two daughters, who had been placed in the same foster home. Mother had maintained frequent contact with them during placement and was judged to be concerned and caring about them by the child welfare agency involved. In 1982, however, Beverly again needed a brief psychiatric hospitalization due to depression, and the girls were once again placed in foster care—this time for only three months. No special concerns were raised about them during either of their two foster home placements.

Mother reports that the children were difficult to manage when they were returned to her in 1982. Penny especially has been whiny and clingy and seems never to be satisfied with the amount of attention mother gives her. When the family recently moved, Penny was quite resistant to attending the new school. Mother feels that things have improved somewhat since her boyfriend, George, moved in six months ago. George was a patient on the same psychiatric ward during Beverly's most recent hospitalization, and they have been seeing each other continuously since that time. Both girls seem very fond of George and responsive to him.

Mother has sought no professional help for her children other than several visits and telephone calls to her family doctor, which resulted in the Ritalin prescription noted above.

Marital and family history

Beverly was one of a family of six children and lived in an impoverished rural area until she left home at 16 years of age. She then lived several years with an aunt until meeting and marrying her first husband, Jack. She described her father as a heavy drinker who frequently beat his children and was absent from the home for long periods of time. Beverly seemed better connected with her mother and several siblings but is not in close contact with any family members now. Her marriage went poorly from the beginning, and her husband was also an abusive man who beat her quite badly on several occasions and who seemed totally uninterested in the children.

Little is known about George's family history because he was reluctant to discuss it, seeing no relationship between this information and the current problem. He has not been married before and says that he and Beverly plan to be legally married soon.

Characteristics of family members

Beverly presents as an anxious, easily threatened woman with a chronic history of depression. She apparently functions adequately when not depressed, however, and has a fairly stable employment record as a postal clerk. She has been able to regain custody of her children, supports herself, and is actively reaching out for help. Beverly feels guilty about having placed her children in foster care twice and suspects that she is to blame for their problems. Her parenting skills are limited, and she is uncertain and inconsistent in her management of the children. When their behavior upsets her, she yells at them and occasionally hits one or the other. There is little apparent differentiation in her treatment or perception of the two girls. She seems sincere in her desire to parent Penny and Lisa but showed little warmth to them during the intake interviews.

George, on the other hand, is demonstrative and caring with both girls and seems to be a stabilizing influence on the family. He will not disclose the circumstances of his own psychiatric hospitalization but states firmly that this episode was in the past and that things are working out well for him now. George has been working as a salesman in a men's clothing store but was recently laid off and is currently looking for work. At home, he helps Beverly with household routines and enjoys playing with the girls. Both Penny and Lisa respond affirmatively to him and reportedly are more obedient to him than to Beverly. George presents as fully involved with this family and very intent on making a place for himself in it. He seems to be a likable, easygoing man.

Penny and Lisa are clearly very strongly bonded to each other. Penny seems to take more of a parental role, and her bossiness is often the source of conflict. Penny tries to project an image of a "tough" person who is unconcerned about any family problems and who thinks that coming to the mental health center is "dumb." She seems emotionally closed to the interviewer and is unresponsive to all overtures. She has a very serious, almost adultlike manner. Lisa is more approachable and open and talks easily about her school and home activities. She is very satisfied with George's presence but worried about her mother and whether she will get "sick" again. Lisa is more impulsive and spontaneous in her play, but neither sister appears in any way hyperactive.

Though the family spends time together and enjoys activities as a unit, there is no clear leader. George is affable and supportive, Beverly is anxious, and the girls compete for attention and favors. It sometimes appears that Penny is the dominant member of the family.

School and community

School reports are sketchy because the girls have only recently been enrolled. Penny's first-grade teacher describes her as aloof with both peers and adults, easily discouraged and frustrated, and lacking in confidence. She has gotten into several fights with other children, but it's not clear who instigates these incidents. Lisa's teacher describes her as "very hungry for love" and confirms the attention-seeking picture given by the parents. Lisa usually gets along with her classmates but has been the cause of complaints by other children because of her aggressiveness during recess and after school. Her cognitive development seems age-appropriate.

In the past couple of months, the girls have been supervised by George after they come home from school. Before George moved in, they would stay with a woman in the building who takes in children. The family likes to go shopping and on outings together, but the parents complain that the girls compete and squabble so much that these trips have become unpleasant. The children are not allowed to play outside without adult supervision.

Case discussion

Consultants: Dr. Julian Rubinstein, Ms. Mary Pat Tillman, Mr. William Wetzel

Interviewer: Okay, we are going to talk about the Venter case. What strikes you about the family?

Tillman: The amount of time that these two girls have been separated from their mother is striking. You may want more information about the placement problems and how the kids initially dealt with the separation from mother.

Wetzel: I think that is a crucial issue.

Rubinstein: I may want to assess the family doctor first. I want to know what his problem is. *(Laughter)* One of the first things I would want to do is to find out on what basis he prescribed the Ritalin and for how long. I would also like to know how he has monitored the effect of the drug or had the mother monitor it. There seems to me little good evidence to use it, and I sense that it has been of little value in this case. But I could change my mind depending on what the prescribing physician says. I would like to obtain stronger evidence to confirm a diagnosis of hyperactivity or else get the family doctor's agreement that the medication isn't helpful and stop it. The major effect may be the labeling process that takes place, and this is not helpful to the child or to the family as a whole.

Wetzel: I agree for sure.

Tillman: Fragmentation and separation are themes that certainly run through this case. I am concerned about the way that Penny handles herself at the age of 6, that those separations threaten to happen again. How long is George going to be around? How long is mother going to be around? Penny is developing all kinds of defenses around those issues. Lisa is more vocal in her needs for attention and belongingness, but Penny withdraws and covers up in all kinds of ways.

Wetzel: Commitment is something I wonder about. I wonder about George's resistance to talking about his hospitalization. I would like to know more about his relations with the girls. I am wondering about possible sexual abuse of the girls. That is purely a speculation and something I would want to investigate.

Rubinstein: Something must have triggered that thought.

Wetzel: What triggered it was what seems to be George's complete resistance to talking about his hospitalization. The fact that he is 34, supposedly never married. I don't know about previous relationships, and the fact that the girls are as responsive to him as they have become in such a short period. I can see that they want male attention, but those are the things that make me wonder about it. So I wonder about George's commitment to the family and about Beverly's commitment to the kids. I wonder specifically about her emotional rejection of the kids and its relation to her feelings about the kids' father.

Rubinstein: There are a number of things here that, superficially at least, appear contradictory. In one sense, George is described in a very positive way, caring and involved. He sounds like a stabilizing influence in the home, the best thing that has ever happened to Beverly or the kids. On the other hand, the psychiatric history, or perhaps more important, his reluctance to disclose it, raises suspicions. Is he hiding something? Is it a stand on principle? There may be something a little bit fishy involved here. I would also want to know what is in it for him, if he really is the knight in shining armor that he seems to be. Beverly doesn't seem to have a hell of a lot going for her, although she is really trying very hard.

Tillman: There *is* something curious in terms of the family relationships. Her first husband seemed to represent very much a repeat of the family she grew up in, and then all of a sudden she finds this white knight. Again, I would want to know more about the nature of the relationship between George and Beverly and look for some of the same needs being met in this union as in the previous union.

Rubinstein: I am not clear whether George is just not willing to talk about his hospitalization or whether he would be unwilling to grant permission to obtain records from the hospital where he was treated.

Tillman: What would you do if he wouldn't agree?

Rubinstein: Well, I would have to live with that. It will be a question mark throughout any contacts I have with them.

Wetzel: That is my feeling. As he becomes more comfortable with, and trusting of, the worker, would he be more willing? If after a while, he wasn't more willing, then I would have more serious questions about him. I would also like to explore with the family just how much the girls worry about mom getting sick and leaving again.

Interviewer: How would you work with this family?

Wetzel: In terms of working with the family I would want to know more about the circumstances surrounding Beverly's previous hospitalization, working diagnosis, prognosis, and treatment that had been provided. This information would influence whom I would see in treatment.

Tillman: I would also seek to determine what kinds of nightmares the kids have, what scares them, and look for a family theme, be it the fragmentation or the separation. I would encourage more permissive sharing of fantasies and fears for everybody in the family. One of the first attempts might be to try to create an environment of more permissiveness and fewer secrets.

Wetzel: In terms of treatment, I would go back to the issue of commitment. I get different messages about Beverly. I get one message that she is caring and concerned about her kids, and yet, at the same time, she has given them up on two different occasions. I wonder what kind of commitment and involvement she really has with these two kids. I would want to assess that early on very clearly.

Tillman: She certainly lacks confidence in her role as a mother. I think she tends to address those fears by, on the one hand, thinking somebody else can look after her kids better than she can and, on the other hand, wanting to do everything herself.

Wetzel: I would explore how she feels about the kids being so responsive to George. Does she want George to take over in that way or is she upset that the kids are more responsive to him than to her?

Interviewer: You have mentioned being more concerned about Penny than Lisa. Would you suggest any individual work with Penny?

Tillman: Not at this point. I think it would be better done with the family. Penny strikes me as somebody who must be in real terror inside and yet covers up very competently. There must have been a great deal of rage associated with the abandonment. What strikes me most about Penny is how difficult it is to connect with her. One of my interventions would be for mother or someone in the system to connect more with her. I would be very concerned about how she might exhibit depression later on.

Rubinstein: I think sickness plays a central role in this family. Mother's hospitalization, the child's diagnosis and medication, and George's hospitalization. This orientation to sickness disturbs me. I would like to promote an orientation toward health. One other thing I would like to know about is the nature of mother's depression. Is it thought to be biologically determined? I think there is a pattern of everybody playing sick roles. I am not suggesting that mother's depression is not legitimate, but I am concerned about depression becoming a mechanism to cop out whenever things become tough or difficult. George seems to have a lot going for him and if that is borne out, I would want to use him in constructive ways with both mother and children. I think this is the kind of family with whom I would use a lot of task-setting around behavior management, hopefully using George's apparent competence to advantage. He could be used as a model. By giving him a role and a status, one could test out the commitment you were talking about and ascertain whether he could help Beverly with child management issues. I am also concerned about Penny's adultlike behavior. I would help the parents handle and respond to her in a manner that is appropriate for her age.

Tillman: One thing that strikes me is that this is only a six-month living-together relationship. That is certainly an adjustment period of getting together and forming a commitment. It is hard to know at this point whether George will stay and whether they will marry. I would wonder how many questions mother or George has about their relationship. I would want to create an atmosphere of permissiveness to explore those kinds of things with Beverly and George with the kids. Exploring what can happen if this family breaks up again. I think what is most destructive in this family is what is not said. The lid is on all over the place and attempts need to be made to loosen the structure a bit.

Wetzel: I was trying to figure out how much either of the kids might remember from when Jack and Beverly were together. There are different theories about what kids remember in their first year, and if Jack was as abusive with Beverly as it sounds, I wonder how much of that Penny witnessed and can recall. She may even have been used as a shield at times. I can see Beverly lifting Penny out of the crib to protect herself from Jack. I wonder about the kids' fantasies about daddy and the past.

Rubinstein: Mother's talk suggests that she might have been psychologically unavailable to Lisa during some early critical periods. I wonder what kind of role the biological father had and what happened to Lisa immediately after birth when mother was hospitalized.

Wetzel: There may have been a period when the kids were with Jack after mother went to the hospital.

Rubinstein: I suspect that this information is not going to make much difference in terms of treatment planning, however.

Tillman: I think where you could use that early information might be to have the kids imagine what it was like when they were 1½ years old. I am not sure how relevant it will be at this point in terms of separation and loss. Rather than initially getting into any concrete interventions, I would be tempted to spend a long time in an exploration phase, creating an atmosphere as opposed to making any direct interventions.

Interviewer: Do you have more to say about strategies or ways of working with the family?

Rubinstein: I would like to make this as brief a contact with mental health professionals as possible. As far as the girls are concerned, the problems are not that serious at this point and I would be concerned about the labeling process that seems to have been going on. I would want to give them very clear and specific messages that, in fact, all is going well, unless some information emerges that changes this view. I would probably still want to try and normalize this family and emphasize areas of health and strength rather than sickness or dysfunction.

Tillman: I would agree with that, because I think a worker can get sucked into the system, follow each problem area, and constantly reinforce this family's use of outside people. I think it would take a person who can refrain from responding to the tugs and pulls of each thing about this case and stay out of the role of expert.

Rubinstein: It seems that attention-seeking and insecurity for these kids is to be expected given the recent history of this family, and I don't see that as pathological at all. If there were a sense of stability and commitment in the future, my expectation is that that would go away without major therapeutic intervention, given that George means what he says and nothing untoward emerges in his history. If it looks like it is going to be a steady, warm relationship with some continuity, I wouldn't be worried about this attention-seeking, insecure behavior. I am sure it is based on the kids' anxiety about moving around and who the mother is and if there is going to be a dad in the family.

Interviewer: Would you discuss those concerns with the family?

Rubinstein: Yes, and it could be in that context that I would try and normalize it. I would tell them that I am not surprised about the attention-seeking at this point, that it is a naturally adaptive process the kids are going through given their history. I would predict very emphatically that if things continue to go well, I expect that it is going to go away soon.

Interviewer: Are there any danger signs for the therapist to look for in this case—besides George?

Wetzel: Well, as I mentioned earlier, finding out more about mother's depressive episodes—whether they were reactive or whether there seemed to be something chronic to them—would be useful.

Rubinstein: I agree with your point. I think one would have to keep an eye open for a recurrence of her depression, and I think that could be a problem.

Tillman: I realize I am still stuck on Penny, but I would recommend keeping in touch with any disturbing behavior she may start to exhibit that gets a bit more disturbing or appears to be more disturbed. I suppose you could have periodic phone calls or meetings to see if her parentlike behavior subsides a bit or if we are getting into something else with her.

Wetzel: I wouldn't talk too much to the school about either of the girls. I wouldn't want the school to be labeling them from the beginning as problem kids. I would leave it to the parents to take the responsibility for connecting with teachers and the kids' progress in school.

Tillman: Yes, I would definitely want to minimize panic and concern about something that looks bizarre now because obviously they are in transition and into a new phase which will create all kinds of funny-looking behaviors at this point. In six months to a year that may settle down.

Wetzel: Another even more concrete danger signal might be an increase in mother's yelling and physical and verbal abuse with the kids. It states that her parenting skills are very limited and she is inconsistent and uncertain.

Interviewer: Okay. Are there any special worker characteristics you would recommend?

Tillman: Somebody who is not too helpful, in the sense of wanting to rush in and do something. Somebody who is able to sit back and stay out.

Rubinstein: If I were supervising or consulting on a case like this I would want to have a thorough justification for continuing after maybe eight or ten sessions. Then I would want additional justification after another four or five sessions.

Wetzel: I think the ability of the worker to contract around very specific goals would be useful.

Tillman: I think you could get trapped as a worker into doing that for the family. I would be curious to see what would happen with this family if you could stay outside a bit and just question what is going on or flow with opening them up.

Interviewer: What would be your treatment goals?

Tillman: Flexibility. Looking at them as a family in transition at this point. If anything, the goal I would encourage the therapist to seek is more freedom, flexibility, permissiveness of thoughts, ideas, fantasies and so on in the family and people being able to talk about fears, separations, and commitments. More connectedness among the members in the family.

Wetzel: I have some more specific goals. One is around the family doctor issue and then checking out the use of the Ritalin and more than likely getting the kids off the Ritalin. A clear assessment of Beverly's depressive illness. A clear assessment around George's previous hospitalization and commitment. Helping mother to see that she can be competent as a mother and can manage these kids and care for them. If things pan out with George, helping him to remain a stabilizing influence and to support Beverly's competence. I don't know how that would work because I would question whether he needs her to be incompetent, but if that is not the case, I would want to help him support her competence.

Rubinstein: I agree with all that. I would like, in addition, to find out whether there is any potential for Beverly to reestablish contact with her extended family. There is a suggestion that she did have some kind of relationship with them. I don't know why she is not connected with them now.

Interviewer: What is your prognosis?

Rubinstein: Good, provided that we are not surprised by the information that is unknown at this time. This is the kind of family with which I would want to maintain contact and make it very clear that I was available to work with them at any time. But I feel positive about them.

Interviewer: Other thoughts about prognosis?

Tillman: I would say middle of the road. In terms of the correct things that they are asking for, prognosis is good. I would wonder, in terms of mother's past marriage and family, what is in store for them down the road. I agree with you in terms of being available for them to get back in touch as a good thing, but not to have them depend on it for a long period of time.

Wetzel: I agree very much with what Julian mentioned. If things pan out the way they seem and there aren't other things that come up with George or mother's illness, I would feel fairly hopeful. With this kind of family it might be good, in terms of maintaining some of the gains, to help them build support systems with their extended family or the neighborhood.

SUMMARY

All the families in Chapter 4 contain at least one parent who is suffering significant emotional disturbance. In addition to the therapeutic needs of the parent, the children are experiencing difficulties that are often aggravated by the problems of the adult.

The first family in this chapter, the Bells, includes a son who reports two suicide attempts, a mother with chronic hypertension, and a father with ulcers. While the suicidal 16-year-old is withdrawn, uncommunicative, and doing poorly in school, his sister and parents are high achievers. Mrs. Bell is also observed to be intensely angry and rejecting with her adopted son and very defensive about any role she might play in his problems.

Concerned about the suicide potential of this boy, the consultants suggest the need for a careful individual assessment of him and his state of mind. The work with the family is seen as requiring effective joining with mother, enabling her to shift from her defensive stance. The consultants believe that the therapist must identify concerns that the whole family shares and then emphasize work on these common concerns. Ultimately, treatment objectives should include improvement of this family's ability to allow direct affective expression, a problem for each individual member. The consultants also advise promoting a stronger bond between father and son.

The "identified patient" in the Lopat family is Stefan, a 7-year-old boy who is setting small fires at home, wetting and soiling himself, and behaving in generally defiant and destructive ways. Clearly overwhelmed by his behavior, the parents are resorting to bribery and medicating Stefan. Mrs. Lopat is a highly anxious woman, on medication herself, with a history of two psychiatric hospitalizations. Father presents as a passive and emotionally unavailable man.

The consultants think that it is essential to help these parents assume control of their son and family. Direct instruction in effective child management is recommended, including demonstration and modeling of ways to handle Stefan in the therapy sessions. In particular, mother needs to be more confident and adept in handling Stefan, with her husband supporting and backing her up. In addition, one consultant believes that Stefan would benefit from being seen in individual play therapy in order to help him express feelings appropriately and to improve his self-image. The other consultant stresses the primary importance of the parents working together as an effective team in helping Stefan behave in more age-appropriate ways.

In the Venter family, the emotional problems of the parents are even more pronounced. Mrs. Venter has a long history of severe depressive episodes that have resulted in several hospitalizations and treatment with electroconvulsive therapy. During her last hospitalization, she met George, who was also a patient, but who will not disclose details of his psychiatric history. George is now mother's common-law husband and has moved in with her and her two young daughters. Mrs. Venter thinks that both girls are hard to control and complains about their constant fighting. Consequently, both girls have been put on Ritalin for "hyperactivity." Mother is anxious and unsure of herself and tends to yell at and hit the girls if they misbehave. George, on the other hand, seems to be warm and caring and a calming influence on the family.

The consultants agree that it is important to discontinue the Ritalin and remove the apparently inappropriate label of hyperactivity. It is felt that the family needs to shift from an orientation of illness and "sick" roles to an emphasis on health and positive areas of functioning. The therapist needs to underline the family's strengths and areas of normal functioning. The consultants also suggest that the family needs to discuss openly its past instability, with the temporary foster placements of the girls being identified as a natural source of anxiety and concern for them. Finally, the consultants mention that Penny, the 6-year-old, has to be encouraged to be more of a child instead of a "tough, little adult."

STUDY/DISCUSSION QUESTIONS

1. How can parents be helped to recognize and address their own personal problems when they present their child as the only problem?
2. What considerations should be weighed in deciding whether to provide individual therapy for a child?
3. How can the specific form of a parent's emotional problem influence a child's functioning and problems?
4. What evidence is there that children of mentally ill parents are at greater risk of emotional disturbance?
5. How can a focus on parenting skills help/harm a mentally ill parent?

5

Parents Who Do Not Let Go

Although extreme closeness between two people is popularly attributed to love ("two hearts beating as one"), intimacy and inter-dependency can become a serious problem when carried to extremes. A relationship between parent and child that is lacking in strong caring, closeness, and sharing is deficient. However, some parents become clearly overinvolved with their children in ways that stifle that child's growth and development. Overinvolvement may have positive or nega-tive emotional "coloring" to it. In other words, parents may be over-involved in a protective, concerned, loving way or in a critical, angry way. In either case, the parent's emotional energy is so intensely and exclusively directed at the child that the child is engulfed by it. Such a child finds it difficult to develop an identity as an individual distinct from the parent. The child is unable to separate from the parents and to develop other relationships. Such a child fails to achieve the progressive independence that is integral to maturation and adulthood. This type of overinvolvement is found to varying degrees in many families and is often a contributing or complicating factor in the child's presenting problem. In fact, negative behavior on the child's part may be his or her only available expression of the desire to break free from the constrict-ing relationship.

A major difficulty in treating families with these characteristics is that the parents see their efforts as well-intentioned and devoted. This is as true for the hypercritical parent as it is for the indulgent, overprotective one. Neither wants anyone to come between them and their child, even a therapist! Treatment efforts to alter the parent-child relationship are met with hostility, panic, or despair and tend to expose the parents' as well as the child's neediness. Furthermore, the child is likely to feel threatened by efforts to separate him or her from the parents and can vigorously resist such efforts. Both partners in an overinvolved rela-tionship fear change and may rigidly unite against the therapist. Treatment usually needs to include ways of supporting and mobilizing wishes in both parent and child to grow and be independent. Ambivalence about fusion versus separateness can be found in all three of the families presented as case examples in this chapter.

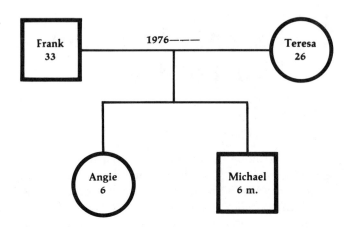

THE DONATELLI FAMILY

Identifying information

Angie Donatelli is a 6-year-old first grader who has been described as "school phobic." The referral was initially made by the school three months ago because they were concerned about Angie's aversion to school and her inability to get along with her classmates and teacher. The parents have since become sufficiently concerned about Angie to follow through with the referral on their own. The Donatelli family consists of Frank, Teresa, Angie, and Angie's brother Michael.

History of problem

The family has always regarded Angie as a dependent child, but the school problem did not develop until she started first grade eight months ago. Angie did not attend kindergarten but went to a neighborhood day care center, which her mother attended with her every morning. As long as her mother was present, Angie's behavior was acceptable, although she seemed to be less mature and socially skilled than her peers. This year mother drives Angie to school and has literally to disengage her from the car and drive off to make sure that she goes. Once or twice a week Angie puts up such a fuss that Mrs. Donatelli either does not take her to school or turns around and brings her home once they are there. Teresa knows that her response is not helpful but is unable to tolerate Angie's tantrums and desperate pleas. At school Angie does not stay in her seat, strikes out at the other children, and is uncooperative with the teacher. On a few occasions the school has called Mrs. Donatelli and requested that she come and pick up her daughter. Angie's teacher regards her as an indulged child who demands too much attention in the class. Since Mrs. Donatelli is now also responsible for taking care of her baby son, she is feeling increasingly overwhelmed and motivated to change Angie's behavior. At home the parents complain that Angie needs more help than she should in dressing and feeding herself, refuses to clean her room and do as she is told, and becomes irate when mother spends time with Michael. Angie's behavior has, in fact, deteriorated since Michael's birth.

Marital and family history

Frank and Teresa Donatelli both came from large Italian families. Frank's parents emigrated from Italy and still speak Italian in the home. His father is a laborer, and Frank works with his cousin in the construction business. His three brothers and one sister are all married and live in the vicinity. The relationships among them are volatile, but they have regular contact with one another through work and on holidays and birthdays. Teresa's family still resides in Italy, although she has cousins who live nearby. Teresa has a grade school education, has never worked outside the home, and speaks only rudimentary English.

The Donatellis left Italy when Angie was a baby. She has learned English by playing with neighborhood children but speaks Italian with her mother, although Mr. Donatelli insists that she speak English with him. Frank and Teresa tried to have other children soon after Angie's birth but were unsuccessful for almost six years.

Characteristics of family members

Frank and Teresa Donatelli come across as emotional, demonstrative people. Frank is impatient, doesn't listen well, has strong opinions, and doesn't understand why he should be bothered about a domestic problem such as Angie's behavior. He claims that Angie is no problem for him and thinks that Teresa should be able to handle her but lets her get away with too much. He seems to lack a clear perception of Angie's fear about leaving her mother. He does not like to hear Angie and her mother shouting at each other or Teresa complaining loudly to him. One of her complaints is that Frank is rarely home, since he works long hours and spends much of his free time with friends from work. When he is home, Angie is under better control. Father's directives are more apt to be followed, and Angie seems afraid of him. On the rare occasions that Frank and Teresa go out together, Angie stays with her grandparents, who indulge her every whim.

Angie is an attractive, dark-complexioned 6-year-old with large, saucer-like eyes and a mischievous grin. When separated from her mother, she seems terrified and breaks into an ear-piercing scream. Teresa's legs and arms are black and blue from Angie's hitting her in protest to her leaving. A typical procedure consists of Teresa gently asking Angie to do something, then increasing her volume and tone until Angie screams back. Lately she has hit Angie a few times and is beginning to worry about losing control. Mrs. Donatelli believes that Angie is "sick in the head." She seems depressed and helpless and complains of getting headaches from her constant battles with her daughter. She undoubtedly does more for Angie than is age-appropriate, such as tying her shoes and picking up her toys.

Angie has a few neighborhood friends who come to play in her back-yard. They frequently end up going home, however, because of Angie's inability to play cooperatively. Angie says she doesn't like school, her teacher, or her classmates. She also does not like talking to other adults. She looks scared, suspicious, and angry, and her favorite response is "No!"

School and community

Angie's first-grade teacher is visibly relieved whenever Angie does not show up for school and looks forward to the end of the term. Because of Angie's high rate of absenteeism and her refusal to cooperate and attend, she is receiving failing grades and will have to repeat first grade. But the school is insisting that Angie and her family receive professional help before agreeing to take her back in the fall. They are also concerned about Angie's primitive social skills and her language development. They believe her intelligence is average but note that her speech is at the 4-year-old level. Angie also occasionally wets her pants at school.

Case discussion

Consultants: Dr. Rudolph Philipp, Ms. Elizabeth Ridgley, Mr. Bruce Stam

Interviewer: What other kinds of assessments would you suggest to a caseworker who was presenting this case to you as a consultant?

Philipp: Somewhere along the line I would suggest a speech assessment of the immature speech that is cited.

Interviewer: Okay, so that is the additional assessment that you'd like to see. Is there any other information lacking that you would want the worker to obtain?

Philipp: Since she failed first grade, you may want to do a psychoeducational assessment as well.

Stam: I had a question regarding Mrs. Donatelli's background and her relationship to her parents. Her parents are overseas and that creates a problem since a lot of this information comes directly from Mrs. Donatelli.

Interviewer: Would you interview her individually or interview her with her family?

Stam: Interview her individually, and retrieve some of her memories from child-hood. The children in the family whom she did and didn't get along with.

Philipp: There is a real problem with that. She doesn't speak English and we might need someone to translate.

Stam: Yes, we will need someone fluent in Italian and familiar with the culture.

Interviewer: What major modalities of treatment would you recommend in this case?

Stam: Basic family therapy with an Italian worker, dealing with the interrelationships between the families, mother and daughter, and father's position. Second, a direct demonstration for mother on how to deal with Angie using positive support and very simple, basic child care techniques. Preferably in the home.

Interviewer: What would you recommend if there were not an Italian worker?

Stam: Basically the same thing, I guess, except that it will be a lot rougher job. But that does not mean it cannot be done.

Interviewer: How about you?

Philipp: In this particular case, ideally one would do family therapy. But I am not sure that you would get that far with this family. I would first want to get the father's approval to work with this Italian family. It isn't easy for them to seek help, so I would certainly commend them for coming. Perhaps I would raise their anxieties a bit, suggesting that failing grade one can have a very negative effect on a child's future. It could become worse if we don't do something now—and with the new baby in the home, the sibling rivalry might result in some harm—to encourage them to become involved. If you couldn't do family therapy because of the language problem, I would suggest that a classmate or another parent take Angie to school. The mother is much too involved with Angie and, of course, that has a bearing on the marital relationship. I might use a behavior chart with the mother and father.

Interviewer: Could you describe how you would set that up?

Philipp: It would be very simple and straightforward. Children that age often use such charts at school. It might involve receiving a "happy face" for getting ready on time, for arriving at school, and for remaining there. The parents would be trained to be agents of reinforcement. I would have the worker or someone familiar with the school system help the teacher as well.

Stam: A good reward system would specify time with mother as positive. Right now Angie is receiving a tremendous amount from the negative behavior, so I would want to start switching the whole system around for her.

Ridgley: I think this is an excellent structural family therapy case. I would speculate that Angie is feeling enormously displaced by Michael and feeling a loss of mother with Michael's birth. I think that probably the relationship between the mother and Angie and father was dysfunctional prior to Michael's birth and that mother was closer to Angie or to her baby than she was to Angie's father. Angie is abruptly required to be 6. She is also in a proper school with the same kinds of demands, and the father is still peripheral and unable to pry mother and Angie apart. The interesting thing to me is that when father is at home Angie is no problem, and father, in fact, is critical of his wife for being incompetent. Father is also seen as less sensitive and as impatient and not listening well. I am wondering where that information comes from. I imagine from mother, so the parents are, in effect canceling each other out and regard each other as incompetent. Each is taking Angie's side, and on various occasions Angie gets stuck in the middle.

I think the prognosis is excellent, because Angie is able to respond to father, and father is able to see what needs to be done. I would work specifically with the father. I would see them as a family, but I would agree with you, Rudy, about getting his permission. Even more than that, I would ask him what he thinks the problem with Angie is and what needs to be done. I would give him the big structural family therapy pitch that his family needs him. That he is the father, his wife is tired, his wife is ineffectual. I would raise his presence in the family, and I would get him to talk to Angie about one change she could make this week. He is to tell her what he thinks about school and how she ought to behave there, that he knows she can manage it. He is not to let her go to mother, he is to do the talking. I would emphasize that his wife is too tired and too soft, and he needs to take over the situation and convince his wife that he can achieve good results with Angie. I would elaborate on the fact that it is a shame for her to fail, for she is a smart girl. I would ask him to get her to talk to him like a 6-year-old, because she talks like a 4-year-old. I think that what happens with the two of them is that father is tougher because mother is softer, and that if he dealt with Angie without mother's interference, his softness and tenderness and all that wonderful, warm Italian family feeling would come out. I think that he can do it because he has a sense of what a 6-year-old should do, and he has more leverage than she does.

Interviewer: Would you have him take Angie to school?

Ridgley: Oh, yes, if it is possible, I would. I would also have him talk to the teacher, because that is very important. At one point when we would be talking about what a shame it is for her to fail and that she sounds like a 4-year-old, I would say "Can you take her to school and can you explain to the teacher that Angie is here to stay in school and that she is now 6 years old?" I would let him deal with the teacher and take over the problem.

Philipp: Since mother is being criticized for not adequately handling her child, aren't you avoiding helping her deal with the issue?

Ridgley: I know I am not helping the family, but I am getting the father to help them. The therapist's job is not to help but to facilitate change in the structure so that the family does the work.

Stam: I am not as optimistic as you are. I get the feeling you aren't going to get very much time from father on this one.

Ridgley: If father is concerned about his daughter, concerned enough that he doesn't like his wife and daughter's relationship, he will help. You know that he thinks his wife is too permissive in letting her get away with things that he would not want.

Stam: I agree with supporting father. I think it would be terrific if we can get that. On the other hand, a lot of the problem concerns the dependency between mother and the daughter and the failure of the marital relationship to fulfill mother's needs.

Ridgley: If you bring father in to help the daughter, it convinces his wife that he knows what to do with her. What mother gets out of this is her husband's attention and she will welcome that.

Interviewer: Bruce, you have talked a bit about some family work and some modeling for mother. Are there other specific strategy suggestions that you want to give?

Stam: I think some individual therapy for mother around her need for affection and closeness would be very helpful. Her husband and family obviously aren't meeting those needs.

Philipp: I would make two suggestions. One is to suggest an English class for mother. Their intentions are to remain in this country and to become Canadians. I assume that the daughter is attending an English school. Another possibility is some kind of activity or social skills group for Angie, because she is a bit immature and doesn't get along well with her peers.

Interviewer: We are certainly getting a nice cross-section of ways of attacking the problem. What kind of worker would you recommend for this kind of case?

Ridgley: I don't think it matters whether the worker is a child care worker or a social worker or whatever. If he or she were to take a structural family therapy approach, I would hope for some experience in that direction or sufficient supervision for a new worker.

Philipp: Ideally, I would like to see a skilled worker with structural family therapy training who speaks Italian! Seriously though, I would want a skilled child care worker. And a male worker might more effectively introduce father to the program. And I am concerned about the fact that they don't have any social life. They rarely go out, and when they do, they leave the girl with the grandparents, who spoil her and————

Ridgley: That is wonderful. Every child should have grandparents who spoil them. The problem is, I agree, that they don't go out.

Interviewer: We are circling back to the case and that is fine because I want to ask you what you would be wanting the worker to look out for if this case gets stuck. What should the worker be worrying about?

Ridgley: The worker, in my opinion, should be worrying about nothing. She should love the family. She should draw out of it Italian traditions that she may or may not know about. She should elaborate and exaggerate how wonderful it is to have such a culture and thoroughly enjoy them because they are a nice family.

Interviewer: Is there anything that you could imagine might happen with this family which would lead you to reevaluate?

Ridgley: Not the way I see it.

Interviewer: Bruce?

Stam: I would be concerned not to push Angie away from mother too quickly. I think it is such an obvious problem that a naturally gung ho child care worker might push to break up this relationship and get the kid to go to school. If that happens too quickly, it will be totally counterproductive. In fact, Angie would withdraw even more and it could produce a difficult situation. I would monitor Angie's emotional state pretty closely.

Interviewer: What is going to happen to Michael in the future? When Angie is on her feet, is Michael going to take on all those problems?

Ridgley: Angie won't be on her feet until the family is on its feet. They may drop out when she starts to go to school, but they will gain an ability to work together and her staying in school would sustain them. I would give them a checkup and tell them I want to see them in six months.

Interviewer: Good. What particular goals should the worker be seeking?

Philipp: I would like to see the two parents working closer together, mother learning more effective skills, and getting out a bit more. This could be for English classes or with her husband for a good time. Finally, I would like to see this girl in school on a regular basis, learning social skills.

Interviewer: Okay, Bruce?

Stam: Father has to gain a major role in the family. Mother has to have her needs met somewhere. You can't simply take away Angie.

Interviewer: What should the worker look for in terms of an outcome for Angie?

Stam: School attendance and doing well there. I think her speech will probably clear up along with it. Doing well academically as well as socially. I believe the prognosis is good.

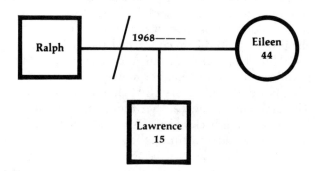

THE YOUNG FAMILY

Identifying information

The Young family consists of Eileen Young and her 15-year-old son, Lawrence. This is a court-referred case. The judicial system became involved when Lawrence was apprehended for the second time in four months for exhibitionism. The only other concerns about Lawrence are withdrawal and a relative lack of friends.

History of problem

Lawrence's exhibitionism was first detected four months ago when a woman in the family's apartment building reported him for knocking on her door and exposing himself. As a result, the family was forced to move. A month ago another woman reported him for running naked through the hall of the new apartment house. After this incident, the court recommended professional treatment for the boy and his family. Lawrence has since revealed that he has been exposing himself periodically for more than a year. Both the mother and her son are embarrassed about the behavior. Mother, in particular, wants to know why Lawrence needs to do this and is angry about having to move again. Her questioning of her son on the subject has not been fruitful.

Marital and family history

Lawrence Young was born out of wedlock when his mother became pregnant by a married man named Ralph. Eileen Young views the pregnancy as her method of breaking away from her own mother. As the fourth of five children it was her role to stay at home, be a companion to her mother, and help to care for her invalid father while the other children married and moved away. Her father died ten years ago, and Ms. Young is still an outcast in her mother's eyes. She sees her parents' relationship as having been unhappy, and she herself has never established a good relationship with a man. She has been the sole support and caretaker of Lawrence for 15 years, while maintaining a stable job as a bookkeeper.

Characteristics of family members

Ms. Young is a neat, plainly dressed woman who appears somewhat older than her age. She is tense and fidgety and smiles nervously while speaking almost nonstop. She acknowledges that Lawrence is her "purpose in life" and finds it difficult to deal with the reality of his growing up. At the same time, she does not want him to stay around for her sake as she did with her mother. Lawrence and Eileen's relationship is close, warm, and mutually overprotective. Eileen has virtually no interests outside the home other than her job. It is important for her to be a good mother, and she goes out of her way to participate in her son's life and to shield him from unpleasantness, such as violence on television and "unsavory" acquaintances. She is currently disappointed in him and becomes tearful when discussing the recent incidents.

Lawrence is a slim, sad, well-groomed, and well-behaved teenager. He appears shy and introverted, relies on his mother to initiate things, and generally complies with her wishes. He probably also finds it difficult to break into his mother's stream of talk. His self-image is poor, and he needs emotional support. Lawrence spends a lot of time at home and is socially immature for his age. He is anxious and guilty about discussing the topic of exposing himself but offers that it is a way of relieving tension and perhaps drawing attention to himself. He is relatively naive about sexuality, although he admits to some masturbation. He has never had a girlfriend. More important, there is no important male figure in his life. He does not like being an only child, and he wishes he had an older brother. Lawrence relates well to adults and, although reticent, can open up when people are patient with him.

School and community

Lawrence is in the ninth grade at school. His academic work reflects his ability, which is average. He is not very interested in school and wants to quit as soon as possible and get a job. He responds to the teacher's questions and interacts appropriately with peers who initiate contact with him. By and large, however, he is passive and isolated at school and has no close friends. He stays away from aggressive kids and prefers to avoid physical activities. He did enjoy the contact with, and support of, a male teacher last year who has since been transferred to another school.

Lawrence has a few neighborhood acquaintances. They collect and trade old comic books and go to the local arcade to play the pinball machines.

Special assessments

A psychiatric interview was conducted with Lawrence prior to his court hearing. The psychiatrist assessed him as mildly depressed but with good reality testing and no serious psychopathology.

Case discussion

Consultants: Dr. Harvey Mandel, Mrs. Marjorie Shore, Dr. Steven Stein

Interviewer: Is there additional information that anyone would want or seek in this case?

Shore: It would be important to get a detailed school report, and I'd like to have the police record.

Stein: Well, I would want more information about the exposure incidents, when they occurred, what was happening beforehand, and so on.

Mandel: Yes, I would want more details about how he ended up getting caught. This is not the first time, it's the second time.

Stein: I think it would also be important to get some flavor from the school, from mother, and from Larry about the quality of the relationship he had with the male teacher whom he lost a year ago, because to me there seems to be some connection between the exhibitionism and the loss of a male figure who supposedly was one of the only people close to him. So I would want to know about the quality of that relationship and how long it lasted, as well as Larry's behavior around the loss of it.

Shore: Along those lines, it would be important to investigate whether there were any other changes during that time. It may well be a male teacher that he lost, it may be that mother brought a boyfriend into the house, or that his best friend found a girlfriend, for example. Anything significant that may have occurred.

Interviewer: Anything else in the way of additional data?

Stein: The only other data I would get would concern some of Larry's thoughts about the incidents of exhibitionism. I know he may be reticent to talk about it, but I would seek some way of finding out what he was thinking at the time that he decided to do it, whether he would get caught, whether he felt guilty, and so on.

Interviewer: How would that be useful to you?

Mandel: Well, I want to find out what's behind the act. Is it attention-seeking? Is it low social skills? Is it that he doesn't know how to communicate with others his age? Is there some kind of sexual problem? I want to get more details about what's actually going on.

Shore: The kind of details that I would want to focus on in this particular kind of problem would be autonomy issues. The thought going through my mind is that mother had to get pregnant to leave her family, and I want to know if this is what Larry has to do to leave his family.

Interviewer: So you're seeing him in some sort of clinch with mother?

Shore: I don't know, but that would be an area that I would want to explore quite specifically.

Mandel: One issue is the bond that exists between mother and Lawrence. Another is the repetitive generational pattern of dealing with questions of separation. The mother having to do something to act-out sexually in order to move away or to separate; Lawrence acting in some way to gain whatever he's gaining at this point. There's an assumption that there may be some need on his part to separate and yet some difficulty in making that kind of transition.

Shore: In a healthy child, separation issues should be coming up at this age. The record suggests that Lawrence is mother's whole life, and it's very difficult for children to leave a mother who's been that good, that giving, and that wonderful.

Mandel: Something else that I'd want to explore is Lawrence's motivational level for the change that may be coming. I'd also want to assess what will happen to mother as the separation process begins. I think these questions would be better answered as the therapy process actually unfolds.

Interviewer: What would you use as an index of that motivation for change?

Mandel: I would start with some very concrete measures such as: (a) Did Larry come in of his own volition even though mother made the appointment? Did Larry come along willingly or did he have to be dragged in? (b) If counseling is going to be a possibility, what flexibility is Larry willing to exhibit around his willingness to come on his own or come with mother? A willingness to sacrifice on his part is an index of his motivational level. (c) Also his attitude toward the assessment process. What sort of attitude did he have toward the people who were gathering information? Was it a hostile attitude? Was it subservient? Was he looking toward something positive that may develop?

Stein: Another basic question is to find out if he knows why he's here. What does he think is going on? Does he accept the fact that this is a problem?

Shore: Adding a step to that is, how severe is his problem? This particular problem in a 15-year-old boy is a very severe problem. It does not speak to a mild behavioral disturbance, and the report states that he's shy and embarrassed to talk about it. Everyone should be absolutely outraged and terrified that this would happen, and so, in terms of assessing his motivation, are they minimizing the problem or are they able to look at it as the severe problem that it is? It is quite severe and very rare for a 15-year-old boy.

Interviewer: Would you want more information about his sexual behavior or his sexual history?

Mandel: I might want to know how he feels about masturbation and some sense of his motivational level for heterosexual activities. In other words, is he interested in females, and in what way is he interested in females? Do they scare him? Does he get excited about the possibility of a relationship? Has he ever tried a relationship? I don't mean sexuality *per se,* I'm talking about some ongoing relationship, and if so, what happened? There are also the more sophisticated questions that I mentioned, such as, does Larry have some sense that there are underlying reasons to the behavior? Now I don't mean, can he explain it exactly, can he nail it from a Freudian or cognitive theoretical orientation, but does he have an inkling that there are some things that are behind the behavior? To me, that would be an index of his appropriateness for insight-oriented treatment.

Shore: I think the other side of the relational issue is important too. I think it would be critical, particularly with this relationship, to have a full understanding of the mother's perception of treatment, why her son is coming in, how she feels about him seeing somebody by himself.

Mandel: What she expects out of treatment.

Shore: Exactly. Her attitude toward having to come for treatment and for having to ask for some help in the first place. Unless you feel very sure that you have mother's full support and she is not going to be a sabotaging influence, you've lost the kid before you've started.

Interviewer: So we're starting to get into treatment now.

Mandel: We're starting to get into some implications for treatment. For me, decisions about the nature of treatment would be based on a more expansive assessment.

Stein: That would depend on who is doing the treatment. My own perspective is a cognitive-behavioral approach.

Interviewer: Can you talk a little bit about that?

Stein: Well, again we tie the assessment to the treatment. His cognitions are central, things that are going on in his mind, his attitude. We mentioned, for example, that he has some shame about the incident now. What other thoughts does he have about what he's doing? The intervention would be to change some of those cognitions that he has. For instance, if it is an attention-seeking behavior, I would try to teach Lawrence that that's not the best way to get attention, that there are other ways that don't bring the same trouble.

Mandel: You're assuming, I guess, that you're going to be doing one-to-one with Larry?

Stein: At this point, it would be either an individual or a family process.

Interviewer: Mother and son?

Stein: Yes, but I wouldn't change my approach that much, depending on whether it's individual or couples or family-focused. I would still focus on the same issues with him. The only reason I might not do this within the family is that Lawrence may be shy about talking about these issues in front of his mother.

Interviewer: Would others of you see the boy individually too, or would mother be included?

Mandel: I think I would plan treatment at two different levels. I would have individual treatment set up one-to-one with a male therapist for Larry. I think there are three important issues: One is the relationship with a male, and I think that there's evidence in here that that's something he needs. The second thing is that it separates him from mother, and I think that's part of the treatment process. The third level that has to be dealt with is mother and the changes that she will go through as Larry begins to go through changes. I would recommend some kind of ongoing, supportive, management therapy initially with the idea that if she begins to get into psychic difficulty as Larry changes, it can shift into more intensive treatment. Structurally, that's how I would deal with treatment.

Shore: I would initially want to do both a family and an individual assessment. And as I mentioned, I'm not willing to focus so much on the sexual issues because I wouldn't see them as a relevant factor at this point. I would see the separation issue as the first issue. I would see Larry and his mother together to deal with that issue. Once some patterns had been changed in terms of Larry doing more autonomous activities and mother doing some autonomous activities, I would then think about moving the boy into individual treatment. But I would want to lay the groundwork for autonomous behavior first to give me a better chance of being successful. If we moved into individual treatment at this point, given the tight bond between mother and son, he would be set to fail because we wouldn't be able to control mother well enough and she would sabotage him. My guess would be that it would be very, very threatening for her son to have a relationship with anyone other than her. I suspect there would eventually be a lot of rage at mom. I think his issue with men probably is quite neutral, I think his issue with women is terrific, so I would begin with a different slant.

Interviewer: So you would also have the worker see the son individually at some point?

Shore: At some point, but the underlying statement would be that this is a case in which treatment has to begin before treatment can begin, if that can make any sense, where some groundwork is laid.

Interviewer: Do you also perceive, as Steve has, that you would be reluctant to deal with the sexual issues with the mother present?

Shore: I wouldn't be reluctant to deal with the sexual issues with the mother there.

Stein: I would only be reluctant if Larry were unwilling to deal with them. I would deal with them with the mother there; but if he's going to clam up and not want to talk, then it's a different story.

Shore: But, you see, I think it's a must to deal with the general issue of sexuality with the mother there, because what Larry feels and thinks is so tied up with mom, that if she has any craziness about masturbation or his relationship with girlfriends or even with boyfriends, I want to know about it. And I want to know about it in front of Larry, so that when I see the boy individually I can say "This is what your mother's been saying to you for umpteen years, where does that leave you?"

Mandel: Margie and I differ on how we would proceed. I think there's some similarity in our conceptualizations of the separation issue. I would force separation to start with, rather than work through the separation between the two of them. I would actually force the issue and thereby raise mother's anxiety level. In other words, I would start by separating the two of them. Raise her anxiety level, start to provide some male support for Larry, and then deal with the fallout as it came. It may involve bringing the two of them back together again at some point down the road to deal with the new tension that has developed as a result of the beginning of that separation. So I think we're talking about a similar issue and two different ways of structuring it.

Interviewer: When you say you would force the separation, you mean you wouldn't see them together?

Mandel: Yes, correct. The rationale for that is to provide Larry with both a male anchor and some privacy in treatment. For me there is a developmental issue at the age of 15 or 16 or 17 that has to be addressed around working within the family to produce the movement toward autonomy, or working individually with the teenager to move toward autonomy and letting the teenager and family reestablish whatever new levels they can establish.

Shore: My experience has been that a physical separation is meaningless without an emotional separation. Over and over again I have found that when a child is physically separated from a parent, it is as if we have his mother beside us because emotionally it makes absolutely no difference. I think one of the things I've learned from that experience is that once an emotional separation has taken place it doesn't matter whether they are there together or not. But I agree with Harvey that separating them right off the bat will certainly raise anxiety levels, and it would be very important to assess whether this is a low-anxiety family. That is, how seriously do they see the problem? If they are coming in with really low anxiety, one would want to separate them and raise the anxiety level because high anxiety is needed to deal with this problem. One of the things I am worried about is the level of affective involvement in this family. I would suggest that they are either highly narcissistic or slightly symbiotic.

Mandel: I would think symbiotic.

Shore: If it is symbiotic, it doesn't matter how little you take him away, it's going to be there.

Interviewer: Can you explain what you mean by that?

Shore: A narcissistic involvement would suggest that this couple's involvement with each other is such that mother's involvement with her son would be meaningful to her in what it meant to her, and the son's involvement with his mother would be meaningful in what it meant to mother about the son. I'm involved in your life because it has meaning in mine. One of the ways to assess narcissistic involvement is to look at the quality and quantity of involvement. In narcissistic involvement the quantity is very high, and quality leans toward the destructive.

There are periods when narcissistic involvement is very helpful. If you have a small child it doesn't matter if you're narcissistically involved with him, it's constructive. At 15, it becomes destructive. A symbiotic involvement is one in which there is a very high quantity of involvement and very low-quality involvement. It's terribly destructive in that it impairs both parties' psychological, biological, and social development.

Mandel: And that's why I said this strikes me much more as a symbiotically connected relationship. I think that can be said about both members of the family.

Interviewer: Let's talk about treatment strategies. For instance, from a cognitive-behavioral point of view, Steve, what might you do?

Stein: Well, unlike Harvey and Margie, I would not focus on separation at this point. The first thing I would probably do is deal with what Larry sees as a presenting problem. He may not see himself as having a problem, so the focus of my time at the beginning would be to convince him that he has a problem and to realize that he will have to deal with it or get himself in a lot of trouble.

He's been dragged here by his ear, so I would want to help him to get out of here. It's no fun coming here, he has better things to do with his time. I would try to get him motivated, to convince him that he really does have a problem, and that he does have to work on it.

Interviewer: And beyond that?

Stein: Once he realizes he has a problem, you can start dealing with it. The first level would be to deal with exposing himself and helping him to realize that that's a nutty thing to do and that there are more appropriate ways of getting what he's after. I would try to determine what he is really after and then get into things like separation issues and helping him to develop his peer relationship skills.

Shore: What about the psychiatric assessment that he's depressed? My experience with depressed kids is that you can talk away to them and not get anything out of them.

Stein: Quite often we work with suicidal kids who are saying nothing and yet manage to get them going. One of the things we use a lot is humor. Sometimes that shakes them a bit. We don't make fun of them, but we use humorous episodes to wake them up and show them that we are on their side and want to help them enjoy themselves a little more.

Interviewer: Would you want to deal with the exhibitionism as a specific behavior as well?

Stein: Well, it is a behavior. I'd want to deal both cognitively and behaviorally. My goal is to reduce that behavior and not have him exposing himself. I may deal with other kinds of issues, but as long as that boy is exposing himself he's going to get in a lot of trouble. So I want to put a lid on that as quickly as I can.

Mandel: We haven't talked about peers and I think that at some point down the road, a peer activity would be crucial for this boy. It might be a therapy group, or an activity group, or a community group, but I would recommend a supervised group experience. I would want it to be a group composed of both sexes.

Shore: Well, first I would want a thorough family assessment, including an individual assessment of both mother and son.

Interviewer: What kind of information would you want?

Shore: First, I would want to know if they agree on the precipitating problem that brought them here. I'd want to know how they have tried before to deal with the problem, given that this is the second time, as well as their understanding of why they weren't successful. I would want a history of the problem, and I would guess that by that time we would have labeled more than just the exhibitionism. I would guess that there would be some mention of Larry having been very different the last little while and of how he has been different so that we could deal with some other kinds of problems, which may or may not relate to the exhibitionism. I would want a history of those problems. I would then want to understand a number of family processes, how they involve themselves, how they tick, how they problem-solve, and how they make decisions. I would want to know about their affective expression, how they show welfare feelings, which are love and caring kinds of feelings, and emergency feelings.

Interviewer: And you would expect that to be done as part of the initial phase of treatment?

Shore: I would not differentiate the assessment from the treatment. The skills needed would be beginning treatment skills. From that assessment I would want to be able to determine the intervention point. I would guess that everything would probably speak to autonomy issues; however, there may be another area where they have more strength. Let's say they are particularly strong in roles that are very rigid. I might start to restructure their roles, while always thinking about autonomy issues, but not necessarily moving in on autonomy issues. Once I set a base from which autonomous behavior was more acceptable, I would give Larry individual treatment. I also agree that it is very important to put a lid on the exhibitionism. And I probably would contract with him around that, including some guidelines as to what we'd all do should this happen again. These contingencies would be agreed on, and we would have discussed them before we ever brought him to treatment.

I would also want to contract with them for a designated amount of time. If no changes have occurred during that time, we would have to restructure the whole business or they would have to go somewhere else. I would want to give them a very clear message that some changes are going to occur quickly and that even though this is a severe problem, things have to change yesterday.

Interviewer: Are there any other strategies that one of you might recommend?

Mandel: I think that Lawrence needs to be offered an alliance in some kind of relationship with the therapist that is qualitatively different from his relationship with his mother. I think it needs to be based on autonomy progress. Generally speaking, teenagers respond to the issue of "you and them against the world." Obviously, this boy is encountering some very specific difficulties in the world. I would use the exhibitionism as a point of entry. Based on the flavor of this report and the depression, anxiety, and guilt that are mentioned, I don't have an impression of Lawrence *not* wanting ever to face this issue.

Shore: How do you assess whether he will?

Mandel: I would have made some assessment of motivational level and if the level is reasonable, the joining will occur.

Interviewer: Any other strategy suggestions?

Mandel: I would also have whoever is working with the mother confront her on the vacuum that gets created when her son is moved from being the entire meaning of her whole life. I would actively work with mother to begin to put in substitutes that seem more appropriate for her.

Shore: But then, of course, a therapist would have to work with the boy as well. He stops his mother from going out because she has to stay home to watch him. It is not only mother stopping Larry, it is Larry stopping mother. It's interactional.

Interviewer: What kinds of difficulties and obstacles might you predict or encourage the worker to anticipate?

Shore: I would be very aware of the effect that each of these individuals would have on the other in terms of Larry growing up and moving away and allowing his mother to grow up, in a sense, and become independent. I would caution any therapist to be very aware of the subtle sabotage that goes on. I feel strongly about this because these people have very set patterns that keep them in that type of bond.

Stein: I would caution the therapist about Lawrence's likely resistance to talking about his exhibitionism and how to get him to talk about it.

Shore: Many therapists would be so cautious of raising the topic that they wouldn't and the family may be so embarrassed that they don't. Even if no one else in the room talks about it, it may be comforting for the therapist to bring it up and talk about it as a way of desensitizing them to view exhibitionism as a problem like any other problem.

Stein: Yes, I agree they have to talk about it, but I would warn against pushing them to the point where they would just clam up again.

Shore: One of the ways that I deal with not pushing is to offer my own thoughts rather than to ask "What do you think? What do you think?" My taking the initiative to speak about it gives permission for others to speak about it as well.

Interviewer: Harvey, do you have anything to add?

Mandel: The caution for me would be around the reticence of a particular therapist or worker to talk about the behavior based on his/her own hang-ups.

Interviewer: What kind of worker would you like to see working with this family?

Stein: Someone who will accept this boy and his behavior and know how to differentiate the act from the person, someone with good verbal fluency, a sense of humor, somebody who is personable.

Interviewer: Does anybody have an age or sex requirement for the worker?

Mandel: I already mentioned that Larry needs a male therapist, based on a developmental point of view. I'd also want the therapist to be willing to structure from the beginning. For me a client-centered orientation would be contraindicated for this particular kind of behavior. I think you need a structured approach to deal with some of the practical, immediate difficulties and issues, then some ongoing sensitivity to the dynamics of where this behavior came from, and for me it lies in the separation area.

Shore: I agree with most of what's been said. I think the therapist's activity level is critical. I think the therapist must be able to take over because this family is clearly out of control, and it should be somebody who is able to learn, or is already at ease with, the whole area of sexuality. I don't have a strong feeling about male or female as long as the worker is good.

Stein: I'd like to second that. I understand why you might want a male therapist. But I also see some advantages for having a female. This boy obviously has a problem relating to women, and a female therapist could probably do some positive things in helping him relate to the opposite sex. It may also diminish some of his anxiety about being with females.

Interviewer: Would you want the same therapist seeing the boy and seeing mother and son together?

Shore: I would probably have two different therapists, basically because it's very hard to switch roles from being a family therapist, where you facilitate and encourage the family, to being an individual therapist where you form a one-to-one alliance with the boy.

Mandel: I would choose a male therapist for Larry, and I think I would choose a female therapist for mother.

Interviewer: How hopeful are you about the outcome?

Stein: The prognosis is pretty good. Some of the earlier factors that were mentioned—some anxiety, some guilt, obviously not too happy with the situation—suggest the likelihood of a motivational change.

Mandel: Although I'm not pessimistic, I have a guarded view of the prognosis. On the positive side are some elements of motivation for change that you and Steve have just mentioned. On the negative side is Larry's lack of connection with peer groups and mother's isolation from her own peer interaction. I see a tremendously tight bond between the two of them and I see a 15-year history that has been brought to that situation, plus the exhibitionism. Again, on the positive side, he has managed to function in school at an average level, and there does not seem to be a long history of this symptomatic behavior. We're also not talking about a family that has been in ongoing treatment for a long time. So I have a guarded view of the prognosis.

Shore: I think my view would also be guarded.

Stein: When we talk about prognosis, we may be referring to different goals.

Mandel: That's a good point. I'm talking about two levels of change. One level is the actual behavioral change for the exhibitionism and the second is the movement toward, and some sense of accomplishment of, the separation between mother and son.

Interviewer: Any guess at how long treatment might go on?

Shore: I would see this as a long-term treatment. Anything over 12 weeks would be long-term treatment.

Stein: I think it depends again on the role that we are talking about and how far they're willing to go. In terms of the exhibitionism, I think it would be relatively short-term treatment. In terms of the separation issues, I see that as long-term.

Mandel: I think the exhibitionism can be brought under a reasonable amount of control fairly quickly. Overall, I see it as a medium-length treatment process. I also see the possibility of some built-in vacation from treatment, with both of them coming back individually to deal with what it's like to live separate lives. I don't mean merely in terms of Larry moving out of the house, but in beginning to form different connections in different groups and coming back to therapy later on with some of the material that that generates. Mother has to make a very significant change. She has to redefine the entire purpose of her life. The son has defined his life as connected to mother, but he hasn't invested the same amount of time in doing so. So I would see a longer treatment for mother and a little less time for the boy.

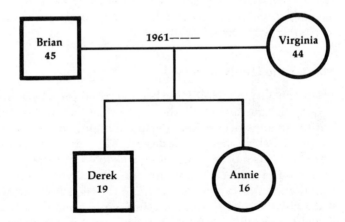

THE HOLT FAMILY

Identifying information

Annie Holt is a 16-year-old, tenth grade student who came to the clinic with her mother, Virginia Holt, age 44, at the recommendation of the school counselor. Mrs. Holt is very upset at having discovered that Annie is 13 weeks pregnant. Other members of the family include Brian Holt, age 45, and a 19-year-old son, Derek. They were not present at the intake interview and are not aware that Annie is pregnant.

History of problem

Annie learned that she was pregnant two weeks ago and confessed to her mother a few days ago. After missing two periods, she became worried but denied her suspicions and waited another month before seeking a medical examination. She was not suspicious initially because her menstrual cycle has always been somewhat irregular. Immediately upset, Mrs. Holt sought the advice of the high school counselor, who made the referral. The current dilemma is that Annie has decided that she wants to have the baby, while Mrs. Holt is encouraging her to have a therapeutic abortion before it's too late. She is convinced that having the baby will ruin her daughter's life.

The father of the child is Annie's boyfriend, Phil Merriweather, an 18-year-old high school senior. Phil reports that he is willing to do "the right thing" but clearly prefers to stay as uninvolved as possible. Annie maintains that her desire to have and raise the child is independent of Phil's decision.

Both Annie and her mother appear to be afraid to tell Mr. Holt about the pregnancy. He apparently has a strict moral code, a bad temper, and strong negative feelings about Annie's boyfriend. They would prefer to solve the problem without consulting him. Mrs. Holt says that she and her husband have both been concerned about Annie's behavior since the onset of adolescence. In particular, they do not like her choice of friends, her nonchalant attitude toward family rules and activities, her temper, and her declining school grades. The interests of Annie's friends are nonacademic and incline wholly toward having a good time, which most likely includes the use of alcohol, drugs, and casual sex. Up to now, Annie's behavior has not resulted in trouble with the authorities.

Marital and family history

Brian and Virginia Holt have been married for 22 years. Mr. Holt holds a managerial position with the post office. His father was a middle-class businessman, since retired. Brian maintains contact with his parents, but the relationship is formal. He describes his father as aloof and authoritarian; he regards his mother as shallow and does not respect her. Virginia Holt's father was a respected government official who died of a heart attack six years ago. Virginia reports that her father was reserved and gentle. She has had a volatile relationship with her mother and feels that her older sister was always the favored child. The Holts met after university when Virginia was working as a buyer for a department store. She quit on the birth of the first child and has never returned to work.

Characteristics of family members

Annie is a fair-haired, round-faced, physically mature adolescent who presents as sullen and truculent. She feels unappreciated and unloved and enjoys the company of only a few friends. She does not think that her choice of friends is the business of her parents and maintains that they are basically nice kids. She believes that her parents' disapproval of them derives from the fact that they aren't the popular, "phony" student leaders. She spends as little time at home as possible, although she has agreed to have meals with the family. She thinks her parents lead dull lives and don't go out enough. Initially she was fearful about the pregnancy but now she has decided that a baby will be a worthwhile goal for her, someone to love and be loved by in return. She envisages finishing high school on a part-time basis and will take whatever job is available to meet expenses.

Annie is reluctant to discuss her feelings or to open up with adults. Her relationship with her mother consists of screaming battles alternating with tearful reconciliations. Their fights usually focus on Annie wanting fewer restrictions or on mother inquiring about Annie's activities. Sometimes Annie and her mother find pleasure in shopping together, but Annie seems increasingly bored with her mother's company. Mrs. Holt is a carefully groomed woman who always appears to be a small nudge away from breaking down and crying. She wants to be closer to her daughter and is confused about Annie's behavior. She does not like it when Annie talks back to her, misses a curfew, or does not do her chores. However, one of her functions is to protect Annie from Brian, who demands strict obedience. Mrs. Holt claims that her marriage is okay and not at issue, although she wishes that Brian could be more flexible and understanding with the children.

Brian Holt leads the family like a platoon sergeant. He has had difficulty lately in accepting Annie's friends, lifestyle, and school performance. He also wants her to show more respect for her mother. Apparently he has threatened to throw Annie out of the house because of her attitude but is dissuaded by the intervention of Virginia. There is some risk that he would throw Annie out if he knew about her pregnancy.

Derek is away at university and comes home on occasional weekends. He is not in any ostensible difficulty. Both parents seem proud of Derek. He and Annie share few interests, and she regards him as somewhat "square."

School and community

Annie will not be able to attend public school as long as she is visibly pregnant. She is welcome to return to school if she decides to terminate her pregnancy. Her academic average is in the low average category. She scores well in the few classes she likes, such as English and art; she does poorly in science and math. Her teachers do not think she is working to her full capabilities. She is often inattentive, comes late, and socializes with a non-academic group with lesser abilities than she has. The school counselor suspects that Annie engages in some drinking and drugs, but she has never been in trouble on that account.

Case discussion
Consultants: Mr. William Carty, Dr. Barbara Dydyk, Dr. Peter Marton

Interviewer: Let's talk first of all about the kind of information that's available to you in the case description and what, if anything, from your point of view is missing.

Marton: Well, one of the things I was concerned about is that the problems begin to appear with adolescence. I'd be interested to know what the relationships were with each parent before that time. The reason is that I would want to know how much of this behavior is a reaction to the parents as a bid for independence.

Dydyk: I'd want to look at the involvement of father. It's reported that he's a bit of a tough guy, a sergeant, but that's just through the report of mother and daughter. It doesn't seem that anybody's contacted him. Also the 19-year-old son. What is his involvement and how is the family taking his being away from home? Is this a natural crisis, with the first-born leaving?

Interviewer: Any other information or assessments?

Carty: I don't have any. I think an assessment has to be done that includes the father, but I think that's a first step in treatment.

Marton: The other point in terms of therapy is to meet with Phil Merriweather to find out from his own mouth what his position is and not just mother's perception of their relationship.

Carty: I wouldn't include Phil. Originally I would look at this as a family unit.

Interviewer: Would you have communication with Phil at all, or do you feel differently from Peter about being in touch with him?

Carty: I see this as Annie's and her family's problem, and how they're going to resolve it. Annie needs something from her parents, the parents have to get together and give her something, or stay out. Then if Annie says, "I'm going to do this," she needs some support to deal with Phil, or the family might want Phil in to deal with the pregnancy crisis. I think there are two issues: first, there's the pregnancy and second, there's the relationship between mother and daughter.

Interviewer: I see, okay.

Marton: That's an interesting point. I guess my rationale would be a bit different. There are two issues: One is the pregnancy, which in a way may not be the real issue; it may be a false issue. Second, there's the relationship between the daughter and the parents. The worry I would have is that in a sense the pregnancy issue is an adult, life decision and to treat it as a family problem means that you infantilize this girl. I think that to bring in the father of the baby is to treat it as a real-life issue. That would be my approach, but I also see your point.

Interviewer: Okay, I'd like you to talk both about the major modalities of treatment that you see indicated here and about some of the concrete strategies that you might use to involve this family. For example, how would you try to get father into the clinic, given the taboos that mother and daughter seem to be presenting?

Dydyk: I would certainly approach it as a family issue, using a systems focus and joining with mother around her difficult problem with Annie because Annie still is living at home. I would emphasize that she can't make this decision on her own, that it is a parental decision and that it's incumbent on her to involve father.

The therapist would, in fact, help both of them in terms of dealing with father and reinforce mother, who seems to have some real power over the father in terms of protecting Annie from him. I'd use that to build up this "inadequate" lady, and then if *she* doesn't talk to father, I'd ask the mother's permission to talk to father myself, not to deal with the pregnancy issue, but to get some contract for involvement with him.

Marton: One tack would be to take a problem-solving approach with the family and say that there's an imminent problem and there's a long-standing one. The imminent problem is that some decision has to be reached about whether the pregnancy should be terminated or continued. I think that given the reality issues, the way to proceed is to have all three of these people sit and discuss it openly and do some problem-solving.

Carty: In a family like this, I'd make a few assumptions. One would be that it might be a family myth that father's so tough, and that he's only as tough as mother is soft. So the first step is bringing father in. I think it's mother's job since it's her spouse, and I'd work with her to bring him in based on her obvious concern and caring for her daughter. The daughter needs both parents together on this issue because it is a very major crisis in her life. I'd work as long as is needed with mother to bring father in because I think you're stuck without him.

Marton: I wonder. This girl discovers that she's pregnant and goes to her mother with the expectation that mother will do something about it. Would you not be tempted to take the other tack and leave it up to Annie to present it to her father as well?

Carty: No, because after the crisis decision, the long-term, ongoing treatment involves getting the parents together again in preparation for their penultimate child leaving home. They have each other, they don't have Annie's infant baby to take care of, and the first step in getting them together is making mother responsible for bringing in her spouse. The daughter is trying to fight and she can't fight mother alone; she has to have a strong front so that she can separate from two parents and the parents can consult each other.

Marton: So you want to place this girl back in the child role?

Carty: I would like to challenge the fact that mother and daughter are closer than mother and father, which I think is evident. I think if you'd explore with them you'd find that though they argue a lot, they also have nice close times and they go shopping. You would, I would think, find mother and daughter are very close and very dependent on each other. For the kid's sake, I would like to get mother together with father. When father comes in I would challenge the myth of his toughness.

Marton: So you see the mother as colluding in the role of older sister rather than mother?

Carty: Yes, or daughter is spouselike to mother. I see it as difficult for a 16-year-old to separate from mother if mother relies so much on her, and she relies so much on mother. Often kids worry about their parents, especially if they are very close to one of them. It's much easier to leave if you're leaving mother and father together.

Interviewer: Peter, would you promote a different kind of strategy?

Marton: I guess I see a possibility that this girl will decide to go through with the pregnancy. If she is having trouble separating, she's dropped a beautiful bomb on her parents, because there is real time pressure. The girl may say "I'm going to go through with the pregnancy" and the parents may reply "You can't do that, we're going to throw you out." This would force a separation, at least physically. If she decides to go through with the pregnancy, I see her as being at risk and certainly the baby as being very much at risk, because at some point this girl may very well decide that she didn't really want to be a mother. She may just want a baby to give her love. I guess one plan would be to accept this attempt to separate from her family and educate this girl for her mom role. I would try to get her into a situation where she can continue her schooling and learn to mother.

Interviewer: If you were doing that, would you be seeing her individually?

Marton: Yes. Well, that's given that the family relationship breaks down and the parents don't want to continue. First you would approach it from a family therapy point of view.

Dydyk: I think that brings up an important issue. Who really is the client? If she's 16 and she says no, then where do you go, how do you handle it? If she says, "I don't want my family involved, I don't want my dad told," what do you do about it? You could continue to bring up the need to involve her parents because she can't function independently. You could stress the need to involve father because her pregnancy isn't going to stay secret long, and when it does come out, mother's going to be in dire straits with her husband.

Carty: I agree with the comments about Annie and the baby being at risk, and that's why I see family therapy as very important to get her parents over the initial crisis. Once there is some sort of decision, the two parents can help their daughter seek and get what she needs in terms of clinics, education, and so on. I think it's very hard for a father and mother to do that by themselves; they need each other to lean on.

Marton: How long do you see that taking?

Carty: I think you have to hook both mother and Annie and, within a very short time, have them bring in father. I think the longer you see mother or daughter alone, the longer you're going with the system. You have to give them a deadline for that part of the work very quickly.

Interviewer: Let's assume that you're successful in engaging the family as a whole and also that the decision is to keep the baby. What other resources, if any, would you want to draw into working with this family?

Carty: I would think, given the history, mother and father would know what was needed and that would be their role with their daughter and that would be a very helpful thing to be able to give her. They know their daughter best, they would know what type of clinic, what kind of support, whether she needs help or not getting there.

Dydyk: I think they would have to know, though, what community options are available in terms of whether to go some place for the period of the pregnancy and in terms of vocational training for the kid because she's talking of leaving school. Those practical kinds of options.

Carty: I think that planning would happen in sessions with the family and then they would be given the homework to do.

Interviewer: We've talked almost exclusively about working with this family around the problem of Annie's pregnancy. Are there other things you'd want to work on with this family?

Dydyk: The marriage hits you in the face, in terms of the reported emptiness or poor quality of communication between the two adults. Through parental issues, however, you're really working on marital issues in terms of them being together as a pair. I see a couple of other issues to touch on. One is the loss of mother's father and the question of unresolved mourning for her. I would want at least to look at that, touch on that area. The other issue is this lady's self-concept. She's losing her two kids, and she hasn't had any career for years. What's going to fill her life? Does she need this crisis with Annie to fill her days?

Marton: That could be why she's willing to collude, protect, and, in a sense, help this girl in her delinquency.

Interviewer: Barbara, how would the worker know when and how to address these other issues?

Dydyk: I don't have a guideline. I think it can be touched on very casually, and if there seems to be something there, exploring it a bit, but not making it a central issue.

Interviewer: Bill, would you keep the focus on parental issues, or would you also go into some of these other areas?

Carty: I think the main task is joining the parents so that they're the partners and their kids are leaving them. I would try to make it short-term, and I wouldn't want to address any particular individual problems that might be hinted about in the family context. I think they're coming for this piece, and they can end with that. Later, if mother called, it could be another case two years down the line.

Marton: Another way to look at it is as a problem of this girl's separation and individuation from the family, especially if she is going to carry through with the pregnancy.

Interviewer: Specifically, what might you do with that?

Marton: I think I would be very practical around preparing for the expected child, learning mothering skills, getting her hooked up with parental care. I think that that allows for the development of a therapeutic relationship. You would want a person who would be able to give some things to this girl so that she could in turn begin to give to the baby. I'm suggesting one-to-one therapy focused around recognizing the separation issues. Meeting the practical needs gives the therapist a vehicle for setting up a supportive relationship.

Interviewer: Are there any particular problems that you might expect to crop up with this family?

Carty: Laying blame anywhere. The crisis is the pregnancy. I think blame, once it's started, is often hard to undo or resolve. The worker needs to unbalance the system without reinforcing blame.

Interviewer: How would you unbalance the system?

Carty: It depends how stuck mother is with Annie to get at father. You might challenge that by just asking her whom she married. Did she marry Annie, or is she going to live with Annie for the rest of her life? And are they planning to move out of the home? You might have to address the real issue, not in a demanding way, but in a very confronting way, because the system excludes father and makes him the big man, a mean character.

Interviewer: Are there other things that might start to go wrong and raise red flags?

Marton: If the father's reaction is that there's no way he's getting involved and he kicks the daughter out, and if the mother colludes with her so that the girl doesn't have to go off on her own, but can maintain a clandestine link with the family through the mother, I think that would be a bad system, one that could go on for a long period of time.

Dydyk: Another issue is the depression that hits you in terms of Annie and the mother and being cautious of that. We don't know what this man's about either and how isolated he may feel from his family. Annie's pregnancy might be a smoke screen for that.

Interviewer: Barbara, are you suggesting that one or more members of the family might become seriously depressed?

Dydyk: Yes, there's some potential. That's something for a worker to be cautious of in disrupting the family system.

Interviewer: What kind of worker would you choose for this case?

Carty: I see the need for a very skilled, experienced worker. A trained, family systems worker because the wrong move might blow it open. When you blow open things like this, it's lifelong because it's the child and the child's child.

Marton: Somebody who is not going to be intimidated by the father. Also, someone who is not going to collude with the mother and daughter.

Interviewer: I'm also curious about whether you would want to pick a female because of the pregnancy issue.

Marton: It would certainly make things easier.

Dydyk: Yes and no. If it was a firm, consistent, but gentle male, you would have mother and the kid dealing successfully with a male authority figure and seeing that that's possible. A male would also be a model for father in trying to deal with this touchy issue.

Interviewer: So there are some arguments for either sex.

Dydyk: Maybe what we're looking at is having two people involved at some point in terms of working as a team. Annie may need something at some point regarding her pregnancy while the other is working with the parents.

Interviewer: What major outcomes and goals ought the worker to focus on in tackling this case?

Dydyk: The immediate things are the resolution of whether she's going to abort or maintain the pregnancy and the involvement of father.

Marton: Another tack would be to help this girl reach a reasonable decision. It doesn't sound like she's going to do it the way things stand. I can think of doing very concrete things, like exposing her to situations that enable her to see what's involved in caretaking and talk to people who just had babies in that kind of situation. This would present a balanced view of what being a young single mother is all about because probably this girl does not have that at this age.

Interviewer: Other outcomes or goals on which the worker should focus?

Carty: The parents being together more generally for both kids.

Interviewer: Any specific outcomes for Annie herself?

Marton: Well, if she decides to go through with the pregnancy, the birth requires a lot of psychological preparation. Also working out a relationship with the father in terms of custody and how he's going to fit into the picture.

Interviewer: What do you think the prognosis is for success around these outcomes with this family?

Carty: Excellent.

Dydyk: Positive.

Interviewer: Peter?

Marton: Again, I'd want to know more what she was like beforehand. If I just read the teacher's report, I would be a bit worried about the outcome.

Dydyk: They talk about her not having been in trouble with any authorities, which I guess is encouraging.

Carty: I think the goal is to get the parents together and let their kids grow up whatever way they're going to grow up. There's a very high possibility to do that in a very short time given their backgrounds and education.

SUMMARY

The three families in this chapter have a closely knit bond between parent and child that is suffocating the child's development and acquisition of instrumental life skills. As is typical in such cases, the families arrive at an agency concerned about the behavior of one or more children, yet they seldom acknowledge the parental enmeshment as a serious concern.

In the case of the Donatelli family the identified patient is 6-year-old Angie, who is described as "school phobic." Mrs. Donatelli has been feeling increasingly overwhelmed by Angie's extreme dependency and her persistent refusal to cooperate, while the school complains that Angie is unable to sit still in class and to get along with her classmates. The mother also feels isolated in the home, since her husband, a construction worker, is often absent and rarely participates in the childrearing.

The consultants point out the advisability of seeking a worker who understands the cultural values of a first-generation Italian family and the strategic necessity to engage father in the treatment process. By drawing on father's input and potential strength, a worker may be able to break up the enmeshed relationship between Angie and her mother. Mother also needs direct help in managing the girl's behavior, while a peer group experience, such as a social skills training group, could be used to increase Angie's autonomy and improve her interpersonal skills.

The Young family, in contrast, is a court-referred case in which the 15-year-old son has been apprehended on two occasions for sexual exhibitionism. The boy was born out of wedlock and lives alone with his mother, who is close and overprotective. At school, he is passive and isolated and has no close friends.

One of the consultants emphasizes the importance of a careful functional assessment of the exhibitionistic acts, and all agree that eliminating this behavior is the first priority. The other consultants focus on autonomy issues. They emphasize the way in which the symbiotic relationship between mother and son is stifling the autonomy of both and accent the need for Lawrence to form normal relationships with peers and adults alike. Strategies range from cognitive-behavioral problem-solving with Lawrence to conjoint work with him and his mother on issues of sexuality and separation. The consultants hope that the exhibitionism, although a very serious indicator, can be eliminated fairly quickly using a structured approach with specific consequences, while more long-term work is needed to achieve separation and individuation.

In the Holt family the identified patient is 16-year-old Annie, who is pregnant and unmarried. Mrs. Holt and her daughter are in conflict over whether to terminate the pregnancy, while both are reluctant to inform Annie's father, a man with a vicious temper, about the problem. The family also includes a favored 19-year-old son.

The consultants identify the immediate issue as the resolution of the pregnancy and advise including both parents in the problem-solving. While therapy might begin with Annie and her mother, it is seen as important to have mother encourage father's cooperation. Such a move would help facilitate the secondary goal of bringing the parents together as resources for their daughter and helping Annie to separate from her mother. If Annie eventually decided to keep the baby, she would also benefit from specific modeling and training in how to become an adequate parent. The consultants are generally optimistic about achieving a positive outcome within a relatively brief period of time.

STUDY/DISCUSSION QUESTIONS

1. How can an enmeshed relationship between parent and child obscure other problems within the family?
2. What are some ways of engaging or eliciting the cooperation and participation of a parent who has the role of outsider in the family?
3. How can a clinical worker facilitate a child's independence and autonomy? How do such issues differ with development from childhood to adolescence?

4. What are some ways of introducing and treating potentially threatening issues, such as sexual disorders and pregnancy, within the family?
5. How does a worker decide who the client is, especially when someone else complains about the behavior of an adolescent?
6. What role do cultural values play with regard to parenting responsibilities, and how should a worker be influenced by them?

6

Children Who Need Protection

Although service delivery systems for children often separate services and agencies concerned with child protection and welfare from mental health services, the real-life problems of children observe no such boundaries. Experience in either type of agency will soon confirm that maltreatment and emotional disturbances of children are often closely intertwined. It is obvious that physical or emotional abuse of a child will result in distress for that child. It is also highly likely that a child who is ignored, unsupervised, malnourished, or otherwise neglected will show signs of impaired development or emotional disturbance. Conversely, research suggests that children who behave or develop atypically are, in fact, at greater risk for subsequent abuse and neglect.

A child suffering both abuse and emotional disturbance needs to be dealt with as a whole child with an interrelated set of needs. This position may present the mental health worker with serious problems. Can the worker assume the role of protector for the child as well as therapist for the family? Is an authoritative stance with regard to child abuse compatible with other treatment activities? What are the limits to confidentiality when child welfare issues arise? Will a team approach to protection and treatment roles result in a well-coordinated and consistent service plan? Finally, can the mental health worker reconcile his/her personal feelings about abusive or neglectful parenting with the need to form a positive therapeutic relationship with those same parents? Unfortunately, these complex issues must be faced more and more frequently in mental health settings. Following are descriptions of four cases in which this problem arises.

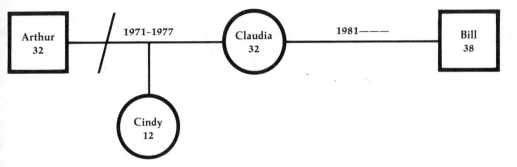

THE STEELE FAMILY

Identifying information

Cindy Worthman, age 12, lives with her mother, Claudia Steele, and her stepfather, Bill Steele. The referral comes from the school, which was concerned about a sexual incident involving Cindy. Cindy is also reported to have poor peer relationships and a history of aggressiveness and stealing. Need for intervention in the family is acute because of an incestuous relationship recently revealed between Cindy and Mr. Steele.

History of problem

Cindy has a history of lying, swearing, and stealing that began at about age 5 when she started school and was living with her natural parents. During the past year, however, Cindy has not been stealing and has become somewhat more cooperative. The incident that precipitated the school's concern consisted of Cindy's allowing three male classmates to disrobe and fondle her in a utility room during recess. A fourth boy who observed the proceedings reported them to the teacher. Confronted by her mother, Cindy angrily confessed that Mr. Steele has been sexually molesting her for almost two years. Although Mr. Steele denies this, Claudia Steele is very upset and inclined to believe her daughter.

Marital and family history

Claudia Steele, age 32, was divorced from Cindy's father, Arthur Worthman, six years ago after a stormy marriage. Cindy was an unwanted child who was often beaten by her father. After the divorce, Cindy lived with her mother for a year, then was shuttled between the homes of her father and her mother's older sister, ostensibly because her mother was experiencing financial difficulties and was returning to school to complete a program in nursing. Apparently mother also resented having total responsibility for her daughter. During this time Cindy's father, a veterinarian, would alternately ask her to live with him and throw her out of his house. Cindy has no brothers or sisters.

About two years ago Claudia remarried and she and her second husband, Bill Steele, a line assigner for the telephone company, took Cindy into
their home. Bill has two boys by a previous marriage who live with his
ex-wife. He has been divorced two years and has contact with her only to see
his boys. Claudia's parents live about an hour away. Claudia does not get
along with her mother, but she and her father sometimes meet for lunch.
Claudia's older sister is married and has three children. She is willing to help
Claudia in emergencies but says that she has enough full-time responsibility
managing her own family. Claudia's younger brother is also married and
works as a logger out West.

Characteristics of family members

Cindy Worthman is a slim, tall, attractive, pubertal girl who presents as
quiet and fearful. She appears distrustful of adults and waits for her mother
to speak. She has certainly experienced a lot of rejection in life. Both her
natural parents gave mixed messages about wanting her to live with them.
Cindy blames herself for the breakup of her parents' marriage and thinks
that their rejection of her was probably justified. She seems frightened of
the world but responds positively to a patient, caring approach. Cindy has
learned to cope with her insecurity and resentment by means of stubborn
defiance. She shows her anger through swearing and back talk, lying about
her actions, and occasional petty theft. Her mother reports that Cindy's
behavior was improving when the disrobing incident took place, and she had
believed that Bill Steele's presence was a very positive influence on the girl.
Cindy says that she does not understand what all the fuss is about and
minimizes the incident.

Claudia Steele is an anxious, frail-looking woman who is currently
depressed. She works as a registered nurse and is proud of herself for
returning to school and obtaining a nursing degree, although she feels
guilty about having neglected Cindy to do so. She sometimes works evenings, which has meant leaving Cindy at home alone or with Bill. She feels
deceived by her husband just when she had thought she was finally building
a stable home life for herself and Cindy. She has asked Bill to leave the
home, and he is pleading to be accepted back. At this time Claudia is as upset
about her disrupted marriage as she is concerned about Cindy's problems.
She is, however, determined to keep and raise the girl herself this time.

In many ways the Steeles have been a concerned and caring, middle-
class family. Mrs. Steele notes that Cindy has difficulty making friends. She
sees Cindy as a follower who gets into trouble at the initiative of other kids.
She is puzzled about the disrobing incident and views it as an example of
Cindy's excessive compliance with peers.

Cindy reports that she used to be mad at her mother for bossing and
neglecting her. But she hated living with her strict father and prefers her
current home. Cindy is reluctant to talk about her sexual experiences with
Bill Steele. When pushed, she confesses that he would frequently undress

her and touch her and, on a few occasions, force her to perform fellatio on him. She also says she likes Bill, did not want to disappoint him or disrupt the family. Bill Steele has refused to be interviewed. He has said that he and Cindy got along well and denies making sexual overtures to her. He seems to want desperately to save his marriage and certainly to avoid legal charges against him.

School and community

The school sees Cindy as a quiet, passive sixth-grader who is sometimes insolent in sassing teachers and swearing. Her grades are barely passing, yet her academic aptitude is above average. In school she keeps primarily to herself. When she does interact with classmates, she alienates them by being bossy and sarcastic. The school wonders whether Cindy's relative immaturity will create problems for her when she advances to junior high school next year.

In the past Cindy has gotten into trouble in the community by shop-lifting and keeping late hours. Recently she has not run around as much and is behaving appropriately, although she seems to have few friends.

Case discussion
Consultants: Dr. Cynthia Gertsman, Dr. Esther Gelcer, Dr. Paul Spring

Interviewer: What other assessments or pieces of information do you want to find out about this case? Cynthia?

Gertsman: There's a lot of missing information. I'd certainly like to get a much more intensive history of both what's happened in this child's life up to her 12th year and, more significantly, what's been going on within the school for her. I'd like some historical data about when the incest was discovered and what the results of that discovery were. Apparently he was sent away, but I don't know whether it actually went to court, whether Cindy was involved, and all the events around that. I might begin within a family context, although I gather Bill would not be a part of that initially, and I would certainly see Cindy individually, very much so, and not just one session, but perhaps a few sessions to do an assessment. I would also see mom individually, and one of the areas I would like to try and define is whether mom wants this child.

Gelcer: Doesn't she say that she was unwanted?

Gertsman: She was unwanted early on, but that appears to be a major issue at this point as well.

Interviewer: You would try to assess whether there had been some bonding that took place, what attachment there was between mother and child.

Gertsman: Yes. I'd also like to try to get Bill in. I might do that individually, in terms of trying to provide him with some support because I can see that he's probably been treated very hostilely by the community.

Interviewer: That's an important point, I think. The case record tells us that there's been at least an initial attempt to bring Bill in. He's resisted that; he says he won't come in. Any suggestions to a worker about what kind of strategy might be used to try to bring in somebody who's this reluctant under this kind of circumstance?

Gelcer: What about the mother, would she not bring him in?

Spring: No, it's the mother who's objecting. The mother wants this guy out.

Gertsman: She's ambivalent, it seems.

Spring: Well, I got the impression from the report that mother won't have anything to do with this guy anymore.

Gertsman: Cindy's mother reports she believes that Bill Steele's presence was a very positive influence on the girl.

Gelcer: He seems to want desperately to save his marriage and certainly to avoid legal charges against him. I would get Cindy and mother to bring him in.

Interviewer: You would use them as the agents rather than have direct contact.

Gelcer: And the only reason why I would want him in is in order to assess how permanently he's going to be stationed in this family.

Gertsman: I wouldn't do that. My reason for not doing that is because at this point, according to the history, mom has said to Bill not to be involved with the family. If mom is ambivalent, I wouldn't say bring him in, because I'd be concerned about giving mom a message that that's where he should be. So I would attempt to contact him alone. I might check out with Cindy and mom whether they could speak with him as well, but I would not see him in the context of the family at this point.

Gelcer: But what would be the purpose of interviewing him in the first place?

Gertsman: That's a good point because I'm thinking I'd like to know what attachment he had with Cindy in terms of providing some positive support for her and some parenting for her.

Gelcer: Do you think he could ever have been a positive support for her if he's been sexually assaulting her?

Gertsman: That's a good question. It's a possibility depending on his history.

Gelcer: Not even depending on his history. If the guy at 38 is getting sexual gratification from a 10- to 12-year-old girl who's supposed to be his adopted daughter, or a girl who's had a history like hers, he's got very poor judgment.

Spring: Now we don't know whether the sexual incidents are true or not———

Gelcer: Oh, well, we do in a way, although we're not in court. I mean we're not a legal system, and we don't need to have legal advice. From knowing systems that deal with incest, we know that the mother always denies it even when she catches the father and the daughter in the act. She closes her eyes and walks off, and the incest can go on for years unless the girl gets some outside involvement. We know that the mother will deny and will support Bill in his denial, and we know that Bill will deny because he's petrified. He could be put in jail for that, apart from losing the family and losing this little girl.

Spring: Is Bill in or out of the family? Who is the family?

Gelcer: Whom do we assess? What information do we want?

Spring: Well, I would have made some effort to get Bill involved at some level. I would have gone through mother and explored it with her.

Gelcer: Why would you have gotten Bill involved?

Spring: I don't know what kind of a guy he is.

Gertsman: Why? To satisfy your curiosity? Or is there any purpose for the family?

Spring: Yes, Cindy, not surprisingly, has a lot of positive feelings about Bill, and I need to know how that's being reciprocated. It was reciprocated at some level, maybe with poor judgment, but it was reciprocated. The decision to throw Bill out of the family comes at a period of great crisis. I think we should try to understand whether that was a well-thought-out decision. Therefore, I would start working with mother to begin to express the rage and all the feelings that are coming out and explore whether Bill can get reinvolved.

Interviewer: Would you work with her individually or in the family context?

Spring: With respect to this goal, I would do it on an individual basis.

Gertsman: I would assess the role the Children's Aid Society may have with this family because at this point I'm not so sure that either adult really wants this kid. Mom has been described as very frail, very depressed, doing her own thing, arranging her hours at a time when, in fact, the child doesn't have much contact with her. The caring has been very inconsistent and back and forth, and so I see it as an issue to be defined in terms of custody of this child. Bill needs to be a part of that, if only to define whether mom is really going to end up being with him—which is my speculation, and that Cindy is going to have to be removed. I see him as an important person in terms of defining who the family will be.

Interviewer: Before we move to treatment strategy, are there any other assessment issues?

Gertsman: I would want to know whether the Children's Aid Society has been contacted yet and by whom. With the new law, they have to be notified of child abuse and it's best that the mother and not I notify them and the school.

Interviewer: Since laws vary across the U.S., would you recommend that a child welfare agency be alerted, whether or not there was a legal requirement to notify?

Gelcer: No, not yet. Not at this particular point.

Spring: I might disagree. We have a long-standing history here.

Gelcer: But the girl has never been involved in treatment anywhere, has she?

Spring: She's been stealing since———

Gelcer: Has she ever been referred to any other clinical agency?

Gertsman: No, there's no previous history. Although that wasn't documented, there may be some further information you need.

Gelcer: I would want to know a lot more. I would want to know about any previous involvement with the family. I would want to know about the aunt, maybe see her. I would want to know a lot about the natural father. Where has he disappeared to since Bill's appearance in the life of this mother and daughter? How did father disappear?

Spring: I guess we're saying that one cannot rule out getting an agency involved.

Gelcer: Oh yeah, but not at the assessment level. In Canada I would be legally forced to involve the Children's Aid Society right at the start. I don't know whether I will involve Bill in the assessment or whether I will involve the father. I think that I would be prepared on the assessment level to work with the mother and daughter, to get as much information about these male figures —father and Bill—about how they come into the lives of mother and daughter and how they leave their lives, why they come in and why they leave. Why did mother marry Arthur? Why did they break up? What was the marriage like? Why did she marry Bill? Why is she prepared to kick him out now? Is it because of Cindy, or is it because of something that's going wrong between the two of them? I would address myself to the mother and then to the girl. How she came to live with her father and how she saw the breakage of the marriage and so on. I would also want to know from the girl about how she sees herself socially and academically at school. I want to get some more information from the school about past academic performance.

Interviewer: Has anybody addressed whether he/she would attempt to get the natural father involved?

Gelcer: I'm not sure whether I would want to get him involved or not, but I would want to hear about him first. And the question of involving him or Bill, or both, is in my mind dependent on the information that I get from mother and Cindy.

Gertsman: I think that's a good point.

Interviewer: Agreement on that?

All: Yes.

Spring: Would you test Cindy?

Gelcer: Yes, I would, for school purposes. I would test her on our general battery: intelligence, projectives, and WRAT.

Interviewer: Are there some specific things that you're looking for in a psychological assessment?

Gelcer: Yes, I would come back to the school with a report about what this girl is struggling with and some recommendations about areas she could be developing academically, socially, and personally, and with what areas she needs more help.

Spring: I would also like to look at some ego strengths in this girl.

Gelcer: Those things I look for in the interview.

Spring: Oh, yes, in the interview too, but I think the testing can be of some assistance here.

Interviewer: Okay, let's talk about treatment strategy.

Gelcer: From the information that we have, this is a school referral. I'm leaning toward working with the girl individually and my thinking goes this way— she doesn't have a father who had cared for her consistently. Whatever strengths he had, they're not in parenting. Only the mother has cared for her consistently, but whatever strengths she has, these have not been as a parent. Bill is definitely not acting as a parent. He's dangerous for the girl, and I would keep him as far away from her as possible, if I could. If I would bring Bill into the treatment process, it would only be to help the girl and mother work through this separation. Maybe the mother wouldn't want to separate from him. Maybe the mother has a sadomasochistic relationship with him that she wants to keep, but if I brought Bill and mother in, it would be in order to separate and individuate the girl from this type of relationship. My main focus is long-term work with this girl alone. Leading up to that I might be working with her and mother, or with her and mother and Bill, or sometimes father can drop in to help work on issues relating to him. I see myself working with the girl for another two to three years individually and maybe on a twice- or three-times-a-week basis.

Gertsman: Particularly through adolescence, which is going to be difficult for this girl.

Gelcer: That would be my recommendation and I want a very highly skilled therapist who can accommodate the changes and be prepared to work with the system because this mother will not let go of the girl very easily. She's clearly using the girl inadvertently. I said before that the occurrence of incest in a family is related to the personality of the mother. This is a mother who produces situations that stimulate and promote incest. She has clearly not had satisfactory sexual relations with either of her men, and she's setting the scene for incest with her daughter. As, for example, when she leaves the father alone with the daughter for a long time, and now, repeating it with this guy.

Interviewer: Let's go to some more treatment recommendations and then I want to come back to therapist characteristics.

Spring: I think we have to keep in mind that somewhere along the line this child may have to be removed and you may not have the mother-daughter system to work with. One might have to think in terms of a very extensive program for this girl. Day treatment at least, maybe even residential approaches over a period of time or a group home. I think a therapist right from the beginning has to be aware that these are possibilities.

Interviewer: You would consider milieu kinds of treatments?

Spring: Most definitely, because I agree with Esther that there's no evidence this girl has a father in any real sense, or has a mother in any real sense, and somebody's got to see whether they can fill in the gaps there. I would also make my alliance with the girl.

Interviewer: Would you start out with a day treatment program or residential treatment program, or would you start out with outpatient work?

Spring: I would start with outpatient. I wouldn't rush to day treatment. Again, it's one of those ideas you tuck away if needed later.

Interviewer: And what kind of outpatient work would you initiate? Would it be individual or family or what?

Spring: Well, I have a feeling this is the kind of family of which I would assume ultimately I'm going to be making my alliance with the girl and it would be outpatient work. She may even end up in some foster home or something like that, but I would continue to see the girl on an outpatient basis through the teenage years, right through to age 15 or 16.

Interviewer: So you're also seeing a long-term treatment?

Spring: Yes. I would not be surprised if it's long-term, and a lot of ego building, as I see myself as a sort of auxiliary ego for this girl, structuring realities for her. Again, that's why I'd like to know what ego strengths she has. I'd like to see her through that developmental phase.

Interviewer: Cynthia?

Gertsman: Yeah, I would support individual work with her and I would also want to have some ongoing contact with mother and daughter to reevaluate the relationship constantly. My speculation would be similar to Paul's, that this child will probably be removed from the family system. Again, it's speculative.

Gelcer: A group home, day treatment would be better in the long run.

Gertsman: Depending on the age at which that decision may have to be made, you're right.

Spring: I think what we're really saying is we're going to help mother to free up.

Gertsman: To help her to accept the fact that her daughter needs the treatment.

Spring: So I see a therapist being involved with mother in the early phases of therapy, but the likelihood is it will move to Cindy.

Gertsman: I would also see the need for this girl to develop some peer relationships, and there are different ways of doing that. She may require a therapeutic group to do that because at this point she doesn't seem to have any peers, either male or female. She'd need some help with that eventually, but I would certainly start with the individual focus and then move into a group focus for her. There's a question from the school about junior high. That seems to be an immediate question in terms of her immaturity and whether in fact she could cope with junior high school. That may result in her going into a day treatment program for the subsequent year to provide her with auxiliary support.

Interviewer: All of you feel that this looks like a long-term case. All of you are seeing Cindy as a seriously deficient girl. Could you briefly specify what some of the indicators for that seriousness that you're feeling about her are? What is it about this case that says this is long-term, probably separation from the family, and some kind of milieu treatment as well?

Spring: Okay, the first thing that struck me was the early history. The first two years of life were a mess for this girl. Unwanted child; family life characterized by fights; she was abused; she was a rejected, deprived child and later in life she was shunted around. That, to me, is the first big, red flag.

Interviewer: Other cues?

Gertsman: Significant problems within school since she began in school, and with no treatment available to her, she really has had minimal supports since she entered school.

Gelcer: I would say she's been unwanted and abused all along, so I would be dealing with a character disorder. This requires long-term treatment and a very structural format. I'm more in favor of a group home than day treatment because I would want to structure the night as well rather than send her back home for the night. Whether to recommend junior high would probably depend on the psychological test results. I would recommend some kind of occupational training to get her into a career interest and pursue her training toward that career.

Interviewer: What would you be trying to do with Cindy in individual work?

Gertsman: I think initially trying to form a relationship with her, accept her, and reinforce her strengths. I wouldn't necessarily see her in my office, I think I would do some community work with her, spend some time out with her. Being involved in her areas of interest to try to develop that relationship. I would see her more than once a week as well, probably twice a week.

Gelcer: And be prepared to take a beating psychologically. She's defiant, she's angry. This is not a case that I would recommend to be treated by a student or intern because this girl needs a mature staff member, someone who is prepared to commit himself/herself to working with her for three years. In the past when I've referred such a case to a student, he had to commit himself to that case on a long-term basis. As he moved in his training to other agencies he transferred the case with him. Although supervisors varied in such instances, it is very important, in terms of the expectations of the therapy process, that there be consistency in the relationship. I would see her in my office, but I would expect her to miss some sessions, to come late for some sessions, to storm out of some sessions, and sometimes I would get angry and sometimes she would try to get me angry and I would have to work through those periods with her because, having been shunted around, she would try to shunt the therapist back and forth quite a bit. I have questions about this girl's level of intelligence. I think that if she were above average in intelligence or if she were bright she would probably be much more disturbed and would have shown signs of disturbance earlier. So I would digest my work very slowly with her. I wouldn't go into bright, deep-seated interpretations with her but rather structure the sessions very, very slowly through games and play.

Interviewer: What kind of play therapy?

Gelcer: I think that she would get into playing with games. Most kids 12 years old, if they play at all, play more grown-up games, such as Monopoly and chess and so on. I think that this girl would get into playing with dolls eventually, maybe not at the beginning. She would get into playing with paints, with clay. She would play around with things, and I don't think she would get into cooperative games so soon. In fact, when she does begin to cooperate, it would be a measure of her improvement in treatment. So a lot of work I would do would be through the games she plays. When and if she's ready for group therapy, I would again do activity groups with her rather than insight-oriented group therapy.

Interviewer: Any additional comments regarding technique?

Spring: I agree. I wouldn't do interpretative work with her. That would not be the focus until much later. I think the toughest piece of work would be to develop the relationship, and that's going to take a long time. She's a mistrustful child for a good reason. If an agency is going to get involved again, one would take care that the agency worker is going to make a long-term commitment.

Interviewer: Her whole experience has been with people passing in and out of her life.

Gertsman: Transient.

Spring: And that would be a bottom line kind of thing I would ask from any agency involved. In that sense too, I would make sure that if there's going to be a group home involvement, it is a group home that is prepared to take the child for a long period of time.

Gertsman: And to cope with the behavior she may present which would tend to be rejecting.

Spring: That's right, because there may be a time when this girl, age 14 or so, living in a group home, with things breaking down, has to go for short-term hospitalization. Is that group home going to be available after the discharge? I would be thinking about those things.

Interviewer: Any other suggestions to a worker in terms of strategies?

Spring: The worker should spend a lot of time focusing on the strengths, and what interests this girl. There may be some creative talents. Domestic skills, vocational skills, and life skills have to be looked at. She lies and swears, but does she know how to do basic things, such as get around the city? I think these practical issues are big things for a child like Cindy.

Interviewer: What, if any, danger signals would you warn a worker about with this kind of case? What's likely to go wrong, or could possibly go wrong?

Gelcer: She's going to fall in and out of love all the time. I think a worker should prepare her. A lot of work needs to be done about male-female relationships and about mourning. The girl will become depressed, if the treatment progresses, and angry sometimes. We've talked about the anger and said we should warn the worker about that. She might get depressed and the therapist may think that she's getting worse, though, in fact, if she does get depressed it will be a sign of improvement on her part. Then there will be mourning—mourning of her father, mourning of Bill, mourning of the mother—that needs to be worked through with her. I think that she will resist changes in treatment. Her defenses against such changes will be expressed by introducing others into the treatment. This kind of kid would come in and say "Guess who I met last night at the party, and did he fall in love with me." In the meantime, she would avoid dealing with how lonely she felt at the party. So I guess a worker will have to focus on her quite a lot.

Interviewer: Other possible danger signals, or major problems that would call for a change in strategy?

Gertsman: I think you've focused on the important one of depression and whether, in fact, this girl would experience intense depression that could reach a suicidal level.

Gelcer: I don't know about suicide with her. Impulsive, yes, but speaking intuitively, suicidal danger doesn't come to my mind with her now. I would rather worry about her becoming pregnant and I would make sure that she gets a very clear and good sex education, particularly with regard to the mechanics of how not to get pregnant. Remember that her own mother was pregnant when she married.

Interviewer: What would signal the worker to consider placement outside of the home?

Gertsman: Certainly, no change in her behavior.

Interviewer: So a lack of movement might signal that.

Gelcer: I think the mother will come out. The mother will say, take her out, I can't live with her alone.

Spring: I think the mother will give the cue.

Gertsman: Although mom hasn't said that. I'm not so sure if she will come out with that. The school referred her, the mother didn't.

Gelcer: Who said that she was an unwanted child?

Gertsman: From the history, it would be mother, so it's mother reflecting her own feelings. I think mother will want to get on with Bill and with her other boyfriends.

Gelcer: I wouldn't be surprised if Bill sneaks in first to say that Cindy would be better away from home.

Interviewer: Let's come back to worker characteristics. We've talked about a few in terms of skill level, in terms of permanency or longevity. Are there other characteristics you would recommend?

Spring: The girl needs someone to argue with, and the therapist has to understand that in order to stand firm on many basic issues. Therefore, the therapist must be able to tolerate having arguments with her.

Gelcer: When we started I said that we needed to have a very experienced therapist here. I'm forgetting that it's an incest case. I think we will need to have a very experienced therapist or team for the initial stages of the assessment and so on. Once she is set for individual therapy, probably a young and competent child care worker will do fine as a support for her. Someone who is empathic and can be friendly, but who has solid grounding and receives supervision. The reason why I said "child care worker" is because this girl is very deprived. There would be a period in which she would require a great deal of attention from the therapist. She couldn't make do with one hour a week, a forty-five-minute hour. She would want to know that she could call or drop in on her therapist and so on. So that's why I'm thinking of a child care worker.

Spring: I'm wondering if this is the kind of kid who might butter up the therapist for a time and then comes the "slap in the face." I think a therapist will have to tolerate this coming and going and I think an inexperienced person can get very caught up in it all. These are really transference phenomena. I would support the idea of good supervision, but not if it's by an inexperienced person.

Gertsman: The value of choosing someone being supervised is that it allows two people to be actually involved with this girl: one of them at a distance, who can maintain some objectivity and provide support to the therapist who is actively working with her.

Gelcer: I have two very important words of caution to the therapist. One, children who have experienced incest do not want to talk about it and the therapist who pushes the child would lose the case. So the therapist has to put that aside and wait until she's ready to talk about it, but deal with the issues otherwise. She will probably talk about it if therapy proceeds properly once mutual trust is established. The other point is that this is in a sense a battered child. She has been abused by all the adults around her. These children develop very, very strong loyalties to their parents, and if the therapist implies or suggests that the parents are bad the therapist will lose her. So the therapist must work with the girl's loyalty to her parents.

Interviewer: Does anybody feel strongly about the age or sex of the therapist in this case?

Gelcer: We suggested a young female.

Gertsman: Again, it could be male as well. Because this girl has things to work out with men and to learn more appropriate ways of relating to them, so I can see both being valuable to her.

Gelcer: If it's a male, supervision is definitely required. *(Laughter)*

Gertsman: That's right, because she's very seductive. Availability, I think, is really the key. The girl will quickly pick up if the therapist is not readily available.

Gelcer: Young therapists are more readily available than older therapists. I think that's right.

Interviewer: Let's talk about outcomes and goals. This is a long-term case. What kinds of ultimate outcomes should the worker be looking for?

Spring: Well, I would look for evidence that Cindy feels she can trust the adult world a little bit.

Gelcer: But more concretely, how would that be expressed?

Spring: I would like to see Cindy have a very genuine, real sense of pride in some of the things she can accomplish. I hope she could see herself as an individual. If she believes that she has a place in this world, she might develop trust in the world.

Gertsman: I agree with this, Paul, but we need to focus on more concrete goals for her. That she would settle in a home on a long-term basis. That she would start showing interest in certain things in her life: in a vocation, in some people, in friends, maybe in her parents, some understanding of her parents. That she would show some cooperative endeavors with the people with whom she's living and working and that she would succeed in the employment she has. I would want to see her employed by the time she's 17 or 18, getting good references and having some social life.

Interviewer: Anything else?

Gertsman: Some care and concern for herself, I think that's something to look for. That she would begin to take an interest in how she's dressing and looking.

Gelcer: I think it's important that she would be able to draw on some support from her parents, if that is at all possible. That she would come to understand that they may be available to her, albeit on a very limited basis, but to be able to reach out and not completely close herself off from them.

Spring: If she's 16 or 17, I would want to know how she's making friends, how she's selecting them, and how she's conducting herself with them. I'd like to have a handle on that before stopping therapy.

Gelcer: With regard to stopping therapy, I would see termination as being very gradual and I would want to see her moving toward doing things herself rather than through the therapist. But she would probably require some more contact afterward. In other words, the therapist has to be available two or three years later, so that if she has some trouble and wants to contact the therapist, she will know that she can. If she knows that she can, that's an indication of treatment success for this girl.

Interviewer: At the point when regular therapy terminates, would you recommend setting up something formal in terms of coming back or would you leave a more open-ended invitation to her?

Gelcer: An invitation to her. I would use the last year to educate her toward getting some help generally. In other words, no therapist can commit his whole life to the patient. He needs to help her see that she can, in fact, invite herself back to the agency or to some other agency.

Interviewer: Comments about prognosis?

Spring and Gertsman: Mine is guarded, very guarded.

Gelcer: If everything goes as we've discussed it, great. But given the reality of our society and the helping professions and the agencies' involvement and the group homes, guarded.

Gertsman: She'll need ongoing help for years to come.

Gelcer: She may get much worse.

Gertsman: Which would be my speculation, as well.

Spring: That's why I'm saying we need a little bit of humility in our work. You touch wood when a few of these goals are actually achieved.

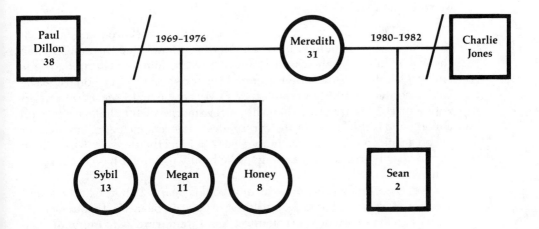

THE DILLON FAMILY

Identifying information

The Dillon family consists of Meredith Dillon and her four children. According to her teacher, Honey has a very limited attention span. She is unable to sit still and is so overactive that she sometimes falls off her chair. She doesn't listen well, and questions have to be repeated to catch her attention. Other children's belongings cannot be left unattended because Honey may take them or deface them. When mother shared her own concerns about Honey, the school advised her to seek treatment.

History of problem

The Dillon family has been in frequent contact with social service and child welfare agencies during the past several years. All the girls have been identified at one time or another as behavior problems and as suspected victims of neglect by their mother or of physical abuse by mother's male friends. At this time Mrs. Dillon reports that Honey is her biggest problem. As a baby, Honey appeared alert and normal, but since the age of 2 she has been very difficult to control. The school reports that her behavior has always been a problem and that she has been particularly disruptive this year. Mrs. Dillon claims that Honey is attention-seeking and agrees that her daughter probably doesn't get enough positive attention from her. Mother has relied primarily on loss of privileges and groundings to get cooperation. Honey does not respond positively to punishment. She is quite blatant about the fact that nothing scares her. Mrs. Dillon was particularly upset to learn recently that Honey has been coming home with small amounts of money, some of it apparently "earned" by agreeing to fondle men who exhibit themselves in a neighborhood park.

Marital and family history

Meredith Dillon comes from a deprived and abusive background. The eldest child, she has two younger brothers. Her father deserted the family when she was in her early adolescence, and she recalls him as a charming rogue but a physically abusive father. Her mother and she never got along, and she has no contact with her parents today. At the age of 16 Meredith ran off with a man 20 years older than she. A few months later she married Paul Dillon, who is the father of the three oldest children, including Honey. But Dillon drank and was physically abusive to her and the children. Mrs. Dillon obtained a divorce seven years ago. The family no longer has contact with him.

A series of men followed, one of whom is Sean's father, Charlie Jones. Meredith terminated the relationship shortly after Sean's birth, but up until a year ago Charlie would break into the house during drinking bouts and attack her. Meredith's current partner is Rod Carter, who has been more or less living with the family for almost a year. Meredith is about four months pregnant by him at this time and intends to have the baby. Mr. Carter has been married previously and operates a filling station.

In terms of previous professional treatment, Sybil has seen a school counselor in the past and has quieted down as a result. Megan has gone to summer camp for two consecutive years and her behavior improves for a couple of months on returning home. Honey has been sent to the school counselor repeatedly but refuses to share her thoughts and feelings with him. Mrs. Dillon has drawn extensively on social agencies for financial and emotional support. She has attended a therapy group off and on for some years but is uninterested in returning at this time.

Characteristics of family members

The Dillons live in a crowded but clean and organized three-bedroom apartment. Meredith Dillon works only occasionally at Rod's service station. The rest of the time she is either home or visiting friends in the neighborhood.

Each of the children has at one time or another been a behavioral problem. Although Mrs. Dillon is a well-intentioned mother, she often leaves the girls unsupervised and there is concern about their potential for acting-out. Sybil is physically precocious and very interested in boys. She is attractive, loud, and flirtatious. Megan is a little overweight, a tomboy, and the most withdrawn of the children. Megan and Honey have a close relationship. Both Sybil and Megan have been difficult to control at home and in school, and now Honey is following in their footsteps. At this point, Mrs. Dillon thinks that all her children except Honey are sufficiently well-behaved.

Honey spends much of her time at home seeking her mother's attention, especially when mother is busy with Sean or taking care of the house. Mother responds to Honey by delaying her with "not now" or "after supper." Honey then becomes quite irritating, running around the room, battling with her sisters, or engaging in some similarly disruptive behavior. Mrs. Dillon tries to ignore acknowledging these behaviors. In addition, she seems to have difficulty giving physical and verbal affection to Honey. Honey, in turn, likes to follow mother around and to help her look after Sean. She does not initiate contact with Rod Carter at all, but when asked about him, she describes him as "okay." She seems to have few opportunities for participating in activities with her mother or him.

Meredith appears ambivalent about her relationship with Rod. She enjoys his company but is reluctant to marry him because of her previous negative experiences with men. It is likely that they do not officially live in the same household so that Meredith can still collect her mother's allowance benefits. She wants Rod to take a greater interest in her children, but he has to be prodded to do so. Unlike her previous partners, however, Rod has not been physically abusive toward her or the children. Her own life has largely been governed by her relationships with men, so that a break-up with Rod could plunge her into depression and self-destructive behavior. She has made at least two low-risk suicide attempts as a result of stress in other relationships. Consequently, she tries to attend to Rod as much as possible, often at the expense of the children. Her level of insight and understanding is high, but her capacity for following through on suggestions is low.

School and community

According to the school, Honey's IQ is in the low average range and her attention span is low especially when marred by anxiety. They report that she doesn't like school and appears anxious away from home by herself. Sybil and Megan have sometimes been difficult to control at school, but they are currently passing their subjects and appear to be of less concern.

The children run freely in the community, and there is concern about their lack of supervision when mother is not home. Both Sybil and Megan have neighborhood friends, and Honey either tags along with them, goes off by herself, or stays home. It is on her ventures alone that she has met strangers in the neighborhood park and augmented her meager allowance.

Case discussion

Consultants: Ms. Sandra Birenbaum, Dr. Joseph Kluger

Interviewer: The Dillon family is a single-parent family with four children. What are some of the striking features that stand out for you?

Birenbaum: Well, what stood out for me is that this is a fairly typical family in the sense that they're a single-parent family in today's society. I suppose that Honey's problems are not unique to the rest of the siblings. So it seems to be a long-standing, well-entrenched family system for these children, and mother seems pretty uncommitted to change.

Kluger: A multiproblem family: emotionally, instrumentally, behaviorally, financially, whatever. A great deal of emotional deprivation in the immediate family and certainly in mother's family, transmitted down the line, so to speak. All of the kids are showing tremendous needs. The capacity for change, I think, is not great in this family.

Interviewer: What about areas for assessment?

Kluger: I would want to know more about the parent-child interaction. There is an indication that mother does not allow this child to be involved with activities in which mother is engaged, even around chores, which offer a golden opportunity for mother to meet some of the child's as well as her own needs. I think that's inherent in the deprived nature of the mother. That sense of how you can orchestrate that and do things without having to say "I'm busy now, don't bother me." That takes a certain amount of emotional strength and parenting.

Interviewer: How would you find out about the parent-child interaction?

Kluger: I would ask about a typical day. I would want to know from beginning to end and cover a number of areas. It gives the mother and the father something concrete to talk about, and so it's not a threatening situation. That would be in contrast to asking "Do you do anything with your child?" which would be a no-no. I would also want to know whether this child has any friends and what the nature of those relationships is. There is a strong suggestion that this child does not have any friends, that she is off by herself, and that she desperately wants the attention of anybody and everybody. That's one of the most characteristic features about this child. It also shows up in her uneasiness about being away from the home, so there is that striving for reassurance which obviously isn't coming from the family. I would also want to know about the mother's own interests. One gets the feeling that, aside from mother wanting the immediate attention of friends and male companions, she has no interest in relationships. I would want to know if there are any interests for the purpose of seeing if there is some way in which we can meet some of mother's personal needs, some goodies that she can experience that would build her strength to deal more effectively with the kids.

Interviewer: Jerry, can you give a concrete example of how you might open up that topic? How would you get mother to look at her interests for a more meaningful relationship?

Kluger: I would ask her how she spends her time, particularly when the older kids are out. She would probably say that she is looking after Sean, busy with housework. I might ask her to fantasize a bit and say "What do you think about during the day, what things come to your mind that you'd like to do if you could?" I'd possibly get at it through the magazines she reads or programs she may watch and use the content of that to get back to her interests and fantasies in a fairly direct way, not interpretive at all. When she does go out, what does she like about helping out at her boyfriend's gas station? What's good about it for her? I want to know more about her as a person. I'd also want to know how she handles Sean, the 2-year-old. I'd want to know of any past agency involvement.

Birenbaum: There has been a considerable amount of agency involvement.

Kluger: Yeah, the nature of that involvement.

Birenbaum: Financial and emotional support.

Kluger: I would like to clarify the nature of the relationship between mother and boyfriend. I would pursue that in the same vein. "What do you do after work? Does he give you a lift, or do you make your own way home?" What is the nature of the relationship, not just the activities. Those are the main areas I would want to know about.

Interviewer: Sandy, were there major gaps for you?

Birenbaum: No. The only thing I am really interested in knowing is what happened in the previous group. That was kind of significant for me. She clearly did not want anything more after that.

Interviewer: In terms of treatment approaches, what makes sense?

Kluger: I would definitely recommend individual counseling for this child. A fairly developmental orientation and a large activity base component. I would not opt for a strictly interpretive approach with this child. I would be much more activity oriented. I would involve this child with cooking, baking, real-life oriented play, but with interpretation as she is ready for it. But certainly to build a relationship. I'm not saying that I wouldn't try to involve the family as well as talk with them. I certainly would offer individual counseling for the child. The second thing I would do is try very hard to build up mother's positive sense of herself in any way I could. She seems to have chosen someone who is not physically abusive, which is a plus.

Birenbaum: That's a gain for her.

Kluger: Yes, and I think I would at some point want to point that out as one moved along.

Interviewer: What modality would you use to work with her?

Kluger: That's a tricky one. I'm really not sure. Had she not had previous group experience, I would have said group. Some kind of supportive, life skills, group experience. I still would want to know what wasn't good about that for her, because simply hearing that she went through possibly something like that isn't enough to say whether that approach would be helpful or not.

Interviewer: If group were not indicated on the basis of what you found out?

Kluger: I think I'd go individually with the added possibility of some kind of behavioral home-management program.

Birenbaum: Well, this isn't a family therapy case as I see it. I certainly would see home management. It seems to work best with this kind of a lady who, I imagine, is fairly concrete and has been around all kinds of agencies and has had people coming to her home. She's not going to welcome coming into my office, although I'll certainly invite her to come in. She'd be most comfortable, I think, in her own home. She is saying there is something wrong with her kid, so I'd have to reach her on that level. I'm not sure about the individual therapy for Honey. I don't know whether that would be enough, depending on how often it was occurring. My sense is that mother is the key person. She will have to make some changes. She's going to have to give in to this child a little bit. Residence may be an answer. Lord knows how much neglect is going on.

Interviewer: Would you involve the Children's Aid Society?

Birenbaum: I would try working with mother first. If mother were unprepared to make any commitment to change, then I would consider a child welfare agency or residential treatment. With mother's permission, whichever she felt most comfortable with. Lots of parents are terrified of CAS, and they are quite comfortable with residence where they still have the control. Any treatment center that's worth its weight is going to insist on some involvement from mother, so she will have to show me that she is prepared to do something. This child is left unsupervised most of the time.

Kluger: I would immediately take a therapeutic stand and try to see what could be effected to make sure that Honey isn't alone at the park. Either she goes with a sister or there is an alternative place or activity that's spelled out immediately, because the difficulties that may accrue on a number of levels with her becoming involved with these men are potentially very great.

Birenbaum: It's interesting, but I don't think mother perceives it as such a problem. She may be concerned but she is not concerned enough to do anything about it. She lets the child go wandering like a ragamuffin.

Kluger: It's also interesting to note that mom is pregnant again, and she does very well at having kids but very poorly at bringing them up.

Birenbaum: She indicates that Honey wasn't a problem until she was 2.

Kluger: It sounds as if when they become a little more independent she can't deal with it.

Birenbaum: That's right.

Interviewer: Other than possibly the Children's Aid Society, are there any other agencies or resources in the community that you would want to involve with this family?

Birenbaum: I don't know of any group that would lend itself to this kind of situation. Maybe some of the settlement houses—but she has to want something. She's not there. She might come to the realization that her life is not very full and ask herself what she's doing grabbing on to these guys. We know she's a very depressed lady. She's pretty overwhelmed, so if she gets in a crisis we may then be able to move in much more effectively. We can anticipate that if this man leaves she will become depressed and start gesturing suicide. Again, I don't know of any groups in particular at this point that would accommodate her.

Interviewer: O.K. Are there suggestions you would give to someone beginning to work with this family?

Kluger: I think I would see this child in some kind of play therapy, in which the therapist is involved in some of the play directly and immediately. So that if she decides to have someone have breakfast with her in her play, perhaps one sets it up with real food. It's not a traditional approach but it's one that I would be comfortable taking for the purpose of helping this child develop more of a sense of security, giving her an opportunity to understand more about her own feelings, and helping her to find more socially appropriate ways to deal with some of her uncomfortable feelings and thoughts. I wouldn't have her in a group. I think she is too needy to be in a group, and I think, on the other hand, she's still craving individual attention to the extent that she should be responsive to the individual attention she'll get from a therapist. She's different from the kind of child who is so anxious in a close relationship that she's better off in a group.

Birenbaum: I don't put that much hope into individual therapy for a child like this. For a more neurotic child, I feel much better, but this little girl is so empty——— You're probably more of an expert in play therapy than I am, Jerry, so I'll concede to your experience.

Interviewer: But you would be more focused on working with mother?

Birenbaum: I would be more focused on working with mother and child. I would try to get mother's level of anxiety a bit higher, which is what I do anyway when I'm working with families, to get mother to do less talking, and to get her to move more effectively with the child. Instead of just saying "Pick up your glass," she might also move over and stand beside her, so that she can start to establish some limit-setting with the child. The other thing I'd try to get this mother to do is to make some commitment to spend time with the child and to supervise this child. If I can't get those things going, I have no grounds to work on.

Interviewer: How would you try to raise mother's anxiety?

Birenbaum: I guess I'd get mother to start talking about her concerns about the child. She would focus on the child never listening to her, not cleaning up, and so on. Then I'd ask her what she could do differently. So in a fairly nonthreatening way, I would try to get mother to assume more of a parental role. She might worry about the child wandering off with men. I'd say "Is it not possible to stay home? Can you get a babysitter? Is there some way you can set it up so you're not being deprived, but your child gets what you feel she ought to have, which is supervision or safety, whatever it might be?" That's how I'd begin to move with her.

Interviewer: What about a strategy of focusing more on some of her concerns that have nothing to do with her child?

Birenbaum: Yeah. Establish some relationship with her so that she feels understood and cared about. Only at that point is she going to be able to reach out to the child in any way.

Kluger: That's what I mentioned earlier. That's the second part of the general treatment approach. One is individual therapy for the child, the other is some kind of supportive counseling or skills treating for mom that has a home behavioral management component. It's not enough for someone to go into this mother's home and simply talk about behavioral management. The worker has to be helpful in the direct sense of the word. When mom has to go shopping, one needs to be flexible enough to say "Hey, come on, let's go together."

Interviewer: The theme for you seems to be one of "doing."

Birenbaum: I think with this entire family the ability to talk is fairly limited. So I think Jerry is right. You can accomplish much more with feeding the child or feeding the mother by going shopping with her. That says much more than anything you can say to her.

Kluger: It builds up credibility and not just meets the need for nurturance.

Birenbaum: Which is helpful for modeling. If the worker is able to carry on an activity as he's giving to the mother, then hopefully the mother will have a precedent to follow and she can maybe do the dishes and talk to the child, get involved with the child in that way as well.

Interviewer: How much time would you give before you started looking at alternatives with this family?

Kluger: Well, long-term if they begin to show some change. Long-term for me is two years. I think that one would have a sense of where they were after four months.

Birenbaum: I wouldn't go for long-term in the same way that you would. My sense is that the child has a low attention span. Mother has a low attention span also. My inclination would be to establish concrete goals that we would work toward together and maybe give them a break in between goals. Diminishing returns occur after a certain point. But it may exceed a two-year period.

Kluger: That's what I'm thinking.

Birenbaum: I feel that with these families, as the budget gets tighter and tighter we're going to have to figure more innovative ways of reaching them more quickly because they are chronic. They could fill up a worker's whole caseload.

Interviewer: In addition to a lack of movement in this family, what are some other things that you might anticipate going wrong as you are starting to work with them?

Kluger: The boyfriend could leave. Mother may attempt suicide again. She may become depressed to the point where she literally can't even carry the instrumental functioning of being a parent, so that the 2-year-old is literally throwing his food around and fighting with his sisters. The 13-year-old is close to going out with an older man if she isn't already, following in the mother's footsteps. She runs a high risk of getting pregnant, she's flirtatious, attractive. This family really is at high risk.

Interviewer: You both seem to be suggesting that this is the kind of case that can easily overwhelm a worker in terms of the range of problems and the intensity of the demands.

Birenbaum: It's a very difficult case, and unless your goals are fairly specific and your expectations realistic, you can be in there forever and end up "doing" for mother, which I think probably has happened in the past.

Interviewer: How do you move from "doing" for mother and promote her taking a more responsible role if you start by doing a lot?

Birenbaum: I'm not doing *for* her, though. I'm doing *with* her, which for me is basically how it has to start and how it has to finish. I'll plan with her but I'll look to her for suggestions because she is very dependent, and one of the problems she's had is that she constantly puts it onto people who can't do any better than she can. Probably worse than her, given some of the men she's selected. So I would encourage her and support her to use her own judgment, her own skills.

Kluger: And reinforce her good decisions.

Birenbaum: That's right.

Interviewer: Is this a family where you would expect either mother or Honey to follow through with the suggestions you give?

Birenbaum: That would be one of my concerns. I think you can anticipate that she's going to promise to do everything or commit herself to doing it and just not be able to carry through.

Kluger: For two reasons. One, the wish that things be good in her family or with her kids. Second, in order to please you as opposed to pleasing herself.

Interviewer: So that both mother and daughter may become highly dependent on you but not put out very much?

Kluger: Yeah, yeah.

Birenbaum: Yeah. They won't put out much. They'll take what they can get and leave, I think.

Interviewer: What would you do when, as seems very likely, other children in the family start showing serious problems? Would you take them into treatment?

Kluger: I think I would point out the commonality in the difficulties, in other words, what's cutting across the problems that all the kids are having. I would take a therapeutic stance in the sense of always being ready to share with mother the range of options. I would also point out the possible need for Children's Aid Society involvement as a reality. If there are difficulties and she's finding it very, very hard to cope, there are agencies which have a responsibility to help out.

Birenbaum: Any number of single-parent mothers, not unlike Mrs. Dillon, have managed. I don't understand how, with husbands who beat them, with the incidence of alcohol, with child after child, they manage to keep their houses neat and the level of their kids' problems acceptable. The last thing they are going to do is go to the Children's Aid Society. And I don't know if we should encourage it. Mother may even have to be hospitalized, but she'll take these children back and it will only be with great reluctance that she'll submit them to any form of treatment or remove them from the home. I think they are already entrenched. Honey is young enough that I feel we can grab her and maybe Sean, but the others are set in a pattern.

Kluger: Speaking of Honey, if the sexual activity does not stop, that would initiate CAS involvement. It's the nature of the sexual activity that concerns me. If she were playing more with peers, I'd still be concerned but a little less concerned.

Interviewer: What kind of worker would you wish for this case?

Birenbaum: Someone who can teach, who can be gentle, who can use activity, who can be supportive and understanding, but who is going to be very clear and able to confront. Eventually a confrontation will be necessary. "Mother, all you are doing is talking. I'm coming to visit you every week, I'm going shopping with you, we're making clothes and still you're doing nothing in terms of modifying your behavior around your child."

Kluger: I would opt for a female worker.

Birenbaum: Oh yes, I agree.

Kluger: I think that there would be some added difficulties with a male worker going into the home in terms of mother's fantasies and projections and getting in the way of working with Honey. I think somebody who has some experience in play psychotherapy but is able to move out of a strictly passive, interpretative approach.

Interviewer: Would you prefer it if all of those skills for mother and Honey came in the same person or would you prefer different workers?

Kluger: I would prefer different workers. I think that each of them needs to feel like she has people for herself. I think they would compete for the same person because they are so needy.

Interviewer: Let's talk about outcomes.

Birenbaum: We can predict that Honey will continue to go along this way and be not unlike her sisters and her mother, unless there is some kind of major change.

Interviewer: What would you want the worker to be shooting for?

Birenbaum: At least adequate supervision and involvement with mother, and mother being able to set some kind of limits for this child.

Kluger: Well, I would give it 10%/90% in terms of favorable/unfavorable outcome. In general, I think that the family members need to get as much as they can outside the family. It's not enough to rely on what they are going to get within the family. I am talking in terms of whatever success they can experience though schoolwork and through friends. I would be very practically oriented. I would make very direct suggestions. Certainly I would talk with the 13-year-old about birth control. To the 8-year-old I would give a very specific directive about not associating with men in the park. So one goal would certainly be supervision—adequate supervision eliminating the extremely problematic behavior. In terms of case recordings, I would document all the difficulties because it's over time that one needs to help the parents see the repetition in the behavior, in order for them to realize that certain consequences follow from certain changes not occurring.

Birenbaum: There are two points that Jerry mentioned that I'd like to come back to. One is the sexual business. There is no doubt that this little girl is into sex, the sister is into sex, and so is the mother. I'd like to modify or to understand what goes on in the home with these various men and how much this child is exposed to. She's pretty young, and I'd like to encourage mother to be a little private and to see that nothing is going on between her boyfriends and the children. There is no talk of mother being abused in this way, but I think it's important for us to understand it. The other thing is a goal to get these children into the community where they are going to get some nourishment. I see they have been in summer camps. I think any activities that have healthy kids ought to be explored. And summer camp is excellent, as well as community groups where there are healthy, nondelinquent kids, because they are sure to pick up with that very quickly.

Interviewer: Any last comments on this one?

Kluger: There's another point that rarely comes up because it's so hard to build it into a system. The staff needs support.

Interviewer: So an alert to the supervisor in this case that this worker needs some special support.

Kluger and
Birenbaum: Yes.

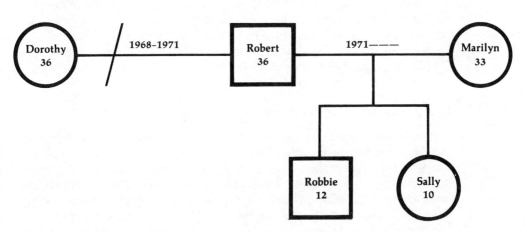

THE MALONE FAMILY

Identifying information

The Malone family consists of Marilyn, age 33, Robert, age 36, and their two children, Sally, age 10, and Robert Jr. (Robbie), age 12. Marilyn Malone initiated contact concerning the negativistic behavior of Sally. She reports that Sally fights constantly with her brother, pays no attention to her, is loud and abusive, and has stolen money from the home.

History of problem

Family problems appear to be long-standing but are becoming increasingly acute. Mrs. Malone sought treatment a few months earlier, but at that time father was unwilling for the family to be involved. At this point both parents have agreed to cooperate with the agency. Mrs. Malone in particular is finding the children unmanageable at home, although she attributes most of the blame to Sally. She claims that Sally provokes her brother when he is working or playing by himself and begins to fight with him. When mother asks her to do something, she neither listens nor cooperates. Sally's most upsetting ploy is to have a long temper tantrum, kicking her feet and screaming. Mrs. Malone has responded inconsistently to these behaviors, so that when she does intervene she usually overreacts, becoming very critical, yelling, threatening, and upsetting herself. She fears that she has lost control of the children. Father appears to have much more effective control over Sally through strong verbal commands backed by occasional spankings.

Marital and family history

The Malones have been married for 12 years. Mr. Malone was married previously and his involvement with Marilyn apparently contributed to the break-up of his first marriage. The Malones are a lower-middle-class Catholic family. Robert Malone was raised in a Catholic group home and had no contact with his own parents. Marilyn Malone comes from a large rural family that was poor during her upbringing. Her closest family contact is with an older sister, who also lives in the city.

Characteristics of family members

Robert Malone works as a welder. He has had drinking problems; then he would sometimes lose control and become violent with his wife and children. He has apparently not had anything to drink for more than a year. He still comes across like a bully, demanding immediate obedience from his wife and children. The children obey, but they are also fearful around him. When they reach out to mother for support, he becomes jealous.

Marilyn Malone is a housewife who spends the day at home or visiting friends in the neighborhood. She suffers from a variety of physical ills, most of which appear to be psychologically based. She feels pressured to be a good wife to Robert, look after the kids, and take care of household chores. She becomes tense and suffers from "bad nerves" when things are not going well.

The Malones' marriage has been rocky from the start. They fight about money, her health, his lack of involvement with the family, and other issues. They fight openly and can be very abusive to each other. On one occasion last year the neighbors called the Children's Aid Society to protect the kids. On several occasions Mrs. Malone has threatened to leave. The parents themselves appear childish in their behavior.

Robbie is a reasonably well-behaved, active boy who seems capable of holding his own with Sally. He teases her and can be a tattletale but is more cooperative than she in following directions and doing his schoolwork.

Sally bears the brunt of the family enmity. She is very physical and has a loud voice, and this in itself generates controversy. In spite of difficulties between her and her mother, they have a closer relationship than she does with her dad. She also plays with her brother, although the play invariably breaks down into combat. Recently, she has been openly challenging her mother's authority, and mother has been buckling under. When father comes home, he is sharp and authoritative with her and Sally complies, although there is little warmth between them. Robbie also has a closer relationship with his mother than with his father. Both children have to witness the fighting of their parents and the competition between them regarding who is hurting the most.

School and community

Sally is in the fourth grade in public school. Her teacher is very concerned about her interpersonal and classroom behavior. Her academic abilities are at least average, but her work habits suffer. She is easily distracted and overly talkative. Her social skills are primitive: she acts silly with her classmates and doesn't seem to have any true friends. She appears quite tense, is very sensitive to minor incidents, and fights at the drop of a pin. She is reluctant to engage in a task at which she might fail. When she does fail, she attributes responsibility elsewhere. Although she bothers her classmates, she also blames them for any incidents. The school has had repeated contact with Mrs. Malone regarding Sally's behavior. Mrs. Malone has always been cooperative but nothing has changed.

In the community Sally has pretty much been ostracized by peers and has withdrawn from them. They call her names like "kooky" and tease her.

Robbie is doing appropriate work in the classroom. He is conscientious in his studies and performs at an average level. He also is a talker and can be disruptive but on a much more minor scale than his sister.

Case discussion

Consultants: Dr. Julian Rubinstein, Ms. Mary Pat Tillman, Mr. William Wetzel

Interviewer: We are going to be talking about the Malone family. Let's start by taking note of any special assessments or information that you'd like the worker to go after.

Rubinstein: One thing I would like to know is whether there are any children from Mr. Malone's first marriage.

Wetzel: It seems as if Robbie is at grade level. I wondered whether Sally is at grade level or a year behind.

Tillman: It might be interesting to know how much, if at all, Dorothy is still involved. Is she an issue or not? Just really around the whole resolution and beginning of this marriage between Marilyn and Robert.

Wetzel: I don't remember any mention of the family doctor. Considering Robert's alcohol problems as well as the fact that he's been abusive with wife and kids, I'd want a good physical on the kids particularly. I'd also like some kind of physical examination for the parents.

Interviewer: Could you say why you are interested in a physical for the children?

Wetzel: I would like to know specifically if there is any evidence of chronic, physical abuse.

Tillman: The only other thing under assessment is that it would be useful to know about the parents' families of origin. What kind of families they come from and their current relationships. Also what the outside supports are. Obviously the community has become involved, the Children's Aid Society and the neighborhood, but possibly there are other people connected with this family who can be used later on as a support system.

Wetzel: I would want to know at what age father was in the group home. It doesn't seem that the Children's Aid Society is involved at present, but I'd like to know more about the history of their involvement.

Tillman: I think I would want to know whether their Catholicism is an issue for this family regarding divorce and remarriage.

Wetzel: I'd like to know more clearly about the current use and/or abuse of alcohol.

Interviewer: What treatment approaches would you recommend to the worker?

Wetzel: The marital conflict seems quite central. There is talk about the marriage being rocky from the beginning and a lot of fighting about different issues. I wonder how much Dorothy is still a figure, at least if not physically present, in some way present. And it seems as though Robert takes a peripheral role and then comes and takes over. I would think that that would be pretty upsetting to mother and undercut her self-esteem. It seems that it is quite a chaotic, underorganized family. So my treatment interventions would certainly take that into consideration.

Rubinstein: I agree. It sounds to me as if both parents have few interpersonal skills and certainly not too much in the way of parenting skills. Those would be the two basic issues. I would consider a home-based plan instead of office treatment.

Wetzel: There is certainly a lot of inconsistent child management. It seems that the marital conflict is reflected in the sibling rivalry and conflict. This is the kind of family with whom I would utilize a pretty structured behavioral management program on a home care basis. A behavior modification program with stars and stripes and the whole bit.

Rubinstein: Yes, I think that could be a good way of approaching it. I think that this is the kind of family that may have difficulty coming to a clinic or to a therapist's office. There are indications that the father has been uncooperative in the past, though he seems willing at this point. My sense is that if he doesn't approve of what is going on in the therapy or doesn't like the therapist and his or her middle-class values, the therapist may have trouble engaging him. The therapy will probably progress further if done in the home. I would start off by providing lots of modeling. I would try to model for mother how to handle the children better. The initial goal would be to improve her parenting skills.

Interviewer: Would you get into the marriage in the beginning?

Rubinstein: I think not. My inclination would be to start with the child—hopefully make some gains, and then test their commitment to doing marital work. I would like to be able to help father see that there are other ways in which he can exercise control than through spanking. I would want to address the issue of parental consistency, both of them giving the children the same messages, the same consequence for noncompliance, helping them to negotiate ways of handling temper tantrums and decide generally who is going to do what under what circumstances.

Wetzel: I think father is the power person to be hooked in this family. If I did a home care behavior management program, I would probably try to have mother as the primary figure in carrying it out. It would give her some semblance of control over the kids' behavior, and it would also increase the opportunities for positive interaction among family members. So I would have her as the primary reinforcer. I would give father the role of supporting mother by helping her with these things, not by taking over, but by being there.

Interviewer: How would he be encouraged to support her?

Wetzel: I would give a specific assignment. I would do a baseline around behaviors, set up specific goals and consequences, and have him there to back up Marilyn dealing with the behavior.

Interviewer: Can you give an example?

Wetzel: Okay. Let us say that one of the targeted behaviors is Sally's lying. I would assign mother a role and if she were having difficulty carrying it out, it would be father's job to assist her and remind her of what she should do.

Tillman: I think the key is what you said earlier, in terms of this being an underorganized family and the need for modeling. I would try to increase Sally's areas of expertise and growing up. What can mother and Sally get positively involved in? It might be cooking or sewing or some sort of positive activity in the home in which the worker could be increasing mother's knowledge and confidence and helping her to teach Sally. They need organizing around more positive activities at home. Right now the only thing they are dealing with is mother's inconsistency and overinvolvement around the negative things that Sally does.

Wetzel: Yes. That would be the way I would develop the behavior program—around appropriate behaviors rather than around negative behaviors and focus on positive reinforcement. I would reward Sally's and Robbie's good behavior, and in so doing the parents' behavior would be modified. For instance, Sally could earn five stars a day if she didn't have a temper tantrum. The reinforcer could be not only the stars but an outing or some special activity that she likes to do with mother or with the family.

Rubinstein: I am not sure I would do that. I think that the first issue is the parents', not the children's, behavior. I would like to focus initially on helping the parents to handle the temper tantrums. My first objective is to get the parents to be parents and to handle the behavior as consistently and confidently as possible.

Wetzel: How would you do that?

Rubinstein: This is where I would have a homecare worker come in. There are some very basic interventions around specific problem behaviors, for example, the temper tantrums. In all likelihood the temper tantrums would occur while the worker is in the home. The worker would take over and model for the parents, explain what he or she is doing and why. The next time the tantrum occurs, mother would handle it under the worker's supervision. It is an active, directive kind of input, instructing the parents how to respond in the context of the ongoing problem in the home.

Tillman: Obviously this family knows that they have failed, so I would search for areas of confidence in both parents. Maybe the father is a boxer, maybe there are some activities he does well that he could be the expert on, teaching one of the kids how to do. The same thing with the mother. I was thinking about cooking or sewing or something that Sally could learn from her mother's expertise.

Rubinstein: Maybe even the neighborhood kids. It sounds as if they are not well integrated into the neighborhood. For example, the neighbor called in the Children's Aid Society. I would try and extend their access to the community. I would have a worker go in there frequently, maybe three times a week in the early stages, in hope of breaking the back of the vicious cycle they are in. I expect that they are going to need more than somebody popping in once a week. It is difficult to anticipate exactly what their needs will be, but I would try to make somebody available on a frequent basis initially and able to be there for a couple or three hours at a time.

Wetzel: Especially around difficult periods like mealtimes.

Rubinstein: Yes, if one identifies that those times are more difficult than others.

Wetzel: It is a family where you are feeding the kids by feeding the parents. I see the homecare worker as not only modeling parenting skills, but developing a giving relationship to mom in particular and to some extent to dad. I can see this homecare worker initially going in three days a week and mother beginning to build a relationship with her and calling her on the off days.

Tillman: You are suggesting that mother would be more married to the homecare worker than to her husband?

Wetzel: Not necessarily more——that is a possibility I haven't thought of in those terms. I think that she needs a caring relationship somewhere. I guess I am assuming that the homecare worker is female. If there were a male, dad would probably be jealous as hell!

Rubinstein: We are developing a program (at Chedoke Child and Family Centre) where we send a couple into the home. This would be precisely the kind of situation where we would do that. There is a possibility that this "big bully" may be an ex-alcoholic.

Wetzel: I would look for some kind of peer group in the neighborhood for the two kids. I would like to check what kind of community activities the kids are in. Get Rob into Scouts, Sally into Guides, those kinds of after-school activities. It might be useful for mother to be in a mother's group. There are a number of types of groups, some of which deal with child care issues, management issues, personal issues. I think that would be .useful.

Interviewer: Julian?

Rubinstein: I would want to be more satisfied that this guy is still not drinking. I would like to get more information about the kind of homemaker the mother is. She is pressured to be a good wife, look after the kids, and take care of the household, but we are not told how effective she is. There is a reference to money problems. Perhaps the homecare workers could do financial problem solving with them.

Tillman: Another thing is that mother is threatening to leave. This gets back to the formulation of the problem. Is Sally's behavior keeping Marilyn from leaving in one way or another and getting more depressed? I think the key for me goes back to the disorganization of the family and the need for organization.

Interviewer: What kind of worker or workers would you recommend?

Wetzel: A couple going in on a homecare basis. If that were available, it sounds to me like the most appropriate.

Tillman: I would recommend a noncritical person. A worker who can search for positive areas, areas of strength. These parents already feel enough like failures, I don't think they need to feel it anymore.

Wetzel: Warm and genuine. I think that the couple should be willing to share some of their own personal experiences in terms of child management difficulties. Something to show that they are human too. Also the worker would have to be someone who wasn't sucked in by the kid's neediness.

Rubinstein: Somebody who understands systems in addition to child management skills so that he or she can intervene when a systems issue arises during the course of the home visit.

Tillman: Would the age of the worker make a difference? I am wondering about somebody with some life experience———

Rubinstein: I have never been impressed that that really makes a difference with most families. Every now and again one runs across a family that challenges a younger or an unmarried person. However, I think the sense of competence and confidence that the worker conveys is much more critical than actual age. I'm not convinced that being able to share personal experiences about child management difficulties is necessarily important either.

Interviewer: What danger signs should a worker be alert for in working with this family?

Rubinstein: Any sign of abuse. Any suggestion that the children are prone to accidents, any evidence of unusual scratches or bruises bears very careful watching. This might apply to mother as well as to the children.

Wetzel: I think it is important for this kind of family to be clear from the beginning that you know that abuse is an issue, not to rub it in their faces, but to state clearly that that is a concern that you are sure they share. One other thing I would want is to establish contact with both kids' teachers in terms of monitoring possible abuse as well as changes in their behavior.

Rubinstein: Well, I wouldn't want to do that.

Wetzel: Why not?

Rubinstein: It might place the family in an untenable situation with another social authority. I don't think that is information that, as a general rule, school personnel need, especially since abuse has not been established. It could easily prejudice the whole case. I think that the family could resent sharing that information with the school and, in my view, quite legitimately so.

Wetzel: I think that is a good point. This is something I would talk to the parents about before doing it. I would be more inclined to establish the connection if the parents want more responsibility in terms of being filled in by the teachers on how the kids are doing.

Rubinstein: Oh yes, absolutely. I don't disagree with that at all. It was the specific point about asking teachers to keep an eye out for signs of abuse that is problematic. In terms of the connectedness with the school and the responsibility for obtaining information about the children's progress, I agree.

Interviewer: Okay, let's talk about objectives and goals. What would you recommend that the worker concentrate on?

Tillman: The key thing is organization, I think, and concrete issues in the family. Trying to increase the positives in the family with concrete issues and concrete areas, to help this family eventually to become autonomous in its functioning.

Interviewer: What would be some examples of better organization in the family?

Tillman: Well, certainly a decrease in angry outbursts, the temper tantrums. Can mother effectively mother these kids without being inconsistent and flying off the handle? You have to look for an increase in the good times this family has together, the parents with each other, the kids with each other, plus how they handle the bad times.

Wetzel: I think a good indicator would be the sibling relationship. I would look for less fighting and bickering and more cooperation between brother and sister.

Interviewer: What would be the overall treatment goals from your point of view?

Wetzel: The big one would be organization. Some consistency between the parents around child management, helping mother feel as if she is a competent parent, diminishing incidence of abuse. I think that a resolution of the marital conflict might begin to develop if they were able to work together in terms of parenting.

Interviewer: Julian, goals or outcomes?

Rubinstein: All the things that have been mentioned. I would also be looking for better school performance, both academically and interpersonally. In the community, Sally's becoming less ostracized and more involved in an appropriate peer group would be very important. I would specifically list improved financial management as a goal, including it under better organizational skills of the family.

Interviewer: How about prognosis?

Rubinstein: With a family of this sort the prognosis may depend as much on the worker's skill as on the nature of the family. The capacity of the worker to become involved with, and then accepted by, the family will be a critical issue in his or her effectiveness, and ultimately, the prognosis.

Interviewer: Does that mean that the prognosis is unlimited?

Rubinstein: I think that the prognosis will be limited by a number of factors. The parents' background, their socioeconomic circumstances, and the history of the problem are likely to be limiting factors. However, I would assume that they have the potential to move considerably from where they are at this point until it is proved otherwise.

Wetzel: I would agree with you and add something to it. I think the prognosis does depend on the agency and on the worker. I think one of the things that would be necessary to build into treatment is a recognition that it may take three or four, maybe more, months to help this family organize. Then there may be a period of no contact. But I think this family would need to know that there is some sort of firm base that they can move away from and move into. I doubt that the Malones could function completely autonomously without support from an agency. I think three or four months is overly optimistic, a year and a half to two years is much more realistic. This kind of family needs an ongoing "executive director."

Rubinstein: If, after a time, they make substantial gains, contact could be cut down to every other week and eventually to once a month. But this is the kind of family that I would want to monitor periodically over an extended period of time. I would be concerned that this is a family that actively seeks help if the situation begins to deteriorate. For this reason I would probably renegotiate the contract with them every three months or so, cutting down the frequency of contact, if appropriate. The children are heading toward adolescence and there could be a recurrence of problems then. So to the extent that resources are available, I would want to keep an eye on them for two years or more.

Wetzel: I agree with a lot of what has been said. My prognosis would depend on a couple of things. One pertains to the severity of the alcoholism. If that were a problem, it would affect my prognosis. The other is the worker's ability to join and connect with the family. If that happens, I think that a fair number of gains could be made. The worker's relationship with the couple may have to continue on a gradually subsiding basis for quite a period of time, perhaps even three to four years. I think that maintenance of the therapeutic gains would depend on the worker's ability to help the family build support systems for themselves and transfer some of what they have established in the relationship to these support systems.

Interviewer: Any last words?

Rubinstein: Yes. If the situation begins to improve, I would start thinking about ways to help mother get out of the home and become more competent in the community, maybe a part-time job or some training. She seems to be very isolated and trapped in the home.

Wetzel: I agree with that because one of the things that strikes me most is the family's isolation. I think that helping them become less isolated in a number of ways is really important.

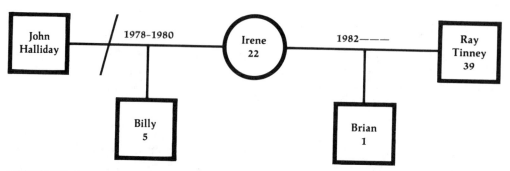

THE TINNEY FAMILY

Identifying information

Billy Halliday, age 5, is suspected of being physically abused by his parents, Ray and Irene Tinney. Billy's kindergarten teacher made the referral to the Children's Aid Society, which in turn involved the mental health center. The teacher bases her suspicions on bruises Billy has on his face and body, on his sad demeanor, and on statements that his parents don't like him. He has not admitted, however, that his parents caused the injuries. The other child in the family is Brian Tinney, who is age 1.

History of problem

Irene Tinney, age 22, admits that she and her second husband sometimes use physical punishment, such as spankings and slaps, to encourage Billy to behave but denies that they have abused him and maintains that he must have hurt himself while playing. A year ago Billy broke his arm, supposedly falling on the ice in winter, although the doctor who treated him suspected abuse from the nature of the injury and the fact that Billy refused to say how he sustained it. Mrs. Tinney thinks that Ray in particular may be too rough on Billy when he loses his temper. She sees Billy as overly demanding and disobedient.

Irene also feels overwhelmed by Brian and can't tolerate his endless crying. She is afraid that the children are destroying her relationship with Ray, who is staying out nights to escape the turmoil at home.

Marital and family relationships

Irene was the product of an unresponsive mother and an abusive stepfather. She is still not certain whether the man was or was not her natural father. She also grew up with a half-sister and half-brother who were children of her stepfather and a former wife. Her entire childhood is painful to her and she doesn't like to talk about it. She left home at 15, worked as a prostitute, had a relationship with John Halliday, a truck driver, and gave birth to Billy. A year later Mr. Halliday deserted them and has not been heard from since.

Irene met Ray two years ago and they were married shortly thereafter. Ray is 39 years old and has been married previously. His family background and life history are fuzzy, although Irene thinks he served time in prison for burglary. Ray has always been resentful of previous men in Irene's life and has never fully accepted Billy. Their marital relationship is characterized by considerable friction and fighting. Irene appears very anxious to please Ray and not get him upset. Ray is very critical of Irene on issues ranging from her appearance to her housekeeping to her personality.

Characteristics of family members

Billy presents as a sad-faced little boy who has endured a lot of grief and rejection in his life. He seems eager to please and afraid of making mistakes. He has an ugly welt over his left eye and bruises on his arms and legs. He says he got them "falling down." Billy appears afraid of Ray and readily runs to his mother for protection and support.

Irene is a very attractive, slim woman who is not currently employed outside the home. She says that her first priority is to make her marriage work. She is alternately cold and warm to Billy and the baby. Their slightest misdeeds can upset her greatly, and she can lose her temper, yell or cry, and lash out at them. She says she tries to avoid physical force but admits to having to spank Billy at times. She thinks that he asks for too much attention and is clumsy around the house. Irene would welcome assistance in giving her relief from the kids. She is not well-versed with regard to basic mothering skills or appropriate expectations for children. Part of the problem may be due to the fact that Irene may have a drug problem. She takes both Valium and amphetamines daily. Most of her acquaintances are women in the apartment building in which they live and men or couples that Ray has met at work.

Ray Tinney is an automobile mechanic. He was soft-spoken and polite with the interviewer and gave the impression of having "no problem" with Billy. He did express concern that Irene is unable to control and adequately care for his son Brian. Apparently he has threatened to take the baby away from her. Ray is very resistant to being involved with any social agencies or therapists.

Brian appears underfed and sickly. Born six weeks prematurely, he has a sensitive digestive system and a number of allergies. He seems insecure and distrustful and cries more than the average baby.

School and community

The school is concerned about Billy and regards him as an unloved and possibly abused child. He appears frightened of adults and other children but has formed a close relationship with his teacher. The teacher regards

Mrs. Tinney as unpredictable and neurotic and resistant to taking the school's advice. The Children's Aid Society is willing to keep the case "open" but does not see itself as having an appropriate service available for this family.

Case discussion
Consultants: Dr. Gerald Casey, Dr. Howard Irving, Dr. Richard Berry

Interviewer: The Tinney family has been referred to the center by a child welfare agency. First of all, I would like to ask you what additional kinds of information and/or assessments you would want to have concerning this case.

Casey: One consideration I would have is that I would insist on a meeting with the child welfare agency because we have a high-risk, abusive family and it is their responsibility to care for these people in a protection sense. I would not want to go too far without having a conference and determining the roles of the child welfare workers to ensure that they haven't opted out of the treatment system. After that conference one would determine roles and, within the context, I think one can talk about assuming that the agency takes the treatment responsibility and the child welfare agency remains involved in certain ways.

Interviewer: How about you, Howard?

Irving: Well, the big thing that is missing for me is an interactional assessment. There is no picture of how these people look as a family or as a unit. I get the impression that you have individual pieces and that the pieces seem headed in the direction of a self-fulfilling prophecy of being defined as an abusive family. The information that follows is typical of a lot of information you get from a child welfare referral with an agenda of high risk. You almost get the feeling that that is the direction you have to move in, and I think part of that is that you don't get a sense of a family here. For example, the information that the teacher gives is very sketchy, just a couple of little physical things, but no real sense of what kind of a kid he is and how the parents are involved in the school. Two things would be useful: less emphasis on abuse and a picture of how these people interact as a family in the here and now.

Interviewer: Plus additional information from the teacher.

Casey: Yes.

Interviewer: Given that that is the situation, what modalities of treatment would you recommend to deal with this family?

Irving: I think I would concentrate more on parenting skills in this situation. The marital relationship would be the second thing that I would concentrate on, along with working with Billy, perhaps in play therapy. I see him as needing some extra kind of support, I see the couple needing some help to work out their difficulty, but I don't see a need for any deep, intensive psychotherapy by any means. I see it as supportive work with giving them some skills around parenting and perhaps the communication stuff between the spouses.

Interviewer: Okay, that is helpful. Gerry?

Casey: That is what I have planned as well, the emphasis on the parents. There are lots of classic indicators of neglect and real difficulty with both children. The fact that one is his and one isn't is another dimension to explore in the early stages. Home care will probably not be indicated, but I would want to monitor the boy at school, to make sure that he is doing okay there.

Interviewer: And you also mentioned a strong involvement through the child welfare agency.

Casey: Well, it sounds as if a very junior worker had the case and got stuck and referred it on, because it says CAS has no program for these people.

Berry: Yes, and it sounds like a classic abuse pattern, and it seems as though CAS is saying that they don't see their involvement in the case, although there are clear protection issues regarding the children. This child is also presenting the kind of temperament with classic predisposing indicators for abuse. He has allergies, he is a whining child, a difficult-to-manage baby. So I would want CAS to maintain involvement with the case.

Interviewer: Let us talk a bit about the kind of strategy that one might take with the family. You could speculate that they may have been pushed to the mental health center through pressure from the CAS. They are not necessarily clear what their goals are or what they want from therapy. What kind of strategies do you try in order to engage such a family?

Casey: There are only two alternatives. One is to say that this is a voluntary agency and we don't see people unless they want to be here. Alternatively one could say "I understand what you are saying, you don't want to be here. I would like to propose that we meet six times, let's say, and see if it is going to be helpful to you. If not, that will be the end of it." I don't know what other options there are.

Irving: I think that makes a lot of sense. You might emphasize Billy, in the sense that the mother is asking for relief from the situation and the father has threatened to take the kid away from the mother because he is worried about her parenting ability. That may be a way to get in with these people.

Interviewer: Okay, let us assume that this family has been hooked through one of these strategies. Could you expand on what you think you would want to be doing or recommending that the therapist do?

Berry: How can we intervene in this family and win the parents over so that it is a nonthreatening intervention for them? My feeling is that what would probably be most helpful for this family is to reduce the mother's child care responsibilities, because she has in essence been left with having to maintain both these children and she has very few parenting skills. My major strategy is to try and reduce her continuous parenting responsibilities. She sometimes goes off the deep end and starts yelling and screaming and hitting the child because she finds the situation so frustrating.

Interviewer: Could you give an example of "relief"?

Berry: Sure, one child is in school. I would look into the possibility of putting the second child into some kind of daycare program. Second, I would look at mother getting some kind of outside interest. I was specifically thinking of a job, something that is going to build up her feelings of self and give her a chance to be involved in activities outside her immediate home environment. Third, I was looking to build up the husband-wife cooperation and their sharing of the parenting responsibilities. I would like to pull the father in, too, so he is just not going out nights. I would turn their interaction into fun events, getting them to go out and do things as a family with their children and also getting just the marital couple together to do things, making use of babysitters. Why should she be at home when he is going out? You have to make interventions early in the game and they have to be in a nonthreatening style. The Children's Aid Society is always viewed as child snatchers, and they have one strike against them from the beginning. So your worker has to be able to overcome that image, and not being from the CAS is in his or her favor.

Interviewer: Gerry, would you approach it that way?

Casey: I was thinking of the possibility of a subsidy for daycare, but certainly the relief, support, and all the other positive ingredients that have been mentioned are key.

Interviewer: The emphasis that I am hearing in both Dick's and Gerry's approach is very much activity-oriented or action-oriented, a focus on very concrete behavior rather than looking at or talking about the process that is going on between family members. Am I reading you accurately?

Berry: Yes, those are the major strategies that I would adopt. That doesn't necessarily comprise a total treatment package; the marital therapy is certainly another component. I was also thinking of getting a public health nurse in because the mother doesn't seem to have many parenting skills and the baby presents a lot of concern. It would be an easy way of having somebody in who can help and be in a teaching role and also check if the kid's being mistreated.

Irving: I would agree with all that has been said and would want to move very quickly into building trust with this family. It sounds like a family that has been bounced around quite a bit, and before you can offer all these concrete services, you have to make them feel that there is caring going on between you and them and part of that caring can be demonstrated by these concrete things.

Interviewer: When you talk about building trust, what do you do?

Irving: There has to be an understanding that the family is going to be working with somebody who is going to get involved and they are not going to be shunted from one place to another—that they can rely on this person and whoever it is can put in the necessary time.

Interviewer: That leads nicely to talking about the kind of worker you might want for this case.

Casey: I think you would not want to turn this over to an inexperienced person. I think the worker would need to have room to be surprised. We are talking about what we would do, but you may find out that you have only a partial assessment and there are more significant issues to consider. I think you need more than one person. The person with primary responsibility would deal with the adults but we have also talked about providing some support for the 5-year-old and we have talked about homecare service in the form of a public health nurse. That is a lot of staffing.

Interviewer: Dick, do you have any thoughts on what kind of person to recommend?

Berry: Well, I would try and have a Children's Aid Society person involved in one capacity or another, basically to play the "heavy" to make sure that these people put some effort into being engaged. I am assuming that they want the children at home and don't want them taken into care. I would like to have a grandmotherly type coming in and doing the home management program with her. Someone who is soft and nonthreatening and will not hold it up to her and tell her she is doing it the wrong way.

Interviewer: What are some of the major things that you might warn the worker could go wrong in this case?

Berry: I think marital breakdown is a real possibility here. Once interventions are begun, they may pull the parents further apart. The family has all the classic characteristics of a child-abusing family, so they are going to be very, very guarded and very, very defensive in the beginning, and I think that they are going to try and cut you off. They are going to look for an escape if you don't get a good relationship going with this lady. There is a suggestion that she has some kind of drug problem, and she may pull away if it becomes too threatening for her.

Irving: It sounds like Brian is very high risk, so you may want close contact with the public health nurse or physician or pediatrician. I would think that that has to be monitored. To me that would be the first thing that I would worry about; it is high risk. Second, the mother seems extremely dependent on the relationship with her husband and if that goes, I think you will see an increase in drug abuse and in the physical violence. So I would watch that relationship. The drug abuse troubles me, and we haven't said too much about that.

Berry: She must be getting it from somewhere. It sounds like these are prescribed medications. I would hope that in the initial material we would get a report from her physician regarding her drug history.

Irving: There is no way this lady is going to tell you about her chemical intake until there is that nice, heavyset woman you talk about putting her arms around her and saying, "Come on, what is happening?"

Casey: I think the worker needs to know that this is a long-term proposition. We are looking at two or three years before we are going to get much change, and they need a lot of support and a lot of feeding.

Interviewer: What would you want the therapist to be shooting for, what kinds of outcomes, what kinds of goals?

Casey: Certainly removing the risk of neglect and abuse will be a major objective. The mother needs to become more productive and satisfied within herself. If the couple busts up, she may need some kind of support for some time. With the kids, I would want them thriving and feeling better within themselves, whatever other symptoms may come along.

Interviewer: Any other thoughts about goals or outcomes?

Irving: You might want to think of a goal attainment plan, one of these monitoring programs with very specific behaviors identified in terms of parenting ability. The key change that you would be looking for with these people is their ability to handle their children more effectively.

Interviewer: Could you give one or two examples of concrete behavior?

Irving: Displaying eagerness in their interactions with the kids, more warmth than rejection. For example, I would want to see the ability to help the infant get proper medical care. If you saw that the parents were at least taking the kid to the doctor for regular checkups, that would be an indication. Actual behaviors.

Interviewer: Any other comments on outcomes?

Berry: Perhaps an increase in mom's outside activities, a job or mother's group, anything outside the home. Hopefully, the parents would be sharing more of the child care responsibilities. In terms of discipline procedures, they would agree on how they are going to do it and there would be consistency in their approach. I have two outcomes that I drew up. One is what I call the optimistic outcome and the other is the pessimistic outcome. My optimistic outcome is that the parents would separate. The mother would get a job and be self-supporting and her youngest child would go to daycare. The pessimistic outcome is that the parents hang in but don't cooperate with treatment. They just carry on with their old ways and all the bullshit. Mother gets into drugs and perhaps suicide and father goes on drinking and the children get admitted to CAS.

Interviewer: Let us end by saying something more about prognosis. Given the information you have, what overall prognosis would you set for this case?

Casey: The history is bad, the complexion of the problems is bad, and we don't have that personal sense of resilience, ego strength, or motivation. We know that father is not interested. In general I have to say that prognosis is not too good.

Berry: I would say the same. The case will require a great deal of supervision, and there will be high and low points. It is a multideficit family and the best the worker can do is grab them when they are down and bring them up to a little higher level.

Irving: I think the prognosis is poor in terms of the characteristics of the family. There is some hope depending on what you consider a good outcome. If the parents could separate there is more hope than in trying to work with them together. If mother can be brought into individual therapy where she can develop a sense of self-worth, have someone to whom she can relate, talk to, and open up to, then I think the prognosis is better. She would not be as tense and anxious and as demanding of the children. If the parents stay together, then she is apt to remain in her present role as subservient to her husband, very passive, seeking all kinds of reassurance from him, then taking out her frustrations on the children. In such a case, prognosis is poor.

SUMMARY

The families in this chapter have experienced instability over long periods of time. The behavior problems of both parents and children are multiple and well known in the community. There is concern about the physical and emotional welfare of the children.

The Steele family consists of Mr. and Mrs. Steele and their 12-year-old daughter. Although the girl has a history of lying, swearing, and stealing, her recent behavior has been noted as greatly improved. However, the survival of the family unit has been threatened by the revelation that the girl is probably having a sexual relationship with Mr. Steele, her stepfather. Mrs. Steele is recently remarried after a stormy marriage to Cindy's father and is feeling devastated.

The consultants agree that it is very difficult to reintegrate with his spouse and family a man accused of incest but disagree on whether to involve him directly in treatment. They also stress the importance of following the legal guidelines for reporting abuse. There is a clear need for long-term individual work with Cindy, based not only on the present issue but also on her deprived and abused history. The goal would be to develop a bonding relationship with the girl and to develop her skills in the areas of self-care, employment, and relating to people. The mother-daughter relationship needs to be reevaluated regularly with regard to its suitability and the need for intervention.

The Dillons exemplify a multiproblem family in which both parents and children have had repeated contacts with mental health agencies. Honey, age 8, is the identified patient this time, having been suspended from school for defiance and disruption. The other three children range in age from 2 to 13 and, with the exception of the youngest, have previously been identified as behavior problems. Mrs. Dillon, a single parent, has been suspected of neglecting the children and, perhaps, physically abusing them.

The consultants agree on the need to focus on concrete goals, use activity-oriented rather than interpretive methods, and draw on existing community resources. Mother not only is lacking in parenting skills but is also emotionally deprived and seems able to give to her children only when in a somewhat nurturing relationship of her own. The success of a behavioral home management program is thus apt to depend on lifestyle factors. Consequently, both consultants recognize the need for long-term treatment and view the prognosis as rather poor.

The Malones have had long-standing family and marital problems but are only now willing to become involved with a professional agency. Mr. Malone is reported to have a drinking history and to be a bully, while Mrs. Malone presents as anxious and hypochondriacal. Their primary concern is Sally, age 10, who is negativistic, abusive, and unmanageable at home and at school.

The consultants recommend assessing for physical abuse and express concern about the stability of the marriage and the disorganization of the family. They point to the need to engage father as a supportive resource while recognizing that mother will carry out most of the child management. They recommend overlooking the marital issues and using a structured behavior management program at home, consisting of modeling appropriate child management and using positive reinforcement to promote change. The children also need to become more involved in community activities. The prognosis is viewed as depending on the worker's skill and ability to join with the family as well as to curb Mr. Malone's drinking problem.

The fourth family in this section is a case of possible physical abuse. Mr. and Mrs. Tinney have a 5-year-old boy who seems frightened and unloved but who is regarded by his parents as demanding and disobedient. Mrs. Tinney, an unpredictable and neurotic woman, admits that her husband may be overly rough and aggressive with the boy. The Tinney family also includes a 1-year-old son.

The consultants maintain that the Tinneys are a high-risk, abusive family and a relevant child welfare agency should be involved in the case. Treatment priorities include clarifying parenting roles and developing parenting skills while offering Billy emotional support rather than intensive psychotherapy. There is also a need to offer Mrs. Tinney some relief from parenting obligations by exploring the possibilities of a job, daycare, and outside interests, while building up Mr. Tinney's role as father. It would also be important to monitor risk indicators such as physical abuse and drugs along the way. The consultants view this as a difficult long-term case.

STUDY/DISCUSSION QUESTIONS

1. When should a worker consider having a child removed from the home and placed in an alternate care facility?
2. What are the criteria for deciding which family members to see in treatment (that is, which parents and children to include)?
3. What are some indicators that child abuse may be present?
4. How and when does one collaborate with and involve other community agencies that are currently involved or have previously been involved with a family?
5. What kinds of community resources are available to utilize in treatment?

7

Closed Families

Many families enter treatment united in the position that they bear no responsibility for the presenting problems and that someone else needs to change, not they. Of course, one mechanism that families employ to deny problems is scapegoating the identified child as the source of all family distress. Other families, however, join with the child and one another to condemn the "outside world" or some portion of it. Often the school system and its personnel are identified as the cause of the child's problem. The community in general, neighbors in particular, or members of the extended family are other targets for blame. Such families are typically isolated from others, distrustful and suspicious and seem to get substantial satisfaction from their relationships within the nuclear family. In addition, they may enjoy and subtly reinforce the child's negative behavior as a way of expressing their own discomfort with, or antagonism toward, others.

Therapists frequently find it difficult to form a collaborative relationship with such families. They approach treatment with little trust, and any suggestion that they may contribute to the problem evokes defensiveness and resentment. Their accusations about third-party blame are often at least partially correct. Consequently, the mental health worker faces the multiple challenge of winning the family's trust, reducing its isolation and alienation, improving the reactions of others to the child, and helping the child as well! The following four families present this type of challenge.

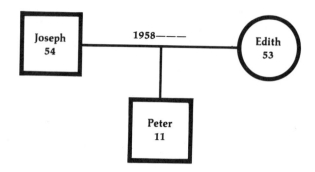

THE CRENSHAW FAMILY

Identifying information

The Crenshaw family consists of Joseph, age 54, Edith, age 53, and Peter, age 11. Peter was referred by his family physician because of his compulsive behavior. Peter engages in a number of rituals such as repeating the phrase "Okay? Okay? Okay?" over and over until his parents respond "Okay, Peter," counting, and refusing to touch items that have been touched by others. He has no friends, won't touch himself in the bath or go to the toilet by himself, and won't eat or go to the toilet away from home.

History of problem

Many of Peter's problem behaviors date back several years. Now that he is approaching adolescence, his behavior is becoming more immature and noticeably inappropriate. His demands, such as requiring his mother to help him in the bathroom and to wash him, are becoming increasingly disconcerting to his parents. His insistence that they respond to him using specific ritualistic phrases also concerns them. If they delay responding appropriately, he panics and becomes highly anxious. Finally, Peter has never had a close friend and has always been relatively isolated in the home. This problem is not of concern to his parents.

The Crenshaw's family physician has been recommending professional intervention for at least three years. Mr. and Mrs. Crenshaw did not seek help for Peter until a year ago, however. At that time the school referred them to a children's hospital outpatient unit which put Peter on a behavior modification program. But the Crenshaws were unable or unwilling to follow through with the program, and no change was reported. Peter's continual demands and immaturity led the parents to contact their family physician again for a referral.

Marital and family history

Joseph and Edith Crenshaw married in their late 30s and gave birth to their only child in their early 40s. They had tried and failed to have children for several years, and Edith became pregnant long after they had given up hope.

The pregnancy and delivery were normal. Edith and Joseph had attended the same grade school in a poor neighborhood. They lost contact for many years, during which Edith finished high school and continued to live in her parents' home while working in a department store. She is a middle child with an older sister and a younger brother, both of whom are married and live elsewhere. Her parents were very much against her marriage, believing that Joseph was not good enough for her. Edith's father died six years ago, and her mother is now feeble and lives in an old age home.

Joseph Crenshaw grew up in a foster home and never knew his parents. He quit school in the tenth grade to go to work. He has had an unstable job history but has now been employed as a security guard by the same firm for eight years. Joseph and Edith met at the wedding of an old acquaintance and were married two years later. The marriage has been stable and uneventful in the extreme.

Characteristics of family members

Peter is a somewhat tense, skinny 11-year-old. He moves stiffly and makes sure he knows where his mother is at all times. His appearance is clean and neat. He relates to adults in a friendly and open manner, although he also seems withdrawn and preoccupied by his own thoughts. He seemed to want to make contact with the interviewer and admitted that he was bothered by his tendency to repeat phrases and count. There is some evidence of thought disorder, his most bizarre belief being that his stereo earphones can make him invisible.

Peter's behavior dominates the Crenshaw household. Whenever he wants to go to the bathroom or wants something to eat or drink, for example, he waits for his mother's help and becomes visibly agitated if she doesn't immediately comply. Peter's primary contacts each day are his parents. He comes directly home from school every day. His favorite hobbies are breeding hamsters and using his chemistry set.

Mr. and Mrs. Crenshaw both look older than they are, move slowly, and speak in deliberate monotones. Joseph appears emaciated and gaunt, and Edith is also extremely thin. They are social isolates who relate almost exclusively to their family, which consists of their son and each other. Their entire existence seems to be wrapped up in Peter and they would not consider leaving the house without him. They have no friends or activities outside the family. Their house is simple, yet clean and ordered, since Edith spends her days cleaning house and watching TV. Joseph frequently works until late at night.

The Crenshaws seem ambivalent about changing their family routine. They complain about how demanding Peter is and how much they have to do for him. Yet they seem terrified about refusing him and, probably, about losing him as the center of their lives. They flatly reject having him hospitalized, which the family doctor originally proposed. Mr. Crenshaw is extremely concerned about not jeopardizing his job by missing work to keep appointments at the clinic or school.

School and community

Peter is in the sixth grade and will begin junior high school next fall. His academic performance is average and acceptable. His rate of absenteeism is high and he sometimes is sent home from school complaining of stomachaches. The school has so far accommodated itself to Peter's peculiarities, but his teacher definitely believes he needs psychological help and worries about his adjustment to a new school with changing classes and schedules. The school has been unsuccessful in pushing Peter to eat lunch and use the school toilets. Other children ridicule him for refusing to touch objects that have previously been touched by someone else, and he remains quite withdrawn from peers. Otherwise, Peter's behavior at school seems normal and he reserves his most bizarre behaviors for the home.

Case discussion

Consultants: Dr. Gerald Beckerle, Dr. Gregor Finlayson

Interviewer: Let's talk about information or assessments that you would recommend the worker to go after with this case.

Beckerle: I'd start with the parents. I'm very concerned about the parents, both physically and emotionally. They both married so late, they're physically thin, almost emaciated, and they have few, if any, contacts outside the home. He's taken a job as a security guard which is very isolative. I want to know how schizoid these people are and if there are even some psychotic elements in their thinking. Could one or both of them be schizophrenic?

Interviewer: Would you assess that through a clinical interview, referral, or what?

Beckerle: I think I'd do it by interviewing them initially. I might see them individually at some point with the ostensible purpose of finding out more about how they view their child, but also assessing them and their mental functioning.

Finlayson: You might also find out by asking if either of them does some of the things their son does. That is, is his compulsive behavior learned from one of them? From his mother perhaps, because she seems to be a very tidy individual. I think usually one of the parents tends to show some of the same kinds of behaviors as the child. I would want to know why the previous treatment attempt failed. I suspect it didn't work because they weren't focusing on the parents' concerns so that the parents weren't invested in the program. I think that would give a picture of potholes to avoid.

Interviewer: Any other areas?

Beckerle: Yes. Why in the world haven't the parents pursued treatment for this child? They've apparently been pushed by the G.P. to do so and they've been reluctant. They don't seem to be bothered by some pretty disturbing aspects of his behavior, and I'd be interested in finding out why they aren't concerned that he doesn't have friends and is so isolated in the home. I think that would also tell us more about their thought processes and how they view the world.

Finlayson: I think it would be helpful, too, to get some information from them about the history of illness in the family. Is either of them ill with some disease that isn't talked about, since this is a family that doesn't talk? This boy keeps going home from school complaining of stomach problems and so it begins to sound a bit like a situation in which he's anxious about what he's leaving behind at home.

Interviewer: Would either of you want any formal assessments of anyone in this family?

Finlayson: Well, initially I would say no, other than what we've already talked about that can be done through an interviewing process, but I would hold that option open as I see how treatment is going and as I get to know the family members better.

Beckerle: The boy's presenting problem seems fairly clear. I think we'd want to know how much thought disorder he's showing, which might be gotten at by something like a Thematic Apperception Test. But he's fairly up front with his symptoms, so I think interviewing might be sufficient.

Finlayson: My sense is that this is a very seductive case. It's a seductive family because there seems to be so much that's not right or the way we think it should be. So I think it's particularly important at the beginning to identify their concerns. There are some things in their son's behavior that they are concerned about, his increasing demands on them, not going to the bathroom without them, and so forth. While there are many things that they don't seem to be concerned about that we wish they were, I think we have to start with what they present in order to find a hook into the family. There's a whole span of symptoms with Peter that we'd be concerned about, having his parents say "okay," counting, refusing to touch things, and having no friends. I would be inclined to pick one thing that concerns them to focus on and to ignore the rest initially.

Interviewer: Would you see them as a family?

Finlayson: I would see them as a family, yes. I don't think they'll leave their son behind to come as a couple. From what I hear they won't leave him at home. I guess one concern is whether Mr. Crenshaw would make himself available because he's expressed a concern about missing work. Is he away every night? When is there time that all three could be together? With these people I would consider reaching out and working with them in their home if they would permit that.

Beckerle: I am concerned about the enmeshment I see in this family and Peter's age. He's preadolescent, and if you don't get to him pretty soon, I think he's going to be so isolated and cut off from his peer group that I don't know if you're ever going to get him. I might start thinking about things that would separate him from his parents even if we started out initially with the family therapy approach. I might bring him into the clinic and have him seen separately part of the time in play therapy. I might also see the parents together part of the time and do some building of their marriage by suggesting they leave Peter and go out as a couple more.

Finlayson: Well, I don't think we are on a different tack. I think these people are going to be extremely anxious about separating from their son and they are going to have to give permission for that to happen, even to be seen in a different room in the clinic. I'm wondering whether the way to do that might be to push them to change their interaction over one issue. For example, the boy insists that they say "okay." What happens when they don't say "okay"? How anxious does he get? Are the parents able, with support, to play that sequence out differently? I think it would be extremely important to give them a lot of support about their concerns, because the concerns the parents express are very appropriate. They're concerned that they are going to be going to the toilet with this boy when he's 25 years old. And I think that they are ambivalent about it, but they have to be supported in being absolutely right about worrying about the spectre of doing that at age 25. "How do you want your son to be when he's 25 years old? Do you want him to be living with you, or do you want him to be off having a family of his own? If that's what you want, then what do you need to do now?" It occurs to me that one way that might help them to make a separation in the clinic is to let him make phone contact from another room with them. He could call his parents after a few minutes when we've talked alone with them and they could answer the phone and then repeat it after fifteen minutes, so that he gradually begins to feel more comfortable being in a separate room.

Interviewer: Who's more anxious about the separation, he or his parents?

Finlayson: It would be a hard race to the finish line on that one.

Beckerle: I think that's what Greg was talking about when he was asking about areas of illness in the family and how much this boy is acting out for them. That's a real issue with this family.

Finlayson: I wonder if the isolation isn't something that one parent wants more than the other. In other words, does one parent want to go out of the home but holds back because of the supposed weakness or anxiety of the other?

Beckerle: From the little history we have, we might speculate that it's more likely to be father who's more isolative, based on his job choices and being raised in a foster home. Or we might have a symbiotic bonding between mother and son, and maybe the son comes home from school on the days when dad's working and mom needs the extra attention and support.

Interviewer: Gerry, were you thinking particularly in terms of some marital therapy? Or would it be more parental counseling?

Beckerle: I'm not very hopeful about this case. I see it as terribly enmeshed and I think I would try that kind of approach over a fairly brief period of time, such as ten sessions, and if I did not see some meaningful movement, I would switch to a different treatment approach. Specifically, I would see if there's any way in which this boy could be physically separated from the parents for a period of time. Maybe in a day treatment school setting or even institution-alization. The reason I'd move fairly quickly with this kind of family is (a) they terminated treatment previously and (b) his age. If he doesn't get decent peer contacts and become somewhat more appropriate soon, I would see him as being set up for failure throughout his life. There's one positive hint in that he is able to control some of his inappropriate behavior in the classroom setting and he doesn't act as weirdly at school as he acts at home. However, it's not a very strong positive outlook.

Finlayson: I think one way we're going to know what to do in this family is by how they respond to the treatment interventions, so I might be inclined to focus on the eating-out problem. I would try having a meal with them in the clinic. I would maybe even set a family task to bring in something to eat, so that the therapist could join the family for a snack and see whether they can work on something as concrete as getting this boy to consume something in a different location.

Beckerle: It would also serve a joining function with the family.

Finlayson: That's right.

Beckerle: I would guess that's going to be the central issue: can they allow somebody else to join, or are they so tightly knit that they're going to end all treatment?

Finlayson: I share your concern about how much one can do with these people, and that's why I would set my sights low at this point without being discouraged. I think the gains are going to be measured in small stages.

Beckerle: I would want a worker who could view small gains as progress and not get discouraged. I think I might want somebody who had previously worked with psychotic people and appreciated the difficulty of that kind of struggle.

Finlayson: There may be a family delusional system operating here, in which these people cling so tightly together that they only see the world in their own strange way. There really isn't any contact with the external world except for this boy going out to school, where he doesn't interact, and the father going out to a job, where he's isolated.

Interviewer: You've mentioned home visits and having meals with them. Are there other things that might facilitate joining with an enmeshed family?

Finlayson: I think one way to facilitate joining and anticipate danger signals is to say to them "You're very concerned about your boy and you have a right to be concerned about him. However, in our eagerness to help you, we may push a little hard, and I want you to be absolutely sure to tell me if I'm going too fast for you." I think that might give them the sense that you understand their anxiety and ambivalence about things changing, and encourage them to speak up.

Beckerle: And appreciating their resistance without getting into a battle.

Finlayson: One other thing I might be inclined to try is seeing whether there are any clubs at school where this boy's interest in science and hamsters can play a part. It would help to have him in the physical presence of peers, although he may not be interacting, but spending a little more time away from home.

Beckerle: Differentiation of any of these individuals seems like a huge but extremely important task. One eventual goal might be to get mother out to a women's group in the afternoon, linking her with some kind of community activity.

Finlayson: Another thing to try is to see whether there is some boy of Peter's age in the school who lives nearby and could be asked to drop by and pick him up on the way to school.

Beckerle: Mother may still be taking him to school, as bonded as they are.

Finlayson: It would be helpful to see what takes place in this family during meals. Supposedly it would be a time when they would be together. Is there any talking? Is the TV on? I would look for any opportunity for them to have a little more interaction with each other. And I think as another strategy we have to look at the extended family system and understand the role of the maternal grandmother. She's frail, she's in an old folks' home, but does she sit on a throne, and does Mrs. Crenshaw feel guilty about her mother being there? That might give a sense of whether this constellation of problems is generational, or whether it started with this generation.

Interviewer: To what extent are either of you concerned about Peter's borderline and possibly delusional thinking—his notion, for instance, that listening to a stereo through headphones makes him invisible? What would you want to do about that?

Finlayson: Well, I'm concerned about it. I found the statement about the stereo head-phones interesting in a symbolic way, because they do make him invisible in the sense that he pulls back into his own world and he can block things out by not being there. I'd want to monitor whether that behavior was increas-ing, whether he was slipping over the edge and withdrawing more and more into his own delusional system. I think that could be a reality if therapy creates enough anxiety in the family. As you said, Gerry, that may be his ticket to getting better. If he becomes more disturbed individually, that may be the way to get out of this family—by becoming hospitalized, by getting treatment that the family isn't prepared to have at this point. I wouldn't suggest you precipitate that, though.

Beckerle: I just wonder about the possible metacommunicational significance of the earphones in shutting his mother off.

Interviewer: How do you reach a kid like this?

Finlayson: I wonder about reaching him through his chemistry or his hamsters. You can get a sense of his capacity for feeling for other people through what he feels about animals. I think having hamsters is a very good sign for him because he has something living that he can care for. I think it is a way of joining with him and getting a sense of what he's thinking and feeling.

Beckerle: One sense of joining that I would not do would be to go along with his crazy behavior. I would not agree to say "okay, okay, okay" or encourage his weird behaviors. I would state very firmly that that doesn't seem right to me and that I can relate to him in a different way.

Interviewer: Why would you do that?

Beckerle: Role modeling for the parents, indirectly teaching Peter that there is a different way of relating, that I'm a separate being from him and I don't have to compromise myself to relate to him and he doesn't have to compromise himself to relate to me about those issues.

Finlayson: I think it's also important for the therapist to be involved with the school. They have picked up on some of his strange behavior and I think they need to get off his back. They need to stop harping about toilets and about not eating at school. I think the way they're handling it is only going to increase his anxiety. He's not going to starve to death because he doesn't eat at school. He's also obviously got very good toilet control. If the worker could educate the school about the nature of the boy's difficulty the school would be apt to respond more helpfully. At this point they're worried and doing what they can do, but they need to relax.

Beckerle: Here's one point that we haven't touched on. I think the word "sex" would blow this family sky high. All these prohibitions and taboos about touching himself and his body are probably a reflection of his parents' very uptight attitudes. I think this is a dynamite area that you probably wouldn't get into in treatment for a year or two down the line.

Interviewer: Any other strategy suggestions for the worker who's going to be tackling this case?

Finlayson: I just had some thoughts about his compulsive behavior, his repetitive counting, for example. Let's say that there's something that he is constantly repeating. I might get him to count his own compulsive behaviors and put him in charge of keeping track of them. Use one compulsion against the other. Now that's coming at it from a different angle. But in this family I would try a whole lot of different things.

Beckerle: That's an interesting thought. One thing we've used with our kids when they've done something for shock value is to have them repeat it twenty times or so. The therapist might be able to get control of the behavior through that kind of a paradoxical maneuver.

Finlayson: I wouldn't give up on the idea of working on the parents' ability to alter their role in maintaining his compulsive behavior. In other words, I would want to explore how they could play a different role and maybe then alter Peter's behavior. But at this point they're not concerned about that compulsive behavior, so I think you have to wait either until you generate some concern or until they begin to express some concern. At this point I think you have to work on the things about which they are expressing concern.

Beckerle: I think for almost any treatment to have an effect, the parents have to become more anxious and more upset than they are. If you can form that initial relationship, join them in some way, then you can gradually start increasing their anxiety and force them to deal with Peter's behavior.

Interviewer: Let's talk about special problems that you might run into with this kind of case. What would you caution the worker about?

Finlayson: I guess it's both sides of the coin of either going too fast and having them drift away, or going too slow and not paying attention to those very real danger signs about Peter's behavior becoming more bizarre and not taking that seriously enough. I think the initial danger is going too fast. They've already shown how impervious they can be through other treatment attempts and through resisting the family doctor. So I think one of the danger signs would be if they stop coming and give excuses.

Beckerle: And I don't know if we've got any legitimate hook for bringing this kid into an institutional setting if they just completely drop out after four or five sessions.

Finlayson: At this point in time, I don't think we do. I think there are families who go crazy together. You might be able to argue that this family is denying their son the treatment he needs if he's in really serious difficulty.

Interviewer: As I'm hearing it, the two major things that you would want the worker to be particularly concerned about are losing the family altogether by going too fast, particularly initially, and, on the other hand, some decompensation on Peter's part.

Finlayson: I think there's another factor. I think this family will show stress internally by developing ulcers, heart problems, or other physical illnesses. If they start to complain about physical symptoms, that may be an indication that you're moving too fast.

Interviewer: Are there any special qualities in a worker that you'd like to see with this case?

Finlayson: Perhaps a therapist who was an older person with a child would help the Crenshaws to bond and engage. I think a female therapist would be helpful in this case. Someone who is prepared to work in a number of different locations, in the home, in the clinic, maybe even go out with them and do something as a family outside the home. And prepared to contact the school and work with them. This family won't do well if the therapist is just going to sit in the office.

Interviewer: Good. Let's turn to major goals and outcomes.

Beckerle: The major goal I see is differentiating these persons from one another. I see the primary problem as enmeshment with the need to loosen the system.

Interviewer: What would some indicators of differentiation be?

Beckerle: Changes in symptomatic behavior where they're not so bound with Peter and his symptomatic behavior. People saying "I" and talking about their own feelings. The ability of mother to go out to a social group by herself, or with the help of the Public Health nurse. The son to join some kind of hamster group after school, that kind of thing.

Finlayson: I wouldn't give up on Mr. Crenshaw yet. This man might like to be in a different kind of job or have some flexibility in his security guard schedule, so he might be around other security guards. Maybe he might want some more information coming into his home, like newspapers. In other words, doing something about the boundaries around this family that are as rigid as the edge of this plate. Something to make them more permeable.

Interviewer: You're talking both about differentiating three people into individuals as one goal and, as a unit, becoming more accessible and connected with the outside world and other people.

Finlayson: That's right.

Interviewer: Any other major goals?

Beckerle: Working on Peter's symptomatic behavior so that he can become more appropriate in relating to his peers. I think that would be an end result of an increased differentiation, but an improvement in his symptomatic behavior might free him to relate better.

Finlayson: We haven't talked much about school other than altering the school's response to his symptoms. I think there's far too much else to be concerned about right now, and it's a good sign that he is able to hold his own academically. It may become harder for him as he goes on in school and can't do all the work that he has. Also, he is going into a rotary system in the coming year and that might be a bad thing for him because he's not going to have as much opportunity to form a relationship with one teacher. It'll be easier for him to get lost in the shuffle and people won't track him and they won't be as concerned about him. I don't know whether it's even possible in the area in which he lives to stay in a school system where he can remain fixed with one teacher. That may be something to look at.

Interviewer: Some comments about prognosis in this case?

Beckerle: I'm quite pessimistic, to be honest. I remember a case I worked on with a 45-year-old man who had very compulsive, ritualistic behavior and had difficulty making it into our day treatment program. Within 72 hours he and both his parents died. The remaining siblings told the therapists afterward that they had always known that when mom or dad died the other one would go, but they had hoped to save Bill, the compulsive patient. That's an indication of how enmeshed some of these families can get.

Interviewer: So you're pessimistic about this family in their potential to respond to treatment?

Finlayson: I'm guarded. However, I think we have to be hopeful about being able to help them. It depends on the therapist's ability to realize that it's going to be painstakingly slow and plodding. There is so little coming back to the therapist in terms of gratification that the therapist will need to bounce ideas off a support group. I think it's important for the therapist to have somebody to talk to about the case.

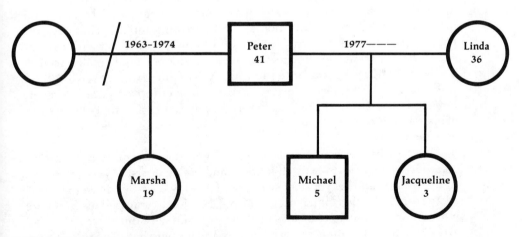

THE REEDY FAMILY

Identifying information

The Reedy family includes Peter and Linda Reedy and their two children, Michael and Jackie. Peter has a child from a previous marriage, who is living on her own and is not in contact with Peter. Michael is attending junior kindergarten this year, and his teacher urged the family to seek help for him. In school, the teacher finds that Michael has a very brief attention span, is highly dependent on adults, and is frequently irritable, frustrated, and nervous. Mr. and Mrs. Reedy deny problems with Michael at home and are angry with the school and teacher for seeing Michael as a problem.

History of problem

Parents describe Michael's birth as normal and without complications. Mother reports that he was a very active baby and a poor eater, but both parents minimize these aspects of his infancy and stress that Michael is a good boy. Mother complains that the school year is more than half over and that this is the first time she has heard that her son has difficulties. She thinks perhaps that the teacher doesn't know how to handle Michael. In the second intake interview, the parents very reluctantly revealed that Michael has a genetic disorder called Klinefelter's syndrome. He is being followed medically by the hospital where he was born but receives no treatment. Parents cannot explain much about this disorder but claim to have been assured that it has no influence on his behavior. They insist that this medical information not be shared with the school.

Marital and family history

Mrs. Reedy was taken into care by a child welfare agency during her infancy. She knows only the sketchiest details about her natural parents and lived in four different foster homes while growing up. She characterizes these experiences as "not bad" and maintains ongoing contact with her last set of foster parents, with whom she lived during most of her adolescence. She confides that she was "into some heavy drinking" from age 18 to 20 and that she was hospitalized once for taking an overdose of pills. However, Linda emphasizes that this was before her marriage and that she has her drinking under control now. She currently works part-time as a hairdresser in a beauty parlor.

Mr. Reedy is a sheet metal worker. His mother was disabled by a joint disorder during most of his childhood, and his older sister was a parental figure for him and his younger sister. His father was a truck driver who was away from home for long periods of time. Mr. Reedy married his first wife when he was 21 years old. He is unable to explain why this marriage ended after 11 years. He simply remarks that he and his wife had been fighting for years and that she finally left to live with another man. There is no apparent emotion attached to these statements.

The current marriage has also known periods of strain. Mrs. Reedy notes that she has been on the verge of leaving several times but has not followed through for more than an afternoon. Arguments have been mostly about how to handle the children and about money. The Reedys report that their relationship has been calm during the past year.

Characteristics of family members

The family seems highly protective of Michael. Father especially minimizes his son's problems and is sharply critical of the school. Mr. Reedy is controlling and authoritarian with both children and appears to relate similarly to his wife. In general, he appears to be a sullen, angry man who resents having to visit the treatment center. He has low expectations of the center and its ability to help.

Mrs. Reedy, on the other hand, appears to be a permissive and outwardly passive figure in the family. She generally looks anxious and fearful and agrees with her husband's condemnation of Michael's school. Both children seem to "walk all over" her, and Jacqueline is especially demanding and clinging with her. Mrs. Reedy tends to avoid looking directly at people with whom she is talking and gives an impression that she is a tired and discouraged woman.

Michael is a heavyset youngster with an oddly shaped head. He moves easily and seems well-coordinated, but his speech and articulation are poor for his age. He is highly responsive to one-to-one attention and shows real pleasure when engaged in a game with an adult. When unsupervised, however, his play is listless and random. He seems to look primarily to his mother for attention and tries to avoid or ignore his father. Jackie is bright and friendly with adults and seems to be developing at an age-appropriate pace. The children do not play together and frequently fight for possession of a desired toy.

School and community

Michael's problems in school have already been described. The teacher's written report conveys concern about him and doubts about the quality of care he receives at home. The teacher notes that Michael is often sloppily dressed and appears tired and listless. She also notes that Michael is a good helper, likes to do special chores for her, and enjoys rough and tumble activities. He tends sometimes to hurt other children through exuberance rather than through malice.

Because both parents work, Michael is cared for, along with his sister, by a babysitter until his mother arrives home. The children spend little time in the community and instead stay mostly in the apartment.

Special assessments

No special assessments have been done with Michael.

Case discussion

Consultants: Dr. Barbara Dydyk, Mr. William Carty, Dr. Peter Marton

Interviewer: Let's take the Reedy case next and start with missing information and other assessments that you would advise the worker to obtain.

    Marton: I would want to do some psychometric assessment with Michael in terms of IQ, fine motor skills, and academic skills. I would be interested in finding out to what extent the teacher is picking up things that are really there. Since the parents are saying that there are no problems and that the teacher's manufacturing them, it might also help to clarify things for them.

Interviewer: What specific things would you want to assess in psychological testing?

    Marton: IQ, partly because he does have Klinefelter's syndrome. The other area is readiness skills for the classroom. Reading, writing, fine motor skills. There's this flag about attention span and the issue of whether this child can't sit still because he has some deficits or whether it's really a reaction to the family. I guess I'd want to assess that.

    Dydyk: I agree with that and I would also look at lags in speech and language. Hearing as well, since that would tie in with speech and language delay.

Interviewer: Any other assessment questions you can think of?

    Marton: I'm concerned about this child walking around, listless and aimless, and I'd want to separate out whether that's a depressive, emotional reaction, or a real skill deficit in this child. I think that's one of the potential issues here. It is mentioned that these kids are being isolated in the apartment and one wonders about parental competence and care-giving. So I'd want to see if there are deficits in terms of this child being able to play at age level. Is he somewhat immature, or is he depressed or anxious?

    Dydyk: Would you want to look at him neurologically in terms of his attentional deficit and difficulty concentrating?

    Marton: I think it would come out in the psychological, because you'd look for soft signs and that would be picked up with those.

    Dydyk: Possibly.

    Marton: I don't think a neurological is going to do it.

Interviewer: Do you feel the psychological testing might be more sensitive than a neurological?

    Marton: Well, to the kinds of things this child is likely to show.

Interviewer: Okay. Any other assessment issues?

    Dydyk: Yes, I would want to pursue what these parents have been told about Klinefelter's syndrome and explore with them the hospital where they have been receiving information. How much information have they received and are they, in fact, following up on the disorder as they say they are?

    Marton: I think that's a good point. I was thinking that that may be the entree into this case because the parents are angry about the school, but they'd bring that up and that may be the way into this case. Another thing I wonder about is whether this woman is depressed.

    Dydyk: Or alcoholic?

    Marton: Yes, the drinking, the suicide attempt earlier, and so on.

Interviewer: How would you assess that?

    Marton: You would ask her about her sleeping and eating patterns. I think you'd want to go to her home. If you saw her home on a regular day, you might get a feeling whether she's depressed.

Interviewer: Let's talk about therapeutic modalities. What would you recommend?

Dydyk: To go back a bit, I wonder about somebody going into the school and looking to see if this kid is dealing with a teacher who's like or unlike one of his parents and having difficulty adjusting because of that. Or does the teacher have a problem handling him in some way? That may also be an "in" to dealing with parents around the kid's problem because that's the issue they're presenting.

Interviewer: Once you have determined that, would you want to work with them as a family? Would you include the children in each session?

Dydyk: Yes, but it may vary. One may want to work with just the parents at some point. If there are issues such as dealing more specifically around Kline-felter's or whatever, you may want to exclude the kids. But basically the whole family.

Interviewer: Bill?

Carty: Oh, I agree, I would work with the whole family. I think all the information mentioned earlier is very important, but I think getting it before you have a family and before you have father is undermining to the father. I would have father and mother talk and tell each other about their concerns about Michael. I'm sure they know what Klinefelter's is.

Marton: I disagree with that. There's a good chance they don't.

Carty: They might not have up-to-date knowledge. They might have it from when it was diagnosed and what the doctor told them. If they didn't, I think they would go to find out because father is very worried about his son. I think he's highly protective of Michael; he minimizes all his problems. I think he's very worried and scared, and he's very scared of experts, so I would not come on as a powerful expert with test results and such. It's the second marriage for father, and he's had more experience raising children. He's raised one to adulthood. There are a lot of issues, but I think the concern for Michael is primary. Both parents have high concern for Michael and I don't think they talk to each other about it. I think father probably dismisses it, and mother goes along with father's dismissals. I might encourage dad and mom to meet with the school and go back to the doctors to find out if anything has come up about the boy's disease. What do the parents do together? Or do they just worry silently, one in the basement and one in the bedroom? I think those are the issues because they're very worried about them. I think father will be very hard to hook in any way other than recognizing his competence, and strength, and knowledge, and his experience raising kids. They feel terrible about themselves as parents. And they think anyone who looks closely is going to find a lot of mistakes. Father's very scared and feeling very ineffectual.

Marton: But I think he's also very angry. I think you'd do well with the father. I think he would respond well to your approach, but I think I would do it a little bit differently. I'd pick up on the same kinds of things that Barbara has, a lot of important things that I don't think are being done. I have a concern that this mother is a depressive alcoholic, that these kids are being looked after by a babysitter, that they're locked up in the apartment and not getting normal socializing experiences. There is a real question about whether Michael is very anxious because he's dealing with a distant, punitive father and a dependent mother who doesn't give him very much. He's plopped into school, and either he has some real handicaps and can't cope or he's not functioning because he's just very anxious and can't deal with social demands. My goal would be to change this family and also to prepare them for future problems, of which there will be a number. This boy has a lot of needs. He needs appropriate peer contacts. Also, he needs some better parenting now. But it's very hard to do that because his father is saying there are no problems in the school. He's not going to want treatment. He's very angry with the school, and he's going to respond to treatment very angrily.

There is a concern in the family around the Klinefelter's. I suspect that might be a sore point for the father because this is a sexual disability. He's been left by one wife, and this wife is threatening to leave or does leave, at least for the afternoon. So there's that whole issue, which he doesn't voice, but there's enough information to make you wonder about that. On the plus side they seem to have at least some positive feelings, and they recognize that the hospital said that there is a problem. As a worker I would try to link myself with the hospital, or their family doctor, as an ally, to get an entree to this family and talk about this child's potential problems around the Klinefelter's syndrome.

Interviewer: What treatment methods would you use? Are you also promoting family therapy in this case?

Marton: Well, slightly differently, in the sense that my aims are not so broad. I recognize the importance of the dynamic changes you want to make, but I think some concrete changes have to be made in terms of how they interact with this child, the opportunities they allow him to have. So I would take that route, changing parenting style and family routines, but if that route breaks down, another approach would be to work with the school. In other words, this child needs a significant figure he can attach to and feel comfortable with. And if he can't do it at home, if the parents resist therapy and get angry, then I would work with the school. I would try to have the teacher or someone in the school be that kind of person and also have them make sure that the child gets remedial help if the assessment warrants it so that he can cope with the schoolwork, and that he gets some help socializing with the other kids, so he doesn't feel terribly threatened. That would be my backup plan.

Interviewer: Other comments about the kind of strategy you would attempt to use with this family?

Dydyk: I agree with Bill about a major emphasis being to join with the parents around their concern about the kid. Dealing with the school may be a good way of getting in and then proceeding from there to the parenting.

Carty: You'll see the parenting issues right in front of you with the two children. If the behavior happens in the sessions, it happens at home, it happens everywhere else. The parents can't dismiss it when it happens in front of you. For example, mother might say one thing, like "I always ask my husband and then he goes over and whacks the kid," and he'd respond "You never asked, you never consulted me." The therapist can do some very concrete work on such incidents in the session. I read the case a little more positively, in the sense that they have a lot to offer. Father has a lot to offer, mother has a lot to offer, but basically they're isolated.

Dydyk: I'm thinking that they're really fragile and that you might have to spend three or four sessions just joining with them because they would see you as wanting to intrude and regarding them as pathological. You might have to take a position almost opposite that of the school as a way of getting in. So I'd really stay away from looking at parenting issues.

Marton: That's a real hot potato.

Interviewer: What would you be looking at?

Dydyk: Their concerns about what's happened with the school, how they see their kid functioning, what pluses he has and what they make of what's going on. Getting into how difficult it must have been to hear that about the school because this is father's firstborn son. So reinforcing the parental caring, things that may not be there, but that every parent should feel.

Interviewer: Other recommendations for tactics and strategies?

Carty: I don't know if we're disagreeing. I do think you work with father and mother, but you recognize strengths, and I think that an obvious strength is that Michael and Jacqueline probably present very well. They're not going to be squirming all over the room. The fact that they bring up Klinefelter's shows concern, rather than rejection or wanting to fight it.

Dydyk: But they did that very reluctantly.

Carty: But it's amazing, this is a second interview. It's apparently the father who resents being in treatment. He wouldn't allow it to be brought up, so obviously there's some hook, there's some concern. Even if he resents the treatment, he's worried.

Marton: My approach would be to say that I know about Klinefelter's, that I know what problems potentially exist for their son. I think these parents are going to blow if you try to blame them.

Interviewer: Peter, you mentioned as a backup plan doing some work with the school. Barbara or Bill, would you want to do any work with the school?

Carty: I would want to work with the parents and follow their direction and ask their opinion. I would say what I thought to the parents as a recommendation, but I wouldn't then go and do something against their wishes just for the kid's sake. I think that would be a devastating experience for the parents. The kid's only 5, and by age 15, he's going to be placed some place by his parents, who will have had terrible experiences with him. It's crucial at this age to go with the parents.

Dydyk: I agree with that. I think your involvement in the school as an agent for the parents, who have obviously had difficulty with the school and are very angry, is a good way of joining with them. It's a nice way of entering into having them deal with other problems once they trust you.

Interviewer: Let's assume that you have successfully joined with this family and built some trust. What would you work on and how would you work on it?

Carty: Mother and father planning and following through with their children.

Parenting responsibilities. Trying to make parenting more balanced between mother and father. I think it will be very hard with their kid, and
they've got to depend on each other. If they learn to do it around concrete
day-to-day actions, they'll be able to plan for his future and any medical or
special treatment he may need.

Dydyk: My sense is that mother's enmeshed with the kids and that while you are
working at one level on whatever they bring up as a problem, you are also
looking at getting father involved in a more active way with the family.

Marton: It would be nice to work on the marital relationship if possible. This is a man
who was left up in the air with his first relationship and now again the wife
is threatening to leave. I wonder if that's not part of his anxiety for this
child.

Interviewer: Are there any special problems that you might anticipate and want to warn
the worker about?

Dydyk: I would bet there would be a lot of threats of their not coming back if they
felt this wasn't working.

Interviewer: So just holding these parents in therapy may be a problem.

Marton: I see that as a very big risk, because the child is only in junior kindergarten
and already they're blowing up at the school.

Interviewer: Any other special problems?

Carty: I think without hooking the father, they won't be there. I think father is the
key and I think if he's hooked, even if his wife doesn't like it, he'll bring his
wife in. He could be hooked by using the fact that he's a man and he could
probably help his wife raise a boy. I could imagine spending the whole hour
with the man and getting his opinions so that he leaves feeling like a very
active father. Then he'll also be able to do things like take his wife out to
dinner. He courted her only six, seven years ago, so he wouldn't have
forgotten how to do it. You might tell him that she looks very tired and
depressed. "Why don't you take her out to dinner, court her, get a bottle of
wine? You've done a lot of work." It would shake up the system somewhat
to recognize both strengths and weaknesses in both parents.

Marton: You're good at recognizing strengths.

Carty: Without father, I think, it doesn't matter if mother wants to come daily,
father wouldn't allow it.

Dydyk: I agree with that, but I think you have to watch because mother has a lot of
power as well and we're making mother the problematic one.

Carty: It's not at the expense of mother, because mother has worked so hard to
bring her child to 5 and the other to 3 and now she needs a little more help or
expertise. I think she'd agree that she's tired. You wouldn't call it depression, you might just call it "tired."

Interviewer: Is there anything that you would advise the worker to look for as a signal
that treatment was not working and it was time to try something else?

Dydyk: If mother canceled and there was a lapse in contact, I would be concerned.

Interviewer: Okay, anything else?

Marton: Again, if the parents blow, I would keep the school as my backup. Also,
raising the children is already a sore point in this marriage, and I would

advise the worker not to get trapped into supporting one parent versus the other. There's a real danger of getting sucked in there.

Dydyk: I would also want to look closely at the kids and be in touch with the school in terms of possible neglect.

Marton: If this lady is not doing her caretaking properly, then some of the time these kids are not getting to bed on time, and as the description indicates, they're going to come in bedraggled some days.

Dydyk: There's another thing I'd be concerned about with this guy; he doesn't show any affect, he has to come on in a very macho way and he is really quite impotent in his marriage. It's his potential for abuse and violence. I would wonder about that and would want to keep my eyes open.

Marton: Certainly in the long run, when this kid starts developing breasts, this father is going to have a lot of trouble dealing with that. These become issues only with long-term contact.

Interviewer: Okay, what kind of worker would you like to assign to this case?

Marton: Someone who's not going to get angry in retaliation. I think these parents invite that. They want you to get mad at them, and they want to fight.

Interviewer: Any other worker qualities?

Dydyk: Yes, somebody who can gently but firmly challenge them and not be afraid of the response or back off. Persistence. Somebody who is not going to set goals too high and expect things to click very rapidly, because in this kind of family you'd have to go bit by bit and have your goals relatively small.

Marton: I think someone who is comfortable about his/her own role, because this family wants to debunk professionalism.

Interviewer: What should the main goals of treatment be?

Marton: I would like to see a specific change in parenting Michael. Consistency is needed. From the sound of things, mother and father disagree. Mother is letting go and is permissive while father is controlling and authoritarian. I think that they have unclear roles regarding parenting. I would also want mother not to allow those children to walk all over her. So, some basic management skills for her. Given her anxiety and insecurity, I think there also have to be some positives. There's no indication of what this family does for fun. A goal would be to structure so many times per week that the parents do something with Michael to have a good time. He appears to be capable of it with other adults.

Dydyk: I would want to set up short-term and long-term goals. A short-term goal would be to make this therapy experience positive for this family. Another short-term goal would be for the parents to allow other helping people to become involved, like specialized day care for the kids or a public health nurse. The long-term goals are what we said about developing skills as parents.

Marton: Also preparing this child for the problems he's going to encounter with the Klinefelter's. The interpersonal problems are going to be greater for him over time.

Carty: The goals I see are getting the parents to work together and take action and to deal with the school problem. I think father is very worried and threatened about this 5-year-old misbehaving at school. I would like the parents to agree on the best plan of action for the problems at school, regardless of their tactics.

Interviewer: Prognosis?

Carty: Good for the short term in terms of resolving the school issue and the parents talking to each other and planning. I think then it has to be up to the family to seek further help. Maybe next time they'd walk in without having been called, or maybe they'd call first.

Dydyk: I would say the prognosis is fair because there are issues concerning the past level of functioning of these parents that I'm just not sure about in terms of their childhoods, their models, and their relationships.

Marton: Particularly because I don't think the father learned from his first marriage. He seems to be repeating the cycle and that's not a good sign to me. I would be guarded also.

Carty: It would be interesting to see, since father's mother was disabled all through his childhood, if he could be very helpful to Michael once he can address the fact that he needs medical attention, or it might be too much for him. He's had a history of working with disabilities and diseases throughout most of his childhood.

Marton: For both of them, there is a glimmer of hope. She maintains contact with her last foster parents, who obviously were significant figures, and he had the sister. On the other hand, both of them had poor parenting experiences, so those are not good signs.

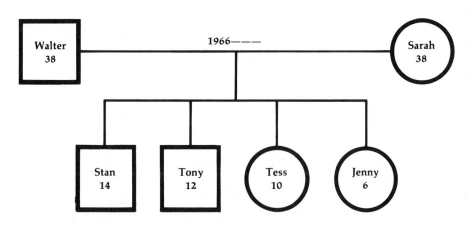

THE SIMPSON FAMILY

Identifying information

The Simpson family consists of Mr. and Mrs. Walter Simpson and their four children, Stan, Tony, Tess, and Jenny. The guidance counselor at Stan's junior high school referred the family to the mental health center when he became concerned about Stan's increasing withdrawal and his potential for violence.

History of problem

Two incidents in the school culminated in Stan's interview with the guidance counselor. An industrial arts teacher became concerned because Stan had been making knives and designing "torture devices" in his class. At about the same time Stan was seen violently throwing everything out of his school locker into the hall. During the interview with the counselor, Stan was very quiet, avoided eye contact, and spoke in a flat monotone. This withdrawn behavior is regarded as typical of Stan, although his teacher claims he has become increasingly withdrawn during the past two weeks. Stan also admitted feeling angry a lot recently and letting off steam by throwing rocks at targets in his backyard. Asked what he was angry about, he would only say that school bored him. He explained the locker incident by saying that a teacher had given him a "C" on an essay that he thought deserved a higher mark.

Informed of the incident, Mr. and Mrs. Simpson seemed more concerned about the embarrassment of being called to the school than about the seriousness of Stan's behavior. They tended to minimize the incidents and to view them as overinterpreted by the counselor and within the realm of adolescent playfulness. They agreed to come to the mental health center but see little need for professional treatment and believe they are capable of getting Stan to "clean up his act." They maintain that Stan has always been very quiet and is well-behaved at home. Mr. Simpson does note that he would like Stan to improve his grades, which are nonetheless above average, and wishes his son were more athletic.

Marital and family history

Walter and Sarah Simpson met in college and married 17 years ago after a one-year engagement. Mr. Simpson's father was an electrician, and Walter grew up in a middle-class neighborhood as the oldest of two brothers. Walter and his father, who is now dead, were not particularly close, although Walter has a grudging respect for his dad's toughness and authority. He felt as a child that his father preferred his younger brother Will. He was emotionally closer to their mother, Mrs. Simpson, who lives about three hours away; they speak on the telephone periodically and see each other on holidays.

Sarah Simpson was an only child, whose father was a successful insurance executive. She grew up in physical comfort and security and saw her father as demanding and aloof and her mother as trying hard to please him. Her parents live a few minutes away, but Sarah avoids contact with them because listening to her mother's complaints depresses her.

According to the Simpsons, their marriage has been satisfactory although they are reluctant to share much about their relationship because they don't view it as relevant to the school's concern about Stan.

Characteristics of family members

Walter Simpson presents as brusque and businesslike and speaks in staccato bursts in a loud voice. Sarah Simpson appears softer and more engaging, has a nervous smile, and clearly defers to her husband. Family roles seem clear-cut. Walter owns an electrical supply company and spends long hours away from home at work. Apparently Sarah's father has a financial interest in the business. Walter expects the house to be run like a "tight ship" and believes that children need strong discipline to develop the necessary survival skills to make it in the world. As such, his stern commands are sufficient to keep the kids in line. Sarah's role is the homemaker, taking care of the kids and seeing that the house is in order. She claims that the children are generally cooperative, but as a last resort she will threaten to report their misdeeds to their father. The family has a cleaning lady who comes twice a week, and Sarah finds time to play tennis and bridge with her friends.

All the children are attractive and well-behaved. Stan is fair-haired and appears physically robust and healthy. However, he has a slouched posture, maintains minimal eye contact, and seems generally unhappy. Privately, he says that he dislikes school and that he feels under considerable pressure there and at home. Although nothing special has happened recently to make life worse for him, he says that he is spending more and more time daydreaming and thinking about getting away. He thinks his parents are stricter with him than with his brother and sisters, admits that he has few friends, and says he prefers working alone on his stamp collection or building models of planes and military weapons. Stan feels he doesn't get much support or encouragement for things that are important to him. He spends little time with his parents and for the most part sees his father only on weekends. He says that he doesn't really like to do things with his dad because he is too demanding and critical. Walter likes to hunt, for example, and has taken Stan on hunting trips. Stan says he wants to join the army after high school but that his parents are very much against the idea and expect him to go to college.

Tony is 12, also attractive, stockier than Stan, and much more gregarious. He seems to have many friends and comes across as somewhat of a braggart. He doesn't know what's wrong with Stan but says that Stan never talks much anyway. Tess and Jenny, although almost four years apart in age, look very much alike and similar to their mother. They are also quiet and reserved but do not appear depressed. They wait for permission to speak and then are eager to share their projects with the interviewer. They both like to spend time with Stan but claim he is ignoring them lately.

School and community

Stan is in the eighth grade. He has scored above average on scholastic aptitude tests and his grades reflect his abilities. The school admits that he is unusually reserved, but they have never been concerned about him in the past. At this time they wonder about his potential for violence. They do not see a deteriorating school performance. They also report that the Simpsons have always felt that Stan could do better at school if he applied himself and that they have been critical of Stan's teachers in the past.

Case discussion

Consultants: Dr. Rudolph Philipp, Ms. Elizabeth Ridgley, Mr. Bruce Stam

Interviewer: What assessment questions or procedures would you recommend to the worker?

Philipp: I would recommend a family assessment to identify where the loyalty is in this family, who is isolated, who is providing support to whom, whether there is affection, and how members relate around major issues. I certainly see this as a family therapy case.

Interviewer: Would you expand on what you mean by a family assessment?

Philipp: I would see the family as a whole for several sessions and ask them how they view the situation that brought them to the clinic. I would certainly do a lot of observing, how they support or don't support one another, how they agree with or contradict one another, how they align within the family. My suspicion is that Stan is isolated in this family.

Interviewer: Would anyone recommend a formal individual assessment of Stan?

Philipp: Not as a first thing, although some of his behaviors are seemingly unprovoked. I would do a formal assessment of Stan if some reason developed to move in that direction.

Interviewer: Okay, let's talk about treatment.

Stam: Basic family therapy. I would see talking with the parents and the children about their relationships and alignments.

Interviewer: Would you use any additional types of therapy or any other community services or do you see it as a straightforward family therapy case?

Stam: I would be tempted to get involved with Stan on a one-to-one basis and get him moving and involved in the community. However, we may be taking away from the family in doing that, and that would be really dangerous at this moment. So despite the temptation, I think I would hold back doing that.

Interviewer: Rudy, what kind of treatment approach would you use?

Philipp: I would start with family therapy, and I would go with it as far as I could.

Interviewer: As far as you could. What does that imply?

Philipp: Well, I wouldn't consider other treatment modalities given the information I have.

Ridgley: I think this case is more difficult than it appears, and so I would have specific strategies ready for the worker who is seeing the family. The father is peripheral and he delegates his authority to the mother to run a tight ship. When she doesn't do that he becomes more demanding and critical of the children to counter her softness. If the kids can't get around mother, they sure can't get around him. The problem is that they don't know him either and only see him on weekends. I don't think this man feels very comfortable with himself despite his success. He was less loved by his father and he outclassed himself in his marriage. His brusqueness probably disguises enormous fears of inadequacy, and his demands on Stan to achieve have a kind of desperateness to them; he is to achieve to make father feel better by having a smart and athletic son. I think that father's fragility organizes his wife, who defers to him and protects him. She does not take this man on about his relationship with his children. And you could speculate that she has reproduced her parents' marital relationship. Given this, I think the father will present as very defensive and controlling because he can't appear inadequate as a father and his children need to reflect his ability by their abilities.

I would agree with Rudy that Stan is an isolated kid. His problem is loneliness and an inability to stand up for himself or assert himself appropriately. He speaks in a monotone, he avoids eye contact, and I would directly relate this to father's distance. I think that father needs to be the initial focus, and Stan's problems need to be exaggerated to counteract the father's minimizing techniques and to engage him in helping his son. So I would ask the father what he thinks Stan's problem is and whatever father replied I would make it worse than what he said. I would point out that he can't look you in the eye, he can't make friends, he can't speak up for himself, and he can't negotiate his marks with the teacher. I would agree that he is underachieving and what a shame that is and how unnecessary because father is an achiever, he has done well, he can talk well, he can handle contact with the world in a truly exemplary fashion, and that this boy could benefit from father's experience. I would place him as the expert on boys growing into men and on achievement. I would emphasize how much Stan needs him as a resource and a consultant. I would start right away with something concrete. Next week when they are having dinner, for example, I might inquire "How often do you have dinner together, by the way?" "Well, you will have to change that because it is not often enough at this time. This family needs you now, not your business." Then I would get him to talk to Stan at the dinner table because Stan is throwing rocks instead of talking. He needs to engage Stan in a conversation and no one is allowed to interrupt. I believe this father could find a way to make this boy talk about anything. Then I would start talking about Rudy's concern about Stan because he doesn't have space in this family. He is the firstborn, the eldest, but Tony is taking all his space. The girls are just like the mother, they talk girl-talk, but Stan is so quiet he goes unnoticed. The emphasis would be on getting the father to help the son, which would confirm his competence and place him in a control position in the family.

I agree absolutely with the Simpsons that the marital relationship does not belong in family therapy. Their relationship will improve as their joint parenting improves, and it is in the interest of the child for them to highlight what a good team they are and not to highlight their conflicts and differences. In order for them to be a team, father first has to be made a full partner, and you can only do this by minimizing mother's impact. Once father is established in there, then mother could come back. She could be given a retirement present or something. As Stan's position in the family is elevated, he will be able to move away and I wouldn't expect any further problems from him.

Interviewer: Rudy?

Philipp: I would question a couple of things. Although the marriage may or may not belong in family therapy, it invariably gets in there somehow. It is in the background or the foreground, and just because they say they don't want to talk about it doesn't mean we can ignore it. Because they say their marriage is satisfactory doesn't mean that we have to assume that it is. One could argue that the acting-out one sees in this family is in response to the parents not getting along. There are a few other minor issues. Stan is displaying periodic outbursts of anger. He feels threatened, and he is making these torture devices. I am not sure where this threat is coming from. When there is anger bursting on the surface, I like to look for the depression that is underneath.

Ridgley: Well, I would elaborate on the torture instruments—you could say "That is wonderful, throwing rocks is bad but torture is mean. How do they work? What kind of torture? How much do they hurt?" You can make them less scary and get father to deal with the specific behaviors rather than what may be, quite accurately, a lot of depression.

Philipp: There is another issue and that is the parents' relationship with their own parents. It is not close for either of them, and in a way that sets the tone for this family. If it wasn't true for them, why should it be true for this family? I would bring this issue into family therapy.

Interviewer: Bruce, would you like to talk about techniques or strategies that you would have the worker adopt?

Stam: The key is the relationship between Walter and Stan. Another factor is that I think Stan can be taught to encourage himself. He is a fairly bright kid. He stated that he is angry, not just covering it up. He is 14. I am guessing he might be able, with father's support, to learn to encourage himself and not be totally at the whim or mercy of his parents. I suspect that both mother and dad don't have a clue at the moment where Stan is at. Mother, as well, is going to have to become more positive in support of Stan and not just father.

Interviewer: What might be some indications that the whole strategy needs to be rethought?

Stam: Father might sabotage the process. If he doesn't withdraw, he might become super-cooperative but, in fact, not change. I would want to be very sensitive to father's attitude and behavior.

Interviewer: What if father does pull out of the case? What would you have the worker do?

Stam: He could probably be challenged again. He is not going to fall apart. He is worth giving a second or third chance to cooperate.

Interviewer: Are there other danger signs or things that could go wrong?

Ridgley: I don't think anything is apt to go wrong, except with the father and the father's competence. I would imagine that this lady outclasses him all over the place. She probably tells him how to eat properly because she is the only daughter of a wealthy insurance executive. But he is supported by the worker and supported to tell his wife, "Enough!" I don't think Stan will get angry anymore once he has the father involved. I think the outbursts will disappear.

Philipp: He needs more than a father. I think there have to be some realistic expectations for him. He may not be able to excel all the time.

Ridgley: He won't get that message. If father feels more competent in the family, father will become more understanding.

Philipp: This father is a workaholic and has done very well. He has to learn that the standards he set for himself are not necessarily good or desirable for his son. If his work still took precedence, that would be a danger signal. He could rationalize it left, right, and center why he had to be at a convention in Chicago or why he has to work until 10 o'clock at night. You have to break through this and I think Libby's suggestion of raising his anxiety to indicate that we need him and the family needs him is very important. I would also like to find out how this family handles anger and sadness. It would give me a clue as to why Stan is feeling pain.

Interviewer: Libby, you said that there is a temptation to at least consider the possibility of adolescent psychosis.

Ridgley: You can tell that the school is very alarmed about the knives and torture devices. I don't think that it is so unusual for a 14-year-old. You can make a big psychiatric case out of that but when you think about it, this kid has only made a couple of knives and a fancy torture device, he is throwing his books out of his locker because he got a "C" instead of an "A," he doesn't look anybody in the eyes, and he throws rocks in the garden in the backyard.

Interviewer: Are there things he might start to do that would cause you to reassess?

Ridgley: I could make them up, but I don't think so.

Philipp: I would want to note all this information and not react to it but just keep it in the back of my mind. Just in case some other behaviors occur that fit in and raise this issue again.

Ridgley: This kind of family therapy follows the symptom very closely—the kid's not talking and his lack of eye contact, for example. If you continue throughout the course of therapy to follow the symptoms you ought not be surprised by anything. It is when you start talking about other issues like whether mother and father have an adequate sexual life that the kid can be developing all sorts of "wonderful" symptoms and you never hear about it.

Interviewer: Okay, what kind of worker would you like to see handling this case?

Ridgley: This worker has to be very sure of himself. This is a very socially conscious family, embarrassed by the problems at school. This worker would have to be able to deal with them without feeling attacked or attacking.

Interviewer: Is this the sort of family that will challenge or question or be skeptical about the worker and about family therapy?

Ridgley: Sure.

Philipp: Especially the father. I would suggest a male worker who has lots of experience and is very sure of himself.

Ridgley: I don't think it matters whether it is a man or woman but there should be a fee for service.

Stam: I think it should be a male. I think Walter has got to be hooked here.

Ridgley: Walter can be hooked by a woman.

Stam: Yes, but in the fathering I think it will help them to relate to a male worker.

Ridgley: But it is wonderful with a woman because you can say "You are the only one in the family who has been a little boy, you are the only one who knows about little boys growing up to become men."

Stam: I would still prefer a male who has his own family and can relate on a business level.

Interviewer: What goals would you recommend to the worker?

Stam: Dad and Stan spending time together, doing things, relating in a positive way. Father taking some time off to spend with his family. You can break that down to a specific number of hours. That would be my primary goal.

Interviewer: Any other goals besides the father-son relationship?

Philipp: One of the important goals I would like to see achieved is for Stan to be able to talk about his feelings. Stan should be able to spend time with his father—time they can both enjoy—so that Stan would not feel that, unless he can meet every expectation, he is a failure. Finally Stan should not have to become a carbon copy of his father.

Ridgley: I would use the father-son relationship in order to help this family function at a more engaged level, having originally diagnosed it as a disengaged family. They are all going in different directions and father is particularly isolated from the family and his wife. But mother is not cleaning her house. She is playing tennis and bridge, so there is an implication that she is a bit disengaged as well.

Interviewer: What would indicate that the family was engaged?

Ridgley: The worker would see, first of all, increased comfort when they are all together in the room and the worker would measure it by the father's ability to talk, not just to Stan but also to Tony and to his two daughters as well. He would be able to individuate among them and talk in different ways to the different children. They would begin to eat together more frequently, and they would begin to do things together. Father might put Tony down and say "You be quiet, Stan is talking now." The whole family would be participating in a more comfortable, easy way.

Interviewer: Is there anything specifically about mother's role in terms of goals?

Ridgley: Part of the initial engaging of father will be at the expense of her competence. I would put mother down and make her presence less important initially in order to make father more important. Mother will have mixed feelings about that, and in order to deal with these feelings you have to encourage father to recognize her needs as well. Take her out to dinner, buy her a gold watch. In other words, she has to have some benefits for retiring from being Stan's caretaker!

Philipp: Isn't there a danger of alienating this woman?

Ridgley: No, because she wants a husband. She wants a husband and lets her kids get away with stuff so that she can tell her husband and bring him back to the family. The only way she can get her husband is by having a problem with the kids. In the end she is going to be delighted because she is going to go to a fancy restaurant for dinner and is going to get what she wants. She wants this to be a family.

Stam: I think there is a bit of danger in retiring mother at this point because she may jump at it and really retire, and then there will be trouble.

Ridgley: She is an expert on raising these kids. She puts them down all the time. So you say to him "Look, you know in your guts what boys need to be doing. Now your wife is telling you that you are too critical, you are too this, you are too that. Tell your wife you know how to be a father and she knows how to be a mother, so in order for you to be a father she needs to stop fathering and mothering. Tell her to cool it."

Interviewer: And what would she be doing?

Ridgley: She would be sitting in silent support of her husband even if she thought he was being terribly hard on Stan. She would not undermine him. If she were able to do that, this man would get a lot softer. He wouldn't be as critical and he wouldn't be as rough on the kids. Because he is compensating for what he thinks is her laxness and she will be surprised to find out that her husband can actually talk to the kids.

Interviewer: What is the prognosis?

Ridgley: Excellent.

Stam: Good.

Philipp: I agree.

Interviewer: How long would you expect to take to complete therapy?

Ridgley: This family is difficult to estimate because it is hard to assess from paper how defensive the father is. It could take just eight sessions and then I would send them on their way, and then I would call him back.

Philipp: There is an unknown fact here and that is the marital relationship. If this is a faltering marriage and father is escaping it through work, it could take longer. Assuming that the marriage is okay, I would say it might take four months working with this family.

Stam: I think the prognosis for Stan is excellent. A couple of months to build a good enough relationship between Walter and Stan. Work with the entire family, especially the relationship between mom and dad, could take a lot longer.

Ridgley: If you don't direct the father to court his wife at the same time, she will get in the way of father's relationship with Stan.

Philipp: You are assuming that there is nothing standing in the way of his courting his wife.

Ridgley: Right.

Philipp: I can't make that assumption, because I don't know.

Ridgley: Well, it is a very important assumption. If you are looking for strength and if you are looking for the highest level of competence from the parents, the assumption is they can look after their marriage. They are stuck right now, and that is why they feel as they do. But they can do it and they want to do it. Otherwise, they wouldn't be in the office and they wouldn't be together.

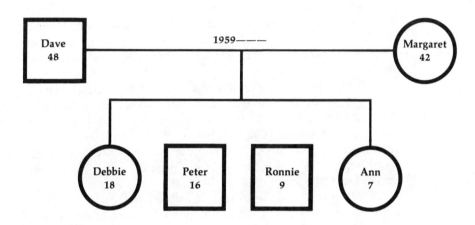

THE BARKER FAMILY

Identifying information

The Barker family consists of Mr. and Mrs. Barker and their four children. The two younger children are adopted.

The parents are seeking help for Ronnie at the urging of his school, which is finding him to be a serious behavior problem. The Barkers describe Ronnie as "no real problem" at home. However, they do acknowledge that he fights frequently with Ann and has stolen small amounts of money from them. Ronnie also is enuretic.

History of problem

Ronnie's school problems were already evident in the first grade. His teacher that year described him as inattentive, easily frustrated, unwilling to try new work, and "rough" with peers. Both first and second grade teachers reported that isolating Ronnie and providing him with one-to-one attention were the only effective ways to help him attend to his schoolwork. Now, in the third grade, there has been a significant deterioration in Ronnie's behavior, which his teacher has labeled as "unmanageable."

Ronnie's parents minimize his problems at school and tend to see the school as inadequate in its handling of their son. They see Ronnie's current teacher as unfair to him and rigid in her disciplinary measures. They deny serious problems at home. Stealing has been intermittent for the last two to three years. Enuresis has been continuous and occurs about twice a week. Other than a physical checkup, parents have taken no measures to correct this problem.

Marital and family history

Mrs. Barker lived in a small Ontario town as a child. She has four older brothers. Both her parents are now dead. Mrs. Barker describes herself as having been "fairly close" to both parents and feels her childhood was happy and unremarkable. Her family moved to Toronto when she was 17 and she met her husband shortly afterward. Mrs. Barker reports that she remained close to her parents until their deaths. Her father died six years ago and her mother two years ago.

Mr. Barker was an only son whose father died when he was 10 years old. Mr. Barker's mother remarried shortly thereafter. He describes his stepfather as a rigid and punitive man whom he feared. Both parents are now deceased. He has spent all his life in Toronto. The Barkers claim that their marriage has had minor "ups and downs" but that their relationship is a happy one. They respond to questions regarding their marriage in a puzzled and defensive way.

Mother required a hysterectomy shortly after Peter's birth. Ronnie was adopted at age 1½ and Ann at 11 months. Both children were in foster homes before adoption.

Characteristics of family members

Mrs. Barker is a full-time housewife and mother. She relates warmly and supportively to all four of her children but especially to Ronnie and Ann. She seems sensitive and tuned in to others' feelings but tends to deny her own feelings, especially negative ones. She seems generally permissive with the children and attempts to manage them with verbal messages and little action. She is easily threatened if unmet needs in the family are mentioned and seems to view questions in this area as a personal "attack" on her adequacy as a mother and wife. Mrs. Barker has few interests outside of her family.

Mr. Barker is a bus driver for the city. He works long hours and rotates shifts from time to time. He has held the same job for the last eight years. Mr. Barker presents as a cool, logical, and rational man who is uncomfortable talking about his feelings. He suffers from migraine headaches and doesn't spend as much time with his children as he would like. The family agrees that father is often tired and hard to reach but emphasizes his devotion to his family.

Debbie and Peter, the Barkers' natural children, are both outstanding athletes and do satisfactory academic work in high school. Debbie remains involved with the younger children and seems particularly warm and empathetic. Peter is heavily involved in hockey. Ann is an attractive, articulate

7-year-old who sometimes seems like a little adult and who can usually charm family members into giving her what she wants. Ronnie, on the other hand, is clearly "odd man out" in this family. He often seems to isolate himself from the family unit on both a physical and an emotional basis. Apart from him, the family unit appears bright, congenial, and articulate. With him, a good deal of family attention is spent on soothing his hurt feelings, meeting his demands and ultimatums, and reassuring him that he is loved and accepted. Parents report that the adoptive status of Ronnie and Ann has been discussed openly in the past and is not an issue.

School and community

Ronnie has recently been suspended from school for a day or two at a time. This has occurred three times in the last four months. In each case, a minor incident escalated into a physical confrontation with either a teacher or the school principal and culminated with Ronnie's hitting, swearing, and spitting at the adult. Aside from these incidents, Ronnie constantly seeks attention in class, clowns and disrupts the classroom, and frequently gets into fights during recess and lunch periods. When confronted, he is belligerent and denies responsibility for any of his actions. His schoolwork is often incomplete. However, it is not known what his current level of academic achievement is. He seems to be working (inconsistently) at a late grade-two level. His strengths include a fascination with science and mechanical tasks, a sense of humor, and some continuing accessibility to one-to-one attention from an adult.

Ronnie spends little time in the community. His father has attempted to get him involved in organized sports (soccer, hockey), but he seems to lose interest quickly.

Case discussion

Consultants: Ms. Sandra Birenbaum, Dr. Joseph Kluger

Interviewer: Why don't we start by talking about the Barker family in terms of the information you have that seems clinically important.

Birenbaum: Well, I was impressed. I think they are a fairly healthy family. What concerns me, of course, is that the problem with this 9-year-old boy has been going on for several years. And there are no indications of any difficulties within the family. They are disowning any concern about him and projecting it all onto the school. For me this is always a dangerous sign.

Kluger: My concerns about the family include their tendency to minimize difficulties. Mother seems to present quite well, talks about close relationships, and seems to be fairly caring, but there is a lax quality to her management of the children. We have the sense that the father tends to be absent from the disciplining. However, when he is there I wonder about the nature of his disciplining. His background suggests that he has had his share of reprimands and criticisms directed toward him from his stepfather. One wonders what his particular approach is. Does he shy away, for example, because of his previous experience with disciplining in his own family? Where, on the other hand, does he lose his cool? He disappears with migraines and complaints of fatigue. His involvement with the other kids seems to be around overtly masculine sports activities. Even though Ronnie, the 9-year-old, has an interest in things that are not particularly athletic, there is no indication that the father tries to promote that interest or share that interest. One of my questions concerns what father and Ron do together. I would certainly want to interview the parents and the child about the kinds of things they do together. The absent father and the lax mother are possible contributing factors in this kid's difficulty with demands that are placed on him in the school situation.

Birenbaum: Also a family that doesn't deal with feelings.

Kluger: Yeah.

Birenbaum: I think you're right about father's behavior at home. I think he does withdraw, and I know this little boy does the same. I assume that they pull back, rather than actually fighting together.

Interviewer: Sandy, you said earlier that one of the first things that struck you was the strengths and the health in this family. Could you explain?

Birenbaum: I was looking at how the family presented. I was looking at the success with the two oldest children and the third. There is a warmth there. And no difficulties until this point in life. For any family that has four children nowadays and doesn't have any major concerns, there has to be some strength.

Kluger: That always makes me think of the vulnerable child. Difficulties in life are 99% multidetermined, and one has to ask why this child is presenting these problems.

Birenbaum: I think you are right. Why is this child vulnerable? He's adopted at a year-and-a-half, and I don't know what kind of a child they got out of the foster home. I'd be most concerned about the foster home and the parents' attitude and response to the child when they first got him. Who wanted the adoption and who did not? It would be fairly stressful, I would think, with a year-and-a-half-old child. I think the parent-child interaction is significant. There is some indication that the mother is a little overprotective with this child for reasons that aren't very clear. So I would assume that not only did he have two parents, but he probably had four who would have already smothered him a little bit.

Interviewer: We have identified two areas about which it would be useful to have more information: current type of contact between the boy and his parents, and the background of his foster home experience and early years in which the family brought this child into their home. Any other major missing areas?

Birenbaum: I thought some psychological and educational testing, including IQ, would be important. I would also want more information medically regarding the enuresis. I was fascinated that a family could have a child of 9 years, well beyond the age of training, and didn't seem a bit concerned about it other than having taken the child for some kind of a medical exam.

Kluger: I am less concerned about the enuresis for a number of reasons. It's a symptom but, first of all, it's occurring only twice a week, which is not in the category of serious in terms of my experience. Second, in terms of the literature, enuresis tends to be associated with generalized immaturity in learning as opposed to a specific neurological or physical condition or problem. So I would second the need for a thorough intellectual and educational or achievement-oriented assessment. This kid may be a year behind academically because he is 9 years old and functioning at a second-grade level, which immediately makes me think of asking what his birthdate is. Are we talking about a child who was born late in the year and started school early? That would augur better for him in terms of his level of academic functioning. On the other hand, we know there is a fourfold greater chance of a male child born in the last quarter of the year starting school early and having maladjustment problems of some kind in school relative to the average child. That information would be helpful to sort out whether we are dealing with a child who is a little more immature across the board, given that he is younger and therefore was faced with academic demands "too early," or with a child who is not early to start school in terms of his age but nonetheless has some learning difficulties. I would look for the connection between the learning difficulties and the enuresis. As for the enuresis *per se*, that's the last thing I would go after in terms of treatment. Finally, enuresis is a self-limiting condition; almost all enuretic children get better with age no matter what you do. Thus, by age 14 only 2-3% of the general population bed-wets.

Birenbaum: I wouldn't treat it either, but, diagnostically, the fact that this family has ignored it or made it less than it is supports my original hypothesis. Twice a week is not the end of the world, except if my kid had it, but I would certainly check into it. For this child, it means no overnights, no camp. Part of my reason for checking out the academics and things of that nature is to sort out how much of this child's problems is related to the school and how much is a symptom of the family dynamics.

Interviewer: O.K. Recognizing that there are some significant areas of information that are not here and that you have to make educated guesses, what do you think is going on here?

Kluger: My feeling is that this kid is presenting with moderate difficulties. He is not serious, he is not mild. My gut-level feeling is that he has some learning problems. I would suspect that he is of low average intelligence, but that's not the major contributing factor. He has some learning difficulties that are independent of, let's say, insecurity *per se*. I suspect that the adoption coming at a year-and-a-half has contributed to some extent to this child's lack of feeling secure, that the relative lack of involvement of the father with this particular child and the father's relative involvement with the older boy, who is very much into hockey, contributes to his feeling like the odd man out. Both the older kids have done well, according to the history. This child is not doing well. He is not doing well academically, he is not involved with sports, and there is not a great deal of information about the nature of his social contacts.

The other kids seem to have friends. There is a suggestion that he really doesn't have friends. I would want to know about the nature of his peer relationships, and I would look to see how one could get him more involved with peers in a practical way so that his self-image would improve. I think the family would be open to concrete suggestions. This is not a family that would go for an interpretative kind of approach either in family counseling or parent counseling. I'll leave it there, and then I'll talk about specific approaches.

Birenbaum: Well, I support what Jerry is saying about this child having a limited IQ and having learning difficulties. I also feel that he has a particular role in the family and was responding to various stresses or things going on in the family system. I don't think it's an accident this child hits out in school or is fighting with his sister. I think he probably builds and builds and then he kind of explodes. I don't see this as being a long-term family therapy case. They may be open to some insight and some opening of communication within the family system, and also some very direct work about the difficulties in school, which are going to create more and more problems for this child.

Interviewer: You said that Ronnie may be serving a particular function in the family. What role is that?

Birenbaum: My guess is that he keeps the family together in some way. People seem to involve with him in that kind of way, giving in to him. I'm not sure what goes on in the marital situation. I don't think they are going to let us in too much. In some way, he meets a need daddy doesn't meet for mother.

Interviewer: Let's talk about some of the major modalities of treatment. What would you recommend with this family?

Birenbaum: I'll go for family therapy. My major goals would be to deal with the symptom that he is presenting in the school, to get this family to stop projecting responsibility onto the school, and to raise their levels of anxiety so that they can start to see what's going on between them and the boy.

Kluger: I think my approach would be at a number of levels in terms of both the kinds of treatment interventions and sequence of the interventions. I agree with something you mentioned earlier. I would want to use a fairly direct approach with the child's behavior in the school situation. No matter what his school placement, I would want to set up some kind of behavior modification system. His behavior problems occur at the point where he is confronted with something he has done. The way that teachers or school personnel approach him perhaps is open to some kind of change through consultation with somebody from the treatment agencies. But I would set up with the child some kind of charting system around behavior. Second, my family approach would be less family therapy oriented *per se*, but I would want to see where the strengths lie in the family. I would want to see if I could get father to spend more time with his boy, even without a lot of interpretation as to why—along the lines of the child's interest, so the child doesn't feel he has to be Bobby Hull in order to divest himself of mother and invest himself a little bit more with the adult male. Now, that's provided the father is reasonably accepting of the child. If it turns out that the father is quite negative toward the child, then I don't think it's a good idea. One would have to look for some kind of substitute.

I've already mentioned that I wouldn't treat the enuresis directly, I wouldn't do anything about it. I think some of my focus would be on the parents, and in particular on mom taking a somewhat firmer stand. However, I say that very cautiously. Using that approach ought to be considered very carefully because they don't see managing the kids as a problem in the home. There are a number of other alternatives that I would think of. There is the nature of peer relations. Is there any kind of supervised activity one could involve this child in? Unsupervised activity would be disastrous. Should some of these more immediate approaches not be successful, I would consider the possibility of a special placement such as a behavior class within the public school system or day treatment.

Birenbaum: I also think we could go for child management. I certainly was less concerned about involving father. You also talked about changing how the teachers deal with the boy. I have the sense that the teachers are probably not unreasonable but that the child has gotten a message within the family system saying "This is not your fault, dear, and those teachers are bad to you." One of the things that I feel would be very significant in bringing about any change in the school would be to make sure the messages from the parents are very different. It may be that this child will do better in a behavior modification program or small class, where the goals may be more realistic for him and there are child care workers who could deal with his inappropriate way of expressing feelings.

Interviewer: How would you have these parents become more allied with the school?

Birenbaum: I would start them with family therapy until I felt they were able to support the school. I would then coordinate and arrange a meeting with the school. I or my workers would work fairly closely with the school and the parents, using a team approach where the parents would become part of the school team. There might be a phone call once a week or twice a week to reinforce Ronnie doing his homework. The parents would start to give the child the message that school is important and they are there to help.

Interviewer: Let's say that the parents remain protective of Ronnie and resistant to expecting him to conform or produce academically. What would you do with that?

Birenbaum: I guess I would start to work with them about how their attitude is preventing this child from growing up into a more functioning young man.

Interviewer: The other thing that I want you to follow up on is the difference in your two perceptions regarding the importance of involving father. Sandy, do you feel that if father, who is a bus driver and is on shift work, proves difficult to get into family therapy, he should be pursued or that he ought to be let go in terms of the sessions?

Birenbaum: I wouldn't let him go. I think that he is an extremely important part of the family. He is the sexual person that this child is going to try to model himself after. To some extent Ronnie isolates himself and withdraws himself a little bit like his daddy, so it would be very important to get father to be part of the helping process. I would do everything I could to arrange a meeting so that he could be there, and to seduce him, coerce him, appeal to him, to be present. In any kind of family therapy I would use a contract specifying a certain number of sessions.

Interviewer: Could we back up a minute and get suggestions from you about how you would initially "hook" this family?

Kluger: In general, I would start with something that concerns them. I might even start with the very thing that we just focused on. The father has tried to get this kid involved in organized sports. I might say "What was it like for you, how did it go, what did you try?" I would do that in the family context.

Interviewer: They are presenting themselves and saying "The school is on our back and they have pushed us to come here and get some help and we think that they are botching up." What would you do to get these people looking at their own family?

Birenbaum: Well, I think this is a common problem. Certainly, most families come in and say "He is the problem. There is nothing wrong with us. What do we need family therapy for? He's just a messed-up kid, or it's that crazy school." They are very clear: something terribly wrong with that school. Except, the reality is he's been suspended three times in the last four months. He is abusive to adults, he swears and spits at them and, granted, maybe the school is terrible. But do they have any thoughts about the child? I would go after that and probably bulldoze my way through.

Kluger: I might want to ask if this happens with the other kids, and why they think it's happening more with him, since presumably the kids attend the same school. I would get them to feel a little more anxious for the purpose of thinking about what's happening.

Birenbaum: I would also support their anxiety even though they are coming in and saying it's a school problem. I think it's completely normal for parents to be worried when their child is into this much difficulty at age 9.

Kluger: If they kept denying it, then I think I would go a little harder and say "O.K., your kid is suspended, what are the options?" and get the school involved in that discussion. "What would you like to see happen? Is it important for your child to finish school? All right, how do you think you can do that?"

Interviewer: What about the sisters and brothers? How much would you involve them?

Birenbaum: I would involve them, and I would keep them involved until such time it becomes apparent there is a marital problem. They are very much a part of this child's problem, and my experience is that they will be helpful in supporting the parents and carrying through any kind of treatment program with the child.

Kluger: I would look at what supports there are in the family for the child, and, in the relative absence of timely and appropriate support from the parents, I would look to the older kids. Debbie, the oldest one, seems to be particularly tuned in. Peter, I gather, is on a high and being well-reinforced for doing well in athletics. He may be supportive if one appealed to him fairly directly.

Birenbaum: I get the impression that the kids are supportive of one another, and I see nothing lost by involving them in the process. It may be that this 18-year-old and 16-year-old are busy with their own lives and out of the home, but my preference would be to have them there if at all possible.

Interviewer: What potential problems might you expect from this sort of family to which you would be especially sensitive?

Birenbaum: I would be concerned that, as we started to pull Ronnie and move him to a different plateau, there would be some shifting around. I am sure we are going to have a fair amount of resistance from the parents denying their part in his problems.

Kluger: With change one would look for some intensification of problems. He might begin to steal again. But there is one thing that's pointed out in the report that I tend to agree with based on the other information there. Ronnie responds well to one-to-one adult attention, and that augurs very well for him. That's a healthy sign and one on which I would certainly want to work.

Birenbaum: I think you are right. He is able to relate to the family members too. The fact that this child can form relationships is critical.

Kluger: I do think that if one confronts this child in a direct way, one is going to get a fairly uptight assaultive response. I would kind of slide it in. I wouldn't let anybody off the hook, but I would put it more in question form as opposed to direct interpretation. I would be very careful about overinterpreting and very careful about just going for feelings. I would use the behavioral equivalent of feelings in my statements. Instead of saying "You feel angry," I might say "You feel like hitting."

Birenbaum: I think you're right. This boy and the entire family are extremely sensitive to any kind of criticism. You'd need a nonblaming, fairly supportive therapist who could also be strong and able to deal with resistance.

Kluger: Somebody who doesn't come on too heavy. I would also opt for a more mature therapist in age.

Interviewer: Why?

Kluger: It's just a gut-level feeling that the parents, being middle-aged, may be more responsive to someone closer to their age than to someone in his or her early 20s.

Interviewer: Any particular feeling that the sex of the therapist would make a difference?

Kluger and
Birenbaum: No.

Interviewer: What outcomes should the therapist be going after, and when should he/she decide that it's time to quit?

Kluger: Certainly the elimination of the assaultive behavior, verbally and physically. Second, an improvement in this child's academic performance, up to capacity, whatever that capacity is. As I mentioned earlier, I would not deal directly with the enuresis at this point. I would also have as a goal the increased readiness for the family to communicate more directly with one another. Again, I would keep coming back to this. I would do it through activity tied to some real situations.

Birenbaum: I have essentially the same three goals. The only difference is that you use activity much more than I do. I would use what's going on in the session, and explore what kind of reaction the family has when Ronnie kicks them or takes the sister's toys, or whatever.

Interviewer: What prognosis do you have for this family?

Birenbaum: I think there is a very good prognosis. Given the goals that we have established for them, I don't think we would have too hard a time. The only thing that would go against that is if we discover some horrible history prior to the age of a year-and-a-half.

Interviewer: How long would it take?

Birenbaum: Under six months, as I see it.

Kluger: I agree.

SUMMARY

The families in this section are generally resistant to becoming involved in treatment for themselves or their children. In each case the child has been referred by the school or the family physician because of some disturbing behavior. The parents minimize the significance of the behavior and attribute responsibility for existing problems to people and institutions outside the family.

The Crenshaw family was referred by their family physician because of 11-year-old Peter's inappropriate rituals and immature behavior. Peter is the only child of Mr. and Mrs. Crenshaw, socially isolated parents in their 50s whose lives revolve around their son.

The consultants express considerable concern for the isolation and possible thought disorder of the parents. They recommend seeing the entire family together to differentiate the members from one another and to encourage Peter's emancipation. It would be critical to join successfully with the parents since they may easily terminate treatment. One idea is to focus on a specific problem behavior, such as Peter's repetitive verbalizations or a compulsive ritual, and use the extent of success in diminishing the behavior as a guide to further interventions. It would also be important to draw on existing community resources to break down the family isolation.

The Reedy family was referred by the school because of their difficulty in handling Michael, age 5, who apparently has a brief attention span, is highly dependent on adults, and becomes easily frustrated. Mr. and Mrs. Reedy deny problems with Michael at home and blame the school for any difficulties there. Michael, however, does have a genetic disorder called Klinefelter's syndrome. The parents, who are highly protective of him, have unstable background histories and a somewhat strained marriage.

The consultants see the need for further assessment of Michael's skill deficits and mental health. They recommend a careful and gentle reaching out to involve the parents in treatment and explore their concerns about Michael's disorder. There is a clear need to engage Mr. Reedy, in part because his wife may be depressed and/or alcoholic. One method would be to involve the school as well and support the parents in communicating with the school. Basic management skills and more balanced parenting would be goals for family sessions.

The Simpson family is another school referral. There are four children, but it is the eldest, 14-year-old Stan, who has drawn attention to the family. He has been increasingly withdrawn at school, and teachers are concerned about his potential for violence, based on a few unprovoked, aggressive incidents. Mr. and Mrs. Simpson minimize the seriousness of Stan's behavior.

The consultants note the need to increase Mr. Simpson's involvement in the family and to develop further his relationship with Stan by arranging opportunities for them to relate. Although the marital relationship is seen as troubled, marital therapy without Mr. and Mrs. Simpson's direct consent would be contraindicated. The consultants believe that the prognosis for Stan is excellent.

Ronnie Barker, age 9, has also been referred by his school because of unmanageability and inattentiveness. Mr. and Mrs. Barker deny any serious problem, although they acknowledge some instances of stealing money in the home and the fact that Ronnie is enuretic. The other family members include three other children, ages 7 to 18, none of whom are viewed as having problems.

The consultants are primarily concerned about Ronnie's possible vulnerability, especially because he is an adopted child. They advocate a family-based intervention to encourage the parents to support the school and each other and explore their relationship with their son. They also suggest a school-based behavior modification approach to improve Ronnie's behavior at school. If it can be substantiated that Ronnie has not experienced an unusual amount of deprivation in his early development, the consultants are optimistic in this case. They believe that the assaultive behavior can be curbed, academic performance improved, and family communication bettered in a relatively brief period of time.

STUDY/DISCUSSION QUESTIONS

1. How can a worker engage uncooperative or resistant parents in accepting family-based treatment for their children?
2. How can fathers be encouraged to participate more in parenting responsibilities?
3. What are some significant indicators of severe (psychotic) disturbance in children?
4. What are some indicators of the potential for violence among children and adolescents?
5. What guidelines may be used to decide whether to disclose to children hidden facts about their adoption, a disease, or other family secrets?
6. At what point, given a pessimistic prognosis, should a worker consider terminating treatment or consider referring a case to someone else?

8

Beyond the Nuclear Family

When a family brings a child's problem to a mental health center, they bring far more than a presenting problem. They may be bringing along critical relationships and problems not included in an examination of the nuclear family. The network of extended familial, social, and business relationships in which families are involved is always relevant to understanding a family's dynamics. However, some families or individuals within them have "external" relationships that bear heavily and directly on the child's problems. Highly conflicted relationships that parents have with their own parents and with ex-spouses subject most exposed children to a high degree of stress. Once again, children are caught in the middle between "warring" or competing parties. Too often, the children represent the most powerful and convenient vehicle for hurting the other adult party. The child's problems, in fact, may be maintained by all concerned because they provide the best grounds for accusing the other adult party. Alternatively, a parent's failure to resolve dependency on his/her own parents or ex-spouse is likely to cripple that parent's effort to be effective with his or her own children.

When nonnuclear family members are actively involved in a child's problem, understanding and effective intervention usually require at least some contact between them and the therapist. In many cases, treatment can be greatly enhanced if this other individual can be positively engaged in the therapeutic effort. On the other hand, failure to involve the "external" person(s) can lead to failure of the entire therapeutic effort. Typical roadblocks the therapist encounters include the reluctance of the nuclear family to allow entry of the other party into the process and the antagonism of the "external" person to a cooperative effort. At the same time, direct ongoing involvement of the other party may be obviously inappropriate or disruptive to therapy. The case examples in this chapter provide opportunities both to generate and to review strategic planning designed to deal with such dilemmas.

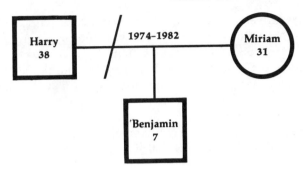

THE SILVERSTEIN FAMILY

Identifying information

The Silverstein family consists of Miriam and her son, Benjamin. Mrs. Silverstein's husband, Harry, deserted the family one-and-a-half years ago. Benjamin was referred by his first-grade teacher for immature, uncontrollable behavior in the classroom. Mrs. Silverstein also reports that Benjamin has a terrible temper, tests all limits, and shows no concern for the possessions or property of others. In addition, he wets his bed almost nightly.

History of problem

Mrs. Silverstein claims that ever since Harry, a chemical engineer, ran off without warning, she and her son have been suffering. Their economic level has diminished dramatically, so that, whereas they were once comfortably middle-class, they now live in a small apartment in a working-class neighborhood. Benjamin does not listen to his mother and is at times extremely withdrawn and at other times very aggressive. As examples of his negativism, he colors on the apartment walls and will not pick up his things. Whenever mother says "no," Benjamin accuses her of not caring about him. She has tried sending him to his room, taking away television privileges, and hitting him, but none of these methods work. Mrs. Silverstein reports that her husband was the disciplinarian and was able to control their son, but since his absence she has been feeling more and more helpless. Her memory of Benjamin's early development is hazy, although she reports him as having been colicky as a baby and toilet-trained at age 2½. For the past year, however, he has been wetting the bed at night and seems unconcerned about it.

Marital and family history

Mrs. Silverstein is the middle child of a reasonably well-to-do Jewish family. She was very close to her father, who died five years ago. Her mother lives in the neighborhood, and although they have regular contact, they fight constantly and do not get along. She is also alienated from her older sister.

Mrs. Silverstein's closest family contact is with her 22-year-old younger brother who continues to live with their mother.

Mrs. Silverstein reports that she was always well cared for by her husband. She knew little about his work but thinks that he gambled quite a bit and that gambling problems may have had something to do with his desertion. His whereabouts at this time are unknown. The couple did not communicate much after Benjamin's birth, and Mrs. Silverstein views her husband as having a nasty temper. She knows very little about his family background, but thinks that his parents are divorced and live on the West Coast.

Characteristics of family members

A very overweight woman who dresses shabbily, Miriam Silverstein moves slowly and spends the day at home watching television and talking to her mother on the telephone. She presents herself as a woman who is harassed and unable to cope. The family lives in a two-bedroom apartment which appears run down and dirty. There are crayon marks on the walls, torn screens, ripped drapes, and clothes lying around. The front door has three locks on it, including one with an alarm to keep Benjamin in and intruders out. Mrs. Silverstein talks a lot about the difficulty of raising a child by herself and quickly moves on to complain about the injustice of her husband running off with their money and her desire to move to a nicer place. She receives aid from a variety of social service agencies and has been very effective at drawing on their resources. Although there are financial problems, she does have some luxuries, such as a late model car and a new color television. Mrs. Silverstein has not worked since her marriage and is thinking about getting a job but doesn't know what she would do and also thinks she must be available to Benjamin.

Mrs. Silverstein's mother frequently gives advice on raising Benjamin, which Mrs. Silverstein rejects out-of-hand. They also argue about money matters. The mother refuses to give Mrs. Silverstein more money, claiming it's time she grew up and took care of herself.

Benjamin relies on his mother a great deal and hungers for her affection. She seems to expect him to know what to do and does not take the time to explain things to him. When mother tells him to do something, such as pick up his clothes, he ignores her, and she eventually gives up. She is inconsistent in her management—for example, pushing him away from her but refusing to let him play with the "delinquents" in the neighborhood. She is very upset about his bedwetting. She wants him to do better and achieve toward the top of his class.

Mrs. Silverstein's resentment toward her husband is mimicked by the boy, who seems bitter at dad's absence. Otherwise, Benjamin does not speak about his dad. When Mr. Silverstein lived in the home, he was a firm disciplinarian, although mother and son spent most of the time together alone while father worked long hours.

School and community

The school's primary concern is that Benjamin is not coping well with the pressures of first grade, either academically or interpersonally. He daydreams and has an explosive temper when pushed or contradicted. He can be friendly and affectionate and relate well to his classmates as long as he has his own way. Otherwise, he lashes out or withdraws. The school thinks that Mrs. Silverstein's academic expectations for Benjamin are unrealistic. She wants him in the advanced stream, whereas his IQ has been tested to be average.

Mrs. Silverstein reports that Benjamin has a number of friends with whom he plays. The boy, however, is unable to name these friends. Both mother and son seem to be cut off from their community and from other people.

Case discussion

Consultants: Mr. Michael Blugerman, Ms. Catherine Jackel

Interviewer: What would you tell the worker to find out?

Jackel: I'd like some interactional description, maybe some home observations as part of the assessment. What Benji's doing that's terrible doesn't seem so terrible. Mother describes him as having a terrible temper and says that he tests limits, shows no concern for property or possessions, and is constantly negative. The example that's given of his negativism is that he crayons on the wall. I want to know more about this very aggressive, negative behavior. When he's withdrawn, what does he do? When he's aggressive, what does he do?

Blugerman: One comment I'd make is that this case is highly detailed in child information, not a lot in interactional information and not a lot in systemic information. I have to read between the lines to get what I want.

Interviewer: Well, I think that there is an important point here. I think that most of the people that come seeking treatment at children's mental health centers tend to present their problems as child-focused, and you can move from there to a systems focus.

Blugerman: I have a thought about that. We make too many mistakes by trying to convert from child to systemic and by so doing insult the family and lose rapport. So I would like to teach the child approach as a way of accepting and joining a family's reality, and have people alert to the system, and interactional, intergenerational work to direct their energy.

Interviewer: What kind of systemic information would you look at?

Blugerman: I would rely a little bit on the live interaction in the consultation. For example, it says that mother thinks her husband's parents are on the West Coast and divorced, and the child can't name his friends. I don't know if that's a lack of information or a lack of rapport in getting information. Now actually there's a phenomenal amount of interactional information here.

Interviewer: Let's stay for a minute with information gathering for assessment.

Blugerman: I think that some of the things that would become important in this case are reality-testing items. So I would like the worker to have information on exactly what Mrs. Silverstein's budget is and just how much the mother gives her. What are her obligations, where did the color TV and the late model car come from? Were they left by him, or acquired afterward? These questions are very critical in this case. Other than that there's more than enough information.

Interviewer: Cathy, are there other areas you'd like the worker to look into?

Jackel: I'm not sure about what she was brought up to be. It sounds like without a man, she's helpless and not prepared for life. I'd like some more information about her educational background. Did she train for any particular profession or was she brought up to be a princess and expect to be taken care of, and now finds herself manless and unable to cope? What are her strengths? What is her training? What do we have to build on because she's alone and she's going to have to handle it.

Interviewer: What kind of treatment approach would you use?

Blugerman: Thinking how to manage is awkward because there's a family intergenerational development problem. There's no mention of how this woman related to her father, or how her mother related to her father, and I think that will become important later. I value creating a different experience between the mother and the kid over time. The problem is that this lady hasn't done much separation or individuation from her mother, and neither have her siblings. So I think that she's had a very sticky mother. I think she needs some differentiation work from her family of origin. And I think that she could also use a good supportive mother worker. I think a mothering female. There's the question of how to mix the mother-child thing with her own work.

Interviewer: So you'd see her in individual therapy and also in mother-son sessions?

Blugerman: Depending on how the material unfolded, there's also room to do grandmother-mother-Benjamin, but I'm not that high on that one, especially with the missing information regarding the father. For sure, she has to have her own supplementary work in order to be able to give to this child. It's like she's waiting for her mother to give her what she deserves before she can give to her kids. I'm thinking that a substitute worker could provide some help in differentiation to enable her to let go of her mother, and then let her get some satisfaction from working with this kid. So I'm thinking concurrently family (mother and child) and individual with the mother. The focus in both therapies wouldn't be cognitive. It would be the division of experience and at the very end an objects-relations focus. That's the individual work. With the parent-child it would be behavior management and a more skill-oriented approach.

Interviewer: Talk a bit more of what you'd expect from mother and what you would try to do in an individual approach.

Blugerman: My hunch would be that as the worker connected with this woman, she would be quite needy and would look for disappointments, look for special considerations, look for special concessions and would challenge the giving and taking relationship between them. She might be suspicious about the worker's interest, she might try to find the limits or boundaries of their mutual involvements. She might try to test that out through phone calls, calls of distress or emergency, or inviting the woman to her house. Maybe reluctance to go for interviews on site. She would play with all the parameters of that treatment model and the worker would constantly have to bring her back to the relationship and the giving and taking and the anticipation of disappointment.

Jackel: Mother obviously needs individual and much along the lines you were describing, except that I'd probably go further if I find that she is not prepared for life. She has some obviously good negotiating skills because she's got a car and a TV and she lives on a hand-to-mouth budget, so I wonder where those things come from. I suspect that either she's got some negotiating skills, or she's getting them from mom. I'd be disappointed if she's getting things from mom because I really like her strength in getting both of those things while managing on handouts. I'd like to work with her around separation and reaching an adult state, a separation from her mother and her husband, whom she obviously saw as father, and helping her achieve some autonomy with regard to who she is. I think that's going to have to be basic skill development. I don't know whether that means she has to seek and train for a career, or that we plug into some of the existing skills that she has and help her get more connected with the community in delivering this. She needs to learn to cope in life outside her family, and she needs to build a life for herself. She's going to go through a period of being very dependent on the worker.

  In a way the dynamics would be very similar to an abuse case or with a single parent where the parent really had to be parented for a specified amount of time, and would greatly test the worker's commitment and consistency. I think mother-son sessions need a basic focus of being a time to play and interact together. Teaching her at the same time as fulfilling some of her needs. Teaching her that he's her son, not someone who is competing with her for attention. I would also, although it may be premature, plug him in for some socialization. Perhaps an activity group set up by the school after hours.

Interviewer: What about things like Cubs, or sports programs, or those sorts of things?

Jackel: Yes, possibly. I'd like some kind of success arena for him having to do with peer negotiation skills outside the family. I don't know from the information we have and the concerns of the school whether he's ready for something like Cubs. I'd like him to have that, but I'd like him to be ready for it. I would not like him to fall on his face, because mother will say "I told you so." She's very needy.

Interviewer: In passing you made some reference to possible vocational training for mother?

Jackel: Yes, she has to resolve her adolescence and get into some adult behavior, and

I really think that one of the vehicles for that is for her to discover some identity for herself outside the identity of being someone's daughter, someone's wife, and someone's mother.

Interviewer: Okay, any other treatments or resources that you might use?

Jackel: I was wondering about someone to help her around basic housekeeping skills. I don't know from the condition of the apartment whether it's something that she can't do, that she can't get herself organized to do, or that she has no motivation to do. If it turns out that she has not been brought up to care for herself and that this is always the condition that she's lived in, no matter what she says about coming from a middle-class background, she may need some teaching about how to care for her house.

Blugerman: It seems like she has a certain attitude. It's not that she doesn't have resources. She has those things you mentioned. She also has a string of social agencies from which she's managed to extract stuff. She manages to extract stuff from her mother now and then, but there seems to be an attitude of "I shouldn't have to do this." So if I moved her to develop her own skills, I would wonder about secondary gains, of an attitude of martyrdom and some natural contempt at using her skill. So I have to do something about freeing that, before I can get onto what you've been addressing.

Jackel: I think it's very important to find out what skills she does have. Are we talking about somebody who basically feels that her needs are not being fulfilled, and who was brought up with an expectation that they always would be fulfilled? Or are we talking about someone who basically does not possess the coping mechanisms to be on her own, to be an adult?

Interviewer: How do you get around the possible martyrlike approach with her? How do you deal with that?

Blugerman: I think the quality of the interaction between her and her worker would make a big difference if she's had a mother who puts strings on whatever was given. The 22-year-old son still lives at home, and other siblings don't get along together. She was closer to her father, who died five years ago, and the mother might have been resentful of that closeness. So I think that she's been used to getting things with strings. The worker would have to be very accepting and have absolutely nothing up her sleeve in terms of demands and expectations. She could steer the woman into certain things as long as the woman felt that she was completely interested in her, rather than reflecting some self-interest on the worker's part. The script seems to read "If I suffer enough, then mother finally will pay attention to me," or "I'm not going to grow up until I get what I want." Until we meet those issues head-on, either through providing the attention she needs, or having her experience some success and accomplishment in doing something differently with her kid, we wouldn't see much change in her.

Jackel: I'd like to work with her on two levels. One, I'd like to give to her without the solid gold umbilical cord that you're talking about and, two, I'd like to see a T.A. contracting approach with her. She would take a look at the things that she wants to change and the way she wants to change and tell you what behaviors you're going to see that indicate changes. She would also tell you how she's likely to sabotage the change from occurring. I think that that keeps you out of the martyr role because you are fostering her own independence and growth. I sense her as a very skillful game player, so the worker will have to be careful about her own games and being hooked by her.

Blugerman: In terms of management of the games that are played, she views all her activity as not doing anything and not being able to do anything. I think you could reframe that passive manipulation into skillful extraction. I would try to convert her passivity into activity.

Jackel: The saying that comes to mind is that the people who created the greatest inventions in the world were usually the laziest people. She's a highly passive person. What I hear you saying is that you'd want her to use that passivity in a more productive way for herself.

Blugerman: If she said, for example, that the superintendent wouldn't fix her window and I ran through how she tried to do it, then I might remember or elicit some information about how she got some other agency to get her something else. Identify the skill component. She may think they gave it to her, because she suffered or cried or begged or whatever, but in fact she was quite skillful in getting some things. So I would try to reframe her intervention with those other helpers, as a skillful, strategy-oriented, active approach to get what she wanted. Could she transfer the skill from that context to the superintendent? I'd try to collect some histories of any kind of successful experiences in her life. If she told me about an event with her kid that she couldn't handle, I would try to collect a strategy or skill that she used in that context and see if she could do it again with the kid.

For example, one time I had a girl come to see me who, I think, at the time was 16, very withdrawn, and who had a large head of hair. When she put her head down it all fell on top of her face like a shield, and her attitude about life was that things happened to her when she wasn't doing anything. She was a victim. So I told her that she was quite obviously getting her hair done nicely, because it was always shining on the days I saw her. That was particularly useful because of the way she used her hair as a screen to keep me away from her. She didn't like the idea that she was doing that, and I said that some people have to resort to things like staring into space, looking away, or turning their chairs, whereas with her technique every word of mine is blocked by her actions. I suggested that with her technique she was managing to keep me away simply by lowering her chin and that she could feel some pride in being skillful about that. I keep going over and reframing passive victim scenarios into active techniques. In other words, for example, let's take the same girl. I would talk to her, she wouldn't say anything back, so I might say "I talk to a lot of kids. I'm usually pretty persuasive, even sometimes charming. You have a tremendous skill at not biting. Where did you learn that? How do you accomplish it? Because now and then, even if I say ten things, one of them must be slightly interesting to you. How do you make sure that you don't talk at those times?" So I'm trying to work by continually converting dependency to responsibility.

Jackel: Like the passive husband whose wife nags him all the time. When it comes time to move in with the husband, you compliment him a lot about how well he listens, how patiently he listens, and ask him what he'd like to say now that he has an opening.

Blugerman: It's critical that this technique comes in an envelope of rapport and acceptance with a fair bit of giving. I would be tempted in this case to do things such as bring donuts if she makes coffee. If she did a bit, I would do a bit. I might even offer some material help to give her an opportunity to manipulate me around it, so that I would have content to work with. For example, let's say I'd brought something that would enable her to fix something that was broken in the house. If she would then push me about something else, we could then fuss about what is expected and what isn't. How does she state her need? In other words, if she responsibly said that she really needed help in something, then we could make an exchange. If I thought I was being manipulated, then I would try to redirect her to a responsible, interdependent approach.

Interviewer: We've talked exclusively about dealing with mother. We haven't talked about mother-son sessions and what one might want to be doing in those, or about how you would advise the worker to deal with Benji.

Blugerman: Let me first back up to the mother. One of the other main themes that I would play in the individual session occurs as she tells me about frustrations with the son. I see a one-to-one correlation or reenactment between what happens with her and her son and between her and her mother. As she talks about what she does with the kid and her disappointment, there's an opportunity to take the point of view of her and her mother. In other words, if she talks about how he doesn't give anything back to her, I'd ask her how she gave back to her mother; if she talks about how mad she gets with him, I'd ask how she thinks her mother felt with her in certain situations. I'd continue to play cross-generational boundaries around the same themes because at any particular point that I can get her to notice a repetition between her and Benjamin, that would be very dissonant with her statements about her mother and she would probably tell me all kinds of disappointments in her relationship with her mother. I'd then focus on how she wouldn't want the same for Benjamin and how she could ensure that that doesn't happen. It seems like she is expecting the boy to be more of a sibling than a son. There's a statement in the record about how she expects him to know how to do things already and not have to explain to him. He's almost protesting the fact that she's not getting to him as a son and resenting the partnership. I think it would be important, by joining with her, to organize the two of them so that he gets what he needs from her. One of the risks of putting him in alternate, outside settings is that I think he's protesting not getting enough from her.

Jackel: I'd like to see Benji's drawing of his family. I'd like to see some basic kinds of assessment with him around things like how he conceptualizes his life and his body. He was age 5½ when dad left. Does he miss him? There's no mention of any kind of resolution for mourning. The father just disappears. He's beginning to have trouble with school and he tries with his peers. As long as they're friendly he's okay, but he doesn't know how to handle conflict. Mother-son sessions need to be used around helping her parent her child more effectively and supporting her in managing and handling. I think that in playing together you're going to see a lot of siblinglike behavior and competition between mother and son. I would hate to see what would happen if they were playing cards and she lost, because I think she might cheat. It's going to be hard to keep her in the parenting role in play sessions. I think that that's an important focus, and she has to be reinforced for it by the therapist. She has to get stroked by the therapist for parenting the kid. It's as if the therapist needs to meet her dependency in these sessions, so it's a very contingent kind of parenting system down the road. I guess that would be the primary focus for me.

Interviewer: Michael?

Blugerman: I think the worker would have to take charge of the sessions to start with and organize the two of them by getting her to, let's say, explain a parable to him, teach him a game, or play something where she isn't a peer of his, but has some parenting function. The worker would then deal with any difficulties that came up between them and demonstrate how to do it. In the next stage the worker would withdraw and coach the mother. So I'd be working on boundaries and parent-child issues. I've changed my view about involving him in other things. I'd like him to learn that he can get things from sources other than mother. Because his demands on her may overwhelm her, she may think she's not up to it. If he started to get some stuff from other places and she was getting things from somewhere else, she would be a good candidate for a mother's group or support group. Then they wouldn't feel as confined together and desperate.

Interviewer: I think that as we have been talking, both of you have labeled some of the ways that mother might test the parameters of therapy. Are there other particular problems that you would want the worker to anticipate in this case?

Blugerman: I think that this is a very tough case for negative countertransference, in the sense that many workers would start to resent the woman and call her *gaming* or *manipulative.* The thing that's really important is to accept whatever she does and to reframe her testing as an opportunity for them both to discover something. Another concern relates to environmental issues. I don't know how much she depends on her mother for financial help. If there were any way to stop that, it would help in assisting the psychological separation between her and her mother and developing a relationship on their own terms. Whatever money she gets from her mother probably isn't worth it. There's a long history of this woman trying to get away from mother and then being seduced back into hoping something is going to change. The worker would have to watch for this, because both of them are bound with each other. As Mrs. Silverstein becomes more confident and withdraws from her mother, her mother would make bids to reengage. So there would have to be a prediction of this on an interventional level.

Interviewer: What kind of worker would you like to see in this case?

Blugerman: Some accepting person for the mother. If I could find some arrangement for the kid to get help external to this system, then I would look for a Big Brother, a male Cub leader, a male teacher, or a volunteer. The kid identifies a little bit with the mother when he talks about the father. He's bought the mother's view of reality a little bit. Some of that may be a protection against getting left by her. He may have some worries about her withdrawal, and siding with her against the father might be a way of building loyalty. It would be nice if he had a male model, especially one that could help mediate between his mother and him.

Interviewer: Cathy, what kind of worker would you like to see?

Jackel: I really am not so concerned about whether the person is a motherly figure, as long as the worker has a pretty stable caseload elsewhere. I think there have to be other cases that feed this person well. The worker is going to have to have good supervision. Also a worker who has worked with emotional deprivation before and understands, on an application level, concepts like countertransference and counterdependency. Someone who is able to work with the passive-aggressive person, so that the knowledge that this lady's pot is never going to be filled will not be overwhelming. I think they're going to need a nice mental health balance through this case, and only one of these kinds of cases at a time.

Interviewer: What kinds of goals would you set?

Jackel: There's all sorts of facetious things you could say like "Mother to write a manual about how to use social services in the metropolitan area." That would be something constructive she could do.

Blugerman: I'm a little bit concerned about mother's lack of empathy for this kid. I don't know if there's some carryover of her resentment about his father with this kid being reminiscent of him, or just not having enough resolved in order to give to the kid. In terms of objectives, I'd like to see some better behavior management and consistency. Participation in some activities or relationships that would give her some support. I'd look for signs of independence between her and her mother. The network management of this case is very important because this mother will withdraw allegiance and go somewhere else. The mother needs to reduce or modify her manipulative use of resources. So reduce her involvement with her mother in terms of financial support, clean up and mature her relationship with other helpers.

Jackel: That's really not speaking to Benji.

Blugerman: Well, my hunch is that a lot of his behavior will clean up as she does more role-relevant things demonstrating that she's more parent, he's more child. So I'm stressing family or system level intervention first, hoping that that'll be enough for some of the kid's misbehavior to fall out.

Jackel: I wasn't thinking so much of his misbehavior as much as of some age-appropriate autonomy from her. He's 7 and should be reaching out to peers, so I'd look for more age-appropriate autonomy for him.

Interviewer: How would you decide that it was present?

Jackel: He'd make friends. I suspect if you saw him, he would look different physically from other kids and he'd belong with the kids in his building, the "delinquents," as mother calls them. He would play with those kids, he would have a social network, and I think that he would connect with and use his teachers more effectively.

Blugerman: So one of the outcomes would be that both of them would take a different approach to their environment—that is, stop marking on the walls and improve the condition of the house and so on. I think that would flow from changes in self-esteem.

Jackel: I think that you should see some redefinition of father from Benji because I think he has unresolved mourning with regard to his father. I'm not sure that mother has a lot to separate from father, because I'm not sure she ever bonded with him. She hasn't even separated from her own home of origin, but Benji obviously saw father as significant. I think we need some kind of a change in the way he sees father, rather than just internalizing his mother's messages.

Interviewer: How successful is the worker likely to be?

Blugerman: I've seen a lot of these cases succeed. If the worker can handle the negativity and manipulation, cover the network issues, and provide nurturance and rapport, I'm fairly optimistic.

Jackel: I'm wondering how strong of a hold the parenting style of her generation, ethnic group, and social network when she grew up will have on her.

Interviewer: So you're more guarded?

Jackel: Yes. I don't see the dynamics as tremendously different from a case of emotional deprivation for a parent, and to me it all depends on how profound the emotional deprivation is and when it happened. A lot of that information is unknown with this lady. It depends on what she got from her daddy and whether they were really close or whether it was just one of those weak absentee alliances.

Blugerman: The worker records that she had a close relationship with her father, so if I can take that at face value, she would have had to have received something from her mother in order to accomplish that. Therefore, I'm not as pessimistic. If I heard that the connection with father was bad or that she had a severe grief reaction to her father's death, then I'd be more guarded.

Jackel: But she looks at her husband's leaving purely in terms of her abandonment and the fact that it's been difficult for her socioeconomic standing. It seems to me if she had bonded that well with her father, she would have bonded better with her husband.

Blugerman: If her early relationship with her mother was lacking, I don't think she would have had a close relationship with her father. As I see the family constellation, there might have been more conflict as she became a peer to her mother, or a threat to her mother's status with her father. She has very high standards for her kid that are unrelated to his needs. Her mother probably had very high standards for her, and she's out of touch with the kid's needs or the mother's needs when she was a kid. If she would mourn the loss of an image of how her life is supposed to be, not so much the guy that left, she might be able to reorient herself to accepting and dealing with what she has now.

Jackel: Yes, I can hear what you're saying. I'm just not sure about her level of deprivation. She's parenting her child in such a way that her demands on him and her level of expectation are far beyond his physical or cognitive ability. It's a repeat of a parenting pattern from her childhood.

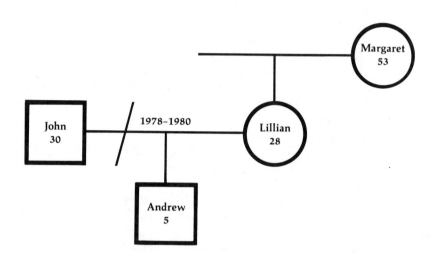

THE CALDERONE FAMILY

Identifying information

Lillian Calderone and her son, Andrew, live with Lillian's mother, Margaret. Lillian is divorced, and her mother's second husband is dead. Lillian is concerned about her son's temper tantrums, swearing, and stubborn, defiant behavior. Mother is seeking treatment on her own initiative.

History of problem

Mother reports that Andrew was a difficult, fussy baby who slept little and was difficult to comfort. She also acknowledges that, during the first two years of Andrew's life, she and her husband fought constantly, and she was often in an agitated, upset state herself. Although mother feels things have improved considerably over the last two to three years, Andrew has become a very willful, demanding child who "flies into a rage" when frustrated, expressing his rage through screaming, kicking, and swearing. On occasion, he has also destroyed household objects and slapped mother. When Lillian attempts to limit or direct him, Andrew usually ignores her, pretends not to hear, or swears and resists. Mother claims that Andrew becomes particularly difficult to manage after visiting with father. Shortly after mother separated from her husband, she saw a psychiatrist for depression. But, after three or four sessions, she stopped going.

Marital and family history

Lillian was the youngest of three children in her family of origin. Her parents were divorced when she was 7 years old, and she and her two sisters lived with her mother. Three years later her mother remarried. Lillian's stepfather was 15 years older than her mother and was often in poor health. Lillian recalls catering to his needs, especially when he became bedridden. He died when Lillian was 17. She feels her mother has always been "the power" in the family and that her mother was constantly critical of her as a child.

Lillian continued living at home until her marriage to John in 1978. She was pregnant at the time. The marriage rapidly deteriorated as John drank heavily, was intermittently unemployed, and physically abused his wife. According to Lillian, he showed little interest in Andrew but then threatened her with a custody battle when she decided to separate. In fact, John did not contest custody but sought and was awarded reasonable visiting privileges when their divorce became final in 1982. Mother reports that her ex-husband visits with Andrew about once every two or three weeks but keeps and cancels visiting appointments unpredictably. She also complains that John takes Andrew to the racetrack and keeps him out late, showering him with toys.

Following her separation from John, she and Andrew lived alone for almost two years. Mother worked as a secretary/bookkeeper, and Andrew was cared for by a variety of babysitters. In the past year, mother felt guilty about and dissatisfied with this arrangement and moved in with her mother. Andrew's grandmother now cares for him while mother is working.

Characteristics of family members

Lillian Calderone works as a bookkeeper at a life insurance firm. In addition, she is attending university courses three nights per week. She presents as nervous and uncertain of herself both as a person and as a mother. She is able to identify some personal strengths, including humor and warmth, but seems generally negative about her capabilities. Although passive and unassertive, Lillian is clearly angry at her ex-husband and, as a parent, feels undermined by him. In addition, she is torn between depending heavily on her mother and resenting her mother's dominance of both her and Andrew's parenting. Lillian states that once she completes her business degree course at university, she wants to move out of her mother's home once again.

Lillian is close and protective with Andrew. She seems highly sensitive and responsive to him and is proud of his brightness and verbal ability. On the other hand, it appears that Andrew intimidates her with his angry outbursts. Lillian's usual response is to give in and placate. As a result, she is frequently inconsistent with limits and expectations, prone to give in and then spank or slap Andrew if pushed to her limit. In many ways, this relationship is more peer-like than like that of a parent and child. They both identify shopping trips and playing games as activities that they enjoy together.

Andrew is an articulate, outgoing 5-year-old who is more comfortable with adults than with children. He is able to describe fights between his parents in great detail and says that he loves them both. He acknowledges that his father disappoints him sometimes by not keeping promises and wishes father could spend more time with him. Andrew feels that he himself has no particular problems except that he sometimes feels frightened at night in bed or has bad dreams. He seems quite attached and devoted to his grandmother. Andrew is quite skilled at engaging and charming adults and is particularly adept at manipulating his mother.

Lillian's mother, Margaret, states she is glad that Lillian is seeking help and hopes it will make her a better mother. She is generally condescending and derogatory about Lillian, her daughter's marriage, her work-life, and her overall maturity. Margaret feels Andrew has no real problems and that Lillian herself is the problem. As far as Margaret is concerned, Andrew is a wonderful child who never creates a problem for her. However, she is concerned that the many changes and instability in his life will hurt him if continued. Margaret is a dominating, controlling woman who is attached to her grandson and treats both Andrew and his mother as equally dependent children.

School and community

Andrew is in kindergarten this year. According to his mother, his teacher is pleased with him. Mother does note that Andrew has had some difficulty with peers and is seen by his teacher as needing to learn social skills such as sharing, taking turns, and so forth. His teacher also feels that he tends to be bossy and get into fights with peers. But she is pleased with his cognitive skills and does not sound overconcerned about his peer problems. At home Andrew spends most of his time with grandmother, helping her with housework or playing alone.

Special assessments

Andrew has had no special assessments but is reported by his pediatrician to be in good health.

Case discussion

Consultants: Dr. Esther Gelcer, Dr. Cynthia Gertsman, Dr. Paul Spring

Interviewer: Let's talk about any indicated assessments or areas of information that you would want the worker to check out at the beginning.

Gelcer: In this case I would want to know what mother wants to accomplish through the referral.

Gertsman: That's the first and most important question.

Interviewer: You would want to clarify with her why she is coming and what she is looking for?

Gelcer: Right. Who she thinks needs help, whether she or grandmother or Andrew, and what she wants to see different. I would also want to know why she's coming now, because he's had problems ever since he was born. If she's really sensitized through her psychology studies, she would have had many reasons to bring him much earlier. He had temper tantrums, was colicky and fussy, and had those frightening dreams. So what does she want now?

Gertsman: That's right, because we don't know when mom went back to school and whether that's tied in with her becoming more aware now.

Interviewer: Okay, any other areas that need assessment?

Gelcer: What else is going on in the mother's life personally and what's going on in the grandmother's life personally, and how do the two of them get along? We know that grandmother patronizes the mother, but we would want to know whether each of them sees the other as a woman in her own right, needing some treatment. What contact does mother have with father, when he comes to pick up Andrew? What precipitated the divorce? His physical abuse? She was pregnant when they married. So they really lived together for fewer than two years. Just a very short time.

Gertsman: And whether that was her way out of the house.

Gelcer: Well, she would have been 23 years old when she got married, 22 to 23. Had she lived at home all the time, until then?

Gertsman: More material about mom's personal history would be important and whether she'd been working before and has continued to do so.

Interviewer: Paul?

Spring: I guess what we're saying is more history. I think that's just an artifact of the brief material we're given here, but in that sense one may have to take several sessions for gathering more history. Not too many sessions. I gather that grandmother actually came in, but it's not stated how that was done. I would like to know this grandmother in some detail, because I suspect she is going to be one of the central figures in therapy. We're going to have to deal with grandmother.

Gertsman: Father as well, because this child does have a relationship with his father. That also brings to mind assessment material in terms of how mother's feeling about father. That would come through in terms of what happens when father comes to pick up the child and whether there's any interaction between the two of them.

Spring: Well, I don't think I'd run to the school. I think I would leave that.

Gelcer: I would leave the boy out of it altogether. I mean, I would assess him once because the mother presents him as a patient.

Gertsman: Would you assess him individually?

Gelcer: Yeah, I would do a mental status interview with him.

Spring: Oh, I would see him alone. There's evidence that he's a frightened kid, and one wants to get a feel of just how frightened he is and what he's doing with this fear.

Gertsman: I think it's very important to assess what the interaction is like between mother and son.

Gelcer: My approach would be to assess all three of them together and then to see the boy alone, to see the mother alone. To see the grandmother alone, maybe to see the father too.

Interviewer: I think you're beginning to get into a treatment approach. What would you suggest to the worker who's on this case?

Gelcer: I would probably focus my treatment on the mother. I have some hypotheses that the mother will pull the father into the treatment. I don't really know, it depends on whether she has any other male contacts at this point. If she does I would work with mother and grandmother. If she does not, then I would work with mother and father. You see, mother is talking more about father than is necessary when she's having trouble with the boy. She's saying "I'm having problems with the boy, and I love him and have a good time with him, but whenever he comes back from father he's having problems." So something needs to be done regarding the father or regarding the father and mother. So I'd work on that level. She's also saying that something needs to be done about the grandmother. It is possible that mother, having regressed back to living with her mother, may now be moving toward a new relationship with a man at this time and want to gain some respect and recognition from her own mother as a woman and not as a little girl. At this point, then, I would work with the mother and the daughter. But I would exclude the boy from treatment altogether. Very gently ease him off.

Interviewer: Cynthia?

Gertsman: Grandmother's become a mothering figure for this child and mother is out working and earning the bread and spending her evenings away from home, and it's almost setting up the pattern of a family. So another approach might be to see mother and grandmother. And initially start with the child as well. I would certainly reinforce mom's being the parent in this position, and allocating some of that responsibility, as she needs to do, to her own mother. It may not be possible if the grandmother is the way that she's described and she's fixed in her relationship with her daughter. However, I think that might be another approach, and I think that would end up with mother and daughter being seen separately without the child.

Gelcer: Why would you include the child?

Gertsman: Because the child as a focus has been the problem. At present the child may also be having some confusion about who he is.

Gelcer: He hasn't been a problem for the grandmother, he hasn't been a problem for the father. He hasn't been a problem for the teacher. Only the mother says that she's experiencing problems, so why would you include him in treatment?

Gertsman: My feeling is that there is confusion about roles within the family and to help this child———

Gelcer: But the confusion is between mother and grandmother, not the boy.

Spring: I agree, but I don't see getting too involved with Andrew.

Gertsman: I see what you're saying. My thought is to start with mother and grand-mother and give mom support in terms of defining her expectations. Initially, this might be helpful for Andrew because the child at this point is not responding to limitations set by his mother and is testing her. Supported by the therapist, mom can be given a clear role that might have an effect on this child.

Gelcer: You don't think that you could do that in the absence of the child?

Gertsman: Yes, I think that could be done also.

Gelcer: So what would the child benefit, or anybody else benefit, from his being there?

Gertsman: Okay, there are two sides to the issue. I can also see that the mother has, at some point, to be clear and stand up to her own mother.

Gelcer: Why do you need the boy there to get her to be clear and stand on her own?

Spring: I can see having the boy involved if therapy is going to move. A lot hinges on what mother is asking for. Mother may want something very child-focused. She may want some child management techniques. If you're going to use some behavior modification approaches, then the whole therapy may go that way and that's all you may get to at this point. In that case, I would involve the boy. However, I think that it's going to go beyond that because already there's enough information that mother's drawing in the other family members.

You have to find out what mother wants; then we can say what shape the treatment is going to take, and that might involve the boy or it might not. I would hope it doesn't involve the boy because that means you're going to involve the other protagonist in the family, and I think that's where the real issues lie.

Interviewer: Cynthia, if you worked with mother and child, what would you work on?

Gertsman: I would work on behavioral components with mother and child and reinforc-ing mom with child management. With grandmother there would be more role definition in giving mom support and being the parent with this child and grandmother assisting her in that parenting position. I see the concerns, Esther, and I'm glad that you pointed them out. This child certainly has strong, good feelings about his grandmother and also about his mother, and that's going to put him in a very, very uncomfortable position where his behavior could escalate to get the focus off the fight between mother and grandmother.

Gelcer: I'm not only concerned about that. I'm concerned also about the process of therapy, because I think that this woman has a hidden agenda, particularly if she's taking psychology. We often get parents who come to treatment in order to learn how to "treat their own kids." I think the hidden agenda here may be for her to become the pseudoprofessional in the family, to use her degrees and the support of these professionals to say "Don't interfere between me and my child because what you're doing is undermining my authority," and in the meantime the kid is getting worse all the time.

Spring: I think that's why the mother went into the profession, not why she came to therapy. I have a feeling that mother studies this profession to get some indirect therapy and she's discovered that it's not working. Many people go into the mental health fields because they really want therapy.

Gelcer: Well, that's a possibility. She goes to university to get therapy and she comes to therapy to get training. Whatever it is, this is not a mature adult and any attempts on her part to assert herself are usually a reaction formation which is pseudomaturity. So I would be concerned about the stamina of this particular therapist. To have constantly to be taking sides between mother and daughter, between mother and father, and between mother and son.

Interviewer: What does that indicate for you in terms of treatment?

Gelcer: In terms of treatment, I would move toward working with the mother alone, ideally; and again, my direction of treatment would be on her relationship with her husband and with her mother.

Interviewer: There's been a nice spectrum of different approaches.

Spring: I think a lot depends on what mother is asking. Probably in the initial stages of therapy, the therapist has to be a good listener. I think we're saying that mother is using Andrew to get herself some help, which is not uncommon. I would start with mother too. I probably would explore whether or not this mother should "boot" the grandmother out of the picture. I think Andrew really is quite frightened about who is in charge of him—grandmother, mother, or father—and I don't think the kid knows the answer. I think Andrew is acting up as a defense against his frightened feelings, so somebody in this family has to let him know precisely who's in charge. Mother may be asking the therapist to help her get grandmother out of the picture. I think the therapist is going to have to decide whether to support the mother.

Interviewer: What would you recommend?

Spring: I don't think there are enough data here to recommend anything specific. All I can say is that it's possible that the grandmother might have to be removed more from the picture or the mother placed more in control of her family.

Interviewer: What would help you decide that?

Spring: Has mother really separated from grandmother?

Gelcer: She has not.

Spring: No, she has not, and if mother is asking for therapeutic help to grow and separate, I think you can move in on that. If you don't get that, you then resort to other things like behavior therapy with Andrew because you're not dealing with the deeper issues.

Gelcer: She says she is having a problem with him, so we help with this problem. It's very straightforward.

Spring: A lot will depend on how she talks about her mother.

Gelcer: Well, she would say "My mother gets in my way, my ex-husband gets him too spoiled and makes me feel like a no-good parent." "Okay, you have a lot of problems, let's work with those. Let's start with one at a time."

Gertsman: I would see going into individual work with mother. I think whatever approach you take, the focus is on the separation between the mother and daughter. It does not have to be a geographical or physical separation, but an emotional one, because she is very much needing her mother and that mother is a very important figure for this child.

Interviewer: Is this a case where you would worry about some special problems or some intensifying difficulties?

Spring: Yes, if we're going to separate mother from grandmother, I'd watch grandmother very carefully. She may get very depressed, she may not tolerate the separation, so I think any therapist has to be very sensitive to this separation and keep an eye on grandmother because she has a lot of power and a hard time letting the strings go.

Gertsman: It's important the grandmother have some involvement outside her home, her daughter, and her grandson.

Interviewer: So if you saw grandmother undermining some of mother's movement, you would work with grandmother?

Gelcer: I wouldn't attempt to work with grandmother. I would attempt to work with mother to help grandmother, not to push her out.

Gertsman: That would be at quite a mature level for the mother to be able to achieve that.

Gelcer: Well, I think that she's already helping her mother, and I would start with that. She complains that her son defies her authority and that she succumbs to her mother's authority. She says, in effect, "My mother is very powerful. She made me take care of her husband until he died, then made me go out and get a job. My son isn't going to do this for me, he's already defiant at the age of 5, so please help me to get my son to be good to me, like I'm good to my mother." If you say that she's bad to her mother, then you lose this case. So I would work to get mother to enlist some help and cooperation from her own son and indirectly build up her confidence and insight. Once this positive relationship is identified and becomes apparent to the grandmother, the grandmother is going to be even more helpful. At that point I would encourage grandmother to find some happiness for herself.

Signs of disturbance in the treatment process would come when mother raises the issue of Andrew. Whenever mother returns the focus to Andrew, I would know that I'm not going in the right direction as a therapist. If she says, for example, "By the way, Andrew was sent home from school yesterday because he hit a kid," then I know the treatment process is not going in the right direction.

Interviewer: What do you do if you get a signal like that?

Gelcer: Well, I'd refocus on the parent. I would wonder how it happened, what happened that morning between Andrew and her. How did she find out? How did she handle it? Had she ever hit a kid when she was Andrew's age? What happened to her when she was Andrew's age? Then back to treating her.

Interviewer: Does anybody think that any other serious problems might arise in the course of this case?

Gelcer: Well, we really don't know about her male-female relations. Some problem may arise in impulsivity in her relationships with males, either back with her ex-husband, or with another male, or at the expense of Andrew.

Interviewer: Okay, what kind of worker would you like to see work with this family?

Gelcer: An older worker, in this case.

Interviewer: How old?

Gelcer: Thirty and up. Life experience is very important in this case. A worker who can tolerate her ups and downs and be flexible with her.

Spring: I may think in terms of a woman in this particular case. She has a lot to work out and she needs a female model to bounce things off. In this case, I think the idea of a woman therapist has some merit.

Interviewer: Any other characteristics?

Gelcer: I never specify male or female. I think that transferences happen with both sexes and they are worked through. We should probably talk about support systems as well.

Gertsman: Supports for mom and grandmother?

Spring: I thought of YWCA, church activities, what the local community offers.

Gelcer: Working through the separation from the husband and the individuation in relation to the mother will have to be accomplished. Those are the two main things. I have a feeling that this woman has been semi-isolated socially, busy working and coming home and taking care of the baby, but not having time for social activities. So I would recommend the Y or singles groups or something along this line.

Gertsman: One of the areas Andrew is beginning to show some difficulty with is with his peers. His relationships with peers consist mainly of his grandmother at home in the afternoon. So I would certainly encourage him to be out in the community, perhaps a swimming class, or involvements in some activity after school.

Spring: He comes home after school to stay with the grandmother until the mother gets home. Maybe Andrew should get involved in a day-care program where they will have activities for him until the mother picks him up at day care.

Gertsman: That would have to be very carefully introduced because grandmother is part of the dynamics.

Interviewer: Cynthia, in terms of outcome for the case, would you be looking for any shifts in the description of Andrew's behavior?

Gertsman: Yes, certainly that's important. I'd like to see the mother feeling more confident in her ability to relate to Andrew. You might check out the presenting problems in terms of temper tantrums and in terms of her comfort in coping with him. Also mom reporting that he's got a friend whom he's bringing home would be very important too.

Gelcer: Sleeping over at some friends' homes, spending weekends together with friends. Taking friends on outings with his father to the racetrack. Also, I think that power struggles and isolation are very, very important in all three generations in this case. There is a struggle with defiance and with feeling isolated. So for all three generations, I would want to see an outcome of finding some social groups to interact with to learn to be tolerant and cooperative. That's why I want to see Andrew bring a friend with him when he goes with his father, so that he's not the sole focus of attention and is able to give and take and to share with his friends.

Gertsman: Further down the road that would involve mom also becoming much more accepting of the relationship between father and son which she resents right now.

Interviewer: Paul, do you have any further comments on outcome?

Spring: Well, first of all I think the outcome should be fairly good. I think there's enough strength here, mother's a fighter. She's been somewhat ineffective but some of her struggling is effective, in terms of her work, for example. I think the therapist can link into her struggling aspect and get some things accomplished. So I think the prognosis is fairly good here.

Gelcer: The most positive outcome would be for Andrew to establish a close relationship with his father. That would relieve mother and grandmother to do their own jobs and allow Andrew contact with a positive male model.

Gertsman: That very much depends on father though. We have a comment that he's inconsistent in seeing his child and sometimes doesn't show. Certainly that would not be something to look for as an ideal.

Gelcer: We don't know. I think the most positive outcome would be for Andrew not to lose a father.

Interviewer: Further comments on prognosis?

Gelcer: I'm going to say guarded to fair. I would rather say fair because this is an impulsive, immature, and deprived woman and she is pointing her finger to a problem in the boy. The boy doesn't have a problem yet that anybody else recognizes, and he's very young, so I would not be 100% sure that there will be a success.

Gertsman: I would have concerns about mom actually being able to separate emotionally from her mother. She's got a lot of resentment from years ago, when mom used to, in some ways, look after her. One thing that could happen is that mother could become ill, and she would be strapped with her mother for years to come and not ever be able to separate. I have concerns about her being able to do that.

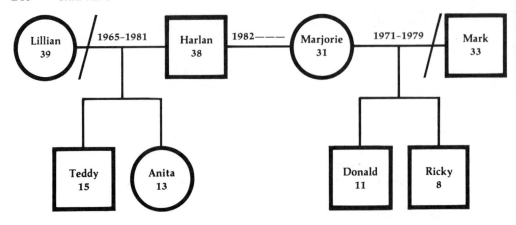

THE WEST FAMILY

Identifying information

The West family consists of Harlan West, Teddy and Anita, his son and daughter by a former marriage, his present wife Marjorie West, and her two boys by a former marriage, Donald and Ricky. The West family is self-referred. They are concerned about difficulties in bringing the children together in a new household since the parents married nine months ago. In particular, Mrs. West and Anita are fighting and not getting along. Moreover, Donald and Ricky fight with each other. According to Mrs. West, her husband picks on them and holds Teddy up as a model.

History of problem

Both parents report that the difficulties with the children began with their courting and deciding to marry. Harlan and Marjorie West have tried desperately to include all four children in their plans and to insist that they get along with their parents. For a long time, however, Anita did not talk to Marjorie at all; now they argue about most things, especially curfews, clothes, and friends. Since the couple has been living together, Donald and Ricky have been fighting more with each other and making increasing demands on their mother's time. Both parents work, so that Teddy has the responsibility to take care of the boys after school. Mr. West is not effective at getting Donald and Ricky to listen and cooperate, and he quickly loses patience with them. Mrs. West is more effective, but she is feeling drained from the constant grousing and lack of cooperation.

Marital and family history

Mr. West comes from an intact middle-class family. His father is an accountant and his mother a housewife. Mr. West has a younger brother who is a petroleum engineer. Mr. West's first wife Lillian left him and their children for another man about two years ago.

Marjorie West's parents are divorced. She was always quite distant from her father, a salesman, and seldom sees him. She has more contact with her mother and their relationship appears to be good. She also has an older sister, who lives in the area, and a younger sister, who lives abroad. Marjorie West and her first husband have been divorced for four years. She says that their relationship grew "tired" and that he was always promising more than he could deliver.

Characteristics of family members

Harlan West works as a draftsman, and Marjorie West is a legal secretary. The family lives in a comfortable, middle-class area in a well-kept house. Teddy and Anita each have their own bedroom, while Donald and Ricky share a room. Both parents seem very motivated for help but do not know how to establish peace in the family. Mr. West is particularly close to Anita and has good control over her. He also is proud of Teddy, who is an excellent student, and expects great things from him. He thinks that Donald and Ricky lack discipline and motivation and resents Mrs. West's ex-husband for not being a good role-model. Mr. West was quite devastated when his wife left him and claims that she just fell in love with another man. There is no contact between them now, or between her and her children. Mrs. West and her ex-husband Mark Cheever continue to have periodic contact, and he sees his sons on alternate weekends. He has since remarried.

Mr. and Mrs. West appear to have a good relationship although there is increasing tension due to their children. Teddy is an excellent student, responsible and soft-spoken, and spends most of his time at home. He tries to ingratiate himself with his new mother and look after her boys. Anita, on the other hand, seems to resent Marjorie's presence and talks angrily about her own mother's desertion of her. She is quite boy-oriented and socially popular. Donald spends most of his time on a model plane collection. He is shier than his brother but tends to bully Ricky. Ricky likes sports and longs for his father's visits, partly because his dad takes him to ball games. Both boys think Teddy is okay but view Anita as a troublemaker. They clamor for their mother's attention and have not yet accepted Harlan West's presence in their lives.

School and community

All the children except Teddy are active in the community. They have many friends. Anita is popular with boys and has been warned by Mrs. West that the guys she hangs out with are too old for her. Teddy thinks that Anita is looking for trouble. The school is not particularly concerned about any of the children in terms of academics or behavior. Teddy and Anita are very good students, but Donald and Ricky work at the average level.

Case discussion

Consultants: Mr. Michael Blugerman, Ms. Catherine Jackel

Interviewer: What would you like to know about the West family that you don't know?

Blugerman: One thing that's missing is a precipitating event. In other words, we have this collection of interrelationships between the various kids, but I don't know whether that has always been the case. It sounds normal. But this is a very trafficky case and it sounds like what you'd expect when you do a *Brady Bunch* reconstitution of a whole mess of people. If I were doing a consultation and somebody presented me with this material, I would start from the beginning and establish who called and why. What is it they want? They say that they are concerned about difficulties in bringing the children together in a new household. Now that's a philosophical problem, not really concrete, and I'm not clear whose problem it is.

Jackel: It seems to me to be an issue of the confusion, arguing, and lack of role definition they are experiencing, plus the family's feeling that they just can't go home to this anymore.

Blugerman: Now let's go to an ideal type. What would you expect to find in a reconstituted family? We have two parents who have each had care and control of two kids. How was that? Were the kids going to school? How was the sibling stuff? A lot of it sounds like normal sibling natterings. Was that the climate before, or is this strictly a factor of a sudden crowd? If you put all these people together, you have to reorganize some social context, and maybe that hasn't been organized. Usually I look to the parent-child interaction. I would expect the parents to set a tone and framework for this new family, so I'd wonder what happened through the courtship period on each side as the kids slowly got the idea that they were going to be melded in with a bunch of other kids. How were the kids introduced to one another? What difficulties were there on various outings that the whole family might have taken together? In a traditional marriage, the couple has a little while together to get to know each other and test limits and establish some kind of nurturing model before the kids put heavy demands on their system. When you do a reconstitution like this, the kids are putting on demands before day one, through the courtship, through the marriage, and when they are living together. Let's assume that the parents want to be together and to set up an organization with the kids feeling secure. What has gone wrong in that process? Information I would collect would be relevant to that question. In other words, how much of the acting-out is just a kids' circus of a few teenagers and a few preteens, and how much is a lack of support by the other guy or lack of involvement or reluctance of involvement due to some insecurity or uncertainty about how that intervention is going to be met by the other partner?

Jackel: I also need more information with regard to Lillian and Harlan. He was abandoned by her in 1981 and married Marjorie in 1982. That's a very brief period of time. Anita seems to be having trouble bonding with Marjorie because of failure to resolve her mother's absence in the first place.

Blugerman: And the history says that the kids started having difficulty when the parents were courting, when they started to get the idea that the mother was being replaced.

Jackel: Yes, and this seems particularly difficult for Anita because she may have felt abandoned. I'd like a history of the initial marital contracts and histories of the marriages, separations, and divorces. And then I'd like more detail with regard to their courtship and marriage. Marjorie's pattern seems straight-forward. She got married, was divorced in 1979 and remarried in 1982, so there was at least some time to work through the separation and mourning issues, plus a chance to adjust to the new single-parent family. With Harlan one wonders, because he was deserted by his wife in 1981 and remarried in 1982. One would suspect that some of the problems that Teddy's having with his "goody two-shoes" role and some of the problems that Anita's having with regard to acting-out against Marjorie relate to the fact that they haven't had a chance to resolve the first mother's departure.

Interviewer: Both of you have expressed some question about how serious a problem there is here.

Blugerman: My feeling is that the people reported a problem that ought to be taken seriously. The data collected is about the kids, whereas the statement we have is that the parents are concerned about the kids. Now we can do all the history-taking, and one advantage of that would be that, during the initial part of the treatment, the couple would come and have private time with someone who could referee or intervene or join or whatever, and that would be seen as supportive, which may give them impetus to do some other work. The risk is that we'll lose the specific interactional information. If everyone were there I could say to the parents "I'd like you two to talk about your concerns and the kids just listen." As I collected hard data from the parents, I could watch what kind of interaction they have. I could also look for nonverbal alliances and disagreements among the kids and then see how the two systems break down.

Interviewer: Would either of you consider working very briefly with this family and possibly supporting them and sending them away?

Jackel: Yes, I think I would lean toward short-term family therapy with all family members present. The only person that I would consider requiring individual assistance is Anita because I'm not sure about her level of distress with regard to Lillian and Harlan. It seems as if the parents are talking about how they can live together and that they are motivated to examine this. To some extent Teddy also concerns me. He's too good for a 15-year-old. It's age-appropriate for him to be breaking loose and seeking more autonomy outside the home. But he's carrying a father role, babysitting Donald and Ricky, and trying to advise Anita on whom she should see socially. I'd like to see a little less pressure on him to be the parent of the family and give him more freedom around being a 15-year-old. But I think this could be accomplished in family therapy.

Interviewer: How about you, Michael?

Blugerman: I don't know what I'm going to find until I get there. For example, Anita says that she resents the new mother's presence and yet talks angrily about her own mother's desertion. The mother thought that her husband didn't deliver the goods. He says that his wife left him. So now when Mr. West tries to discipline the two younger kids, I don't know if he has clear judgment about his wife's abilities. If she were competent, these kids wouldn't be like this. So there's all kinds of room for their marriage to be challenged. I'd start with the family and do boundary work within a family interview. Work with the couple with the kids watching, talk to the kids with the couple watching. I'd be tempted to do couple work to help them manage the kids. For example, if Mr. West has such a good relationship with Anita, can he teach his new wife how to use the same skills? If he can't, then that's a problem on both the relationship level and between the new mother and Anita. All these things would fall into place as I collected more information. I'd be very reluctant to move into any individual work. My rule of thumb is to work from the outside in and do macroorganizational work to see what kind of falloff and symptoms develop when that happens. If it's not enough, then I'd move to individual work.

Jackel: Yes, I see family therapy as the vehicle rather than individual work with the parents. Marjorie and Harlan seem to have different expectations. For example, he believes that her boys lack discipline and motivation while Teddy is the perfect 15-year-old. There are obviously different levels of expectation for how a boy should behave. I'm wondering if it wouldn't be more productive to sort through these different role expectations within the family group, working toward role definitions with all members present.

Blugerman: It's stated that the two younger boys have not accepted Mr. West's presence. Now I don't know if that's because he's tough on them, or has these different standards, or whether they're reading some cues from mother, or whether they still have some loyalty to their ex-father and wish they were back together again.

Jackel: Ricky is the one who really gets off on his natural dad and can't wait for the visits.

Blugerman: All these things would be phenomenally tough on this couple getting together.

Interviewer: It sounds as if you're suggesting that this marriage might be pretty shaky.

Blugerman: I would assume that it ought to be shaky. I'd make sure they got what they're asking. If they said that it's the kid, I'd join them at the level of the kid. I would accept them on the terms they present.

Jackel: I would approach the case as a developmental crisis in the formation of a new family, with perhaps some unresolved mourning. I get a real feeling of strength with regard to their motivation.

Blugerman: The length of treatment ought to be dictated by what they present and how much movement they make. The only other reason for thinking of time is if you believe that it would be repetitive to reenact prior difficulties and open up a whole pile of stuff. Unless there were an agency policy or some other very clear reason to make it short-term, the timing would depend on what was required.

Interviewer: You are both agreeing that family therapy is the primary way you would approach this case. Are there any other modalities to be involved?

Blugerman: Some people are talking these days about groups for kids like this. That might be something to offer. If one or two of the kids are having a lot of trouble, I would try to normalize it by finding a group of children of divorced or separated parents. I would also encourage the family to have family meetings on a regular basis with leadership participation from the couple.

Interviewer: Cathy, you talked about wanting to see Anita individually. What was on your mind?

Jackel: I'm concerned about the escalation of her behavior. She is 13 and, if not there, at least approaching puberty. She has competition with a new woman for father, she has failed to resolve or maybe to mourn a mother who deserted her, and she's expected to bond with this new woman/mother. I don't think her issues are necessarily going to be resolved by family treatment. She's going to need a separate space and permission to sort them through. I initially suggested individual therapy, but listening to Michael's suggestion, I also like the idea of a process group for separated kids, since increased peer group acceptance is part of her developmental stage.

Blugerman: I'm fascinated by the fact that mother and Teddy are worried about Anita but I don't hear father's concern. I would want the mother and father to talk about the mother's concern and let her convince him that there is a problem and then figure out what to do.

Interviewer: If you were running a group of kids all of whom had the common experience of divorced parents and reconstituted families, what would you be trying to do?

Jackel: They wouldn't necessarily need the experience of being in reconstituted families, just having divorced parents. I would have a process-oriented, growth group that explored, shared, and developed coping mechanisms around feelings of abandonment, anger, and guilt that kids go through who have been left by a parent. I think the working through could accomplish this the way any adolescent process group would. You provide an atmosphere in which the kids can do the work and you go with their resistance. It often works nicely, especially if the teens are mixed sexes.

Interviewer: What other specific techniques and strategies would you use with this particular family?

Blugerman: Kids have family romances about the original parents getting back together. They may feel that they have more to say about who the caretaking parent will be than they do and they may test out the relationship between the couple. There are all kinds of challenges to the executive-child process. I'd use the difficult life events the kids go through, complaints such as "He's kinda tough on me," or "She didn't give me my allowance," or "I want to go out with the guys and she won't let me," and challenge both parents to deal with it by having the more aligned or skillful parent share that skill with the other. If the kid presents a problem and it polarizes the parents, then I'd work on the executive function. Can they get together enough to meet the kid's demands? If the parents are together, then it's a question of where this individual kid is stuck. Many unfairnesses or inequalities may emerge. Here are two sets of siblings that have been working to achieve some kind of balance with each other. You put them in a foursome, now you have a whole new constellation of alliances and ground rules that are going to be challenged. They may need assistance in working that stuff out. Again I would pick a family meeting in which to do that. The only other thing that I might do outside the sessions is to orchestrate some contact to challenge some of the alliances and coalitions. So if dad is a favorite with one of the kids, could mom take over some of the parenting of that kid and could dad take over something else? For example, I've heard kids say to me "I try to talk to my mother, I ask her a question, like what time's dinner and Dad answers. Well, it's not his business, and I don't want him to interfere." So there are all kinds of tests and challenges to this new structure that are part of a normal reorganization.

Jackel: For instance, it's perfectly appropriate for the two youngest kids in the family to share a bedroom, but they happen to be the kids from one family. That would be a great topic to bring up at a family meeting. The reality of the bedroom arrangements could be explained in terms of space and time and the new family constellation, rather than leaving kids resentful and feeling that "My brother and I have to share a room but your kid and her brother get separate rooms." Those are the kinds of simple things that are seen with a tremendous amount of jealousy when reconstituted families get together. I think the parents recognizing the strengths of their own union and of their kids is also very important because there's a danger with reconstituted families that rigid communication systems are set up that don't lend to the family bonding and moving on through this developmental crisis. There are some good strengths that can be worked on in the system—for instance, Teddy and Anita are trying to cope with mom's disappearance, while Donald and Ricky have good relationships with their absentee father. There's room in family therapy to have those two kids help the other two kids with their mom's absence. These are strengths in the system that they can use to bond with each other; rather than having to go through mom and dad to resolve that kind of loss, they can go directly to their siblings for this kind of help.

Blugerman: I think it's most economical and elegant to assume a positive outcome, go for it, set up tasks that would challenge that, and then watch for a fallout.

Interviewer: Could you give an example of how you would go about conceiving a task?

Blugerman: If we assume that the parent system ought to decide on parameters for Anita's social life, given her age, then Anita might come and say "I'm going to the show with so and so," and the mother and Teddy would get upset. Then I would say that this is an issue for father and mother to decide. I would ask them to take a few minutes, talk about it, come to a conclusion, and share that with Anita. I would watch Anita's reaction. If she accepts it from dad but not from mom, that would direct me into helping dad assist mom to do better. Or uncovering her objection to getting it. What we may find is Anita may say "Why are you telling me? You may not be around." Then we'd get into a whole pile of material about the absent mother. If Anita said "If dad tells me, okay, but if you tell me, forget it," then I'm back to the couple thing. So the task would direct what happens next.

Interviewer: Are you also interested in assigning family tasks outside the sessions?

Blugerman: Yes, especially around the family council meetings because I want to know if they are going to transfer skills learned in the session around parent- or executive-child structure to their outside world.

Jackel: I think it would be productive to have the family therapy sessions in the home.

Blugerman: Yes, that comes down to economics and style. There's a fallacy among a lot of therapists and clients that the way they are in the office is different from how they are at home. That depends on how you work. If you work for re-enactment or work actively, then you'll get the behavior replicated in the office.

Jackel: Actually, I wasn't thinking on that level. Rather, simply that this kind of structure would make it easier to hold a family council meeting at a living room table where we've had the family therapy session. They are becoming a family and I am looking for anything concrete that will anchor certain experiences to that concept.

Interviewer: What kind of worker characteristics would you recommend for this family?

Blugerman: You have to create a workable reality that requires a fair bit of joining and social skill and authority. I think it would be helpful to have somebody who is older and has had kids. And I think anecdotal material would be helpful in the course of working with these people. I think it ought to be somebody who understands the vicissitudes of divorce, remarriage, and reconstituted families.

Interviewer: What about a co-therapy arrangement?

Blugerman: I'm not high on co-therapy. I'd rather use one person outside as a consultant, able to observe and come in. It would take a long time to test out the balance of co-therapists. In terms of problems, I could expect that some kids, either the two little guys with their misbehavior or Anita with her precociousness, would dramatically escalate a crisis that would challenge the couple before they were ready.

Jackel: Yes, that would be my major concern, too. Right now they're very fond of each other, but the relationship is not as good as it was because they are deeply feeling the tension from the kids. Even though I see them as having a lot of strengths, I don't really anticipate that it would take too many crises at this stage before the desire to bond would be broken. So it's a matter of keeping the strengths ahead of the crises that the kids could precipitate; I think that Anita's probably our key person in that, and the sooner she gets help the better. I think also you might find the two younger boys acting up in school, particularly since Teddy is held up as such a "good" model.

Interviewer: How do you mean?

Jackel: Well, right now Ricky and Donald don't have any trouble in school, but father has high scholastic expectations and Teddy's a model student. Thus, I anticipate that they might act-out around the school in response to the new level of expectations that father will probably place on them.

Interviewer: Could anything happen with this family that would cause you to want to move to a completely different approach?

Jackel: Yes, if Marjorie were looking for the father that she was never close to in Harlan, then it would become very difficult for them to work together on their co-parenting roles.

Interviewer: What would you do?

Jackel: I think I would try a move to marital therapy if this dynamic was very strong.

Blugerman: Another concern would occur if the demands of the kids and the reorganization of the children prevent the couple from getting time away, spending nurturing time together, and having privacy. I would try to make it normal and okay for them to have private times and maybe have them get a babysitter other than Teddy. What would induce me to change my plan about all this? I'm assuming that the members of the family are fairly together, and that it's basically a normal reaction to a crazy situation. If we find out that the father's quick remarriage or some of the mother's unfinished business put them into a symbiotic arrangement in terms of gratification of their needs, I might have to do more marital work. The only other difficulties I can imagine have to do with changes in circumstance. What would happen if Donald and Ricky's father had kids or moved, for example? Another complication would be if the boys' visits to their father reminded Anita of the lack of her mother. If there were blow-ups in any of these areas, we'd have to figure what to do.

Interviewer: What goals and outcomes would you want a worker to focus on with this case?

Blugerman: I'm going back to the initial statement of their concerns about bringing the kids together so I would be working toward a more normalized, optimistic view about that. Less anxiety about the fact that they are having problems.

Jackel: I would probably express it differently, but I would simply see them coming out of this developmental crisis with coping mechanisms that they could apply to future developmental crises.

Interviewer: What do you mean by coping mechanisms?

Jackel: Ability to negotiate with one another, clearly defined roles and ways of facilitating role change, so that as the kids grow and depart, the family can adjust. This family is going to be doing a lot of negotiation around roles and decision-making processes. The fact that they know how to do this because they've done it is going to provide them with adaptive behaviors that they can apply to future crises.

Interviewer: How do you tell whether they have the ability to adapt to role changes or to facilitate role changes?

Jackel: One vehicle is the family council. Another vehicle is monitoring when the parents come together and parent. And the kids beginning to develop their own age-appropriate roles outside the family unit instead of being anchored into it. I think those would all be indicators that things are going well.

Blugerman: And if Harlan asks the boys "How about if we go to the hockey game Saturday night?" they might say "No, we're going with my dad." That may not sit so easily. And these are things that normal kids do. He's going to have to suffer with that and come to terms with it through his relationship with Marjorie and how good he feels about himself.

Interviewer: So you're looking for him to be able to step back from that and cope?

Blugerman: His ability to take disappointment and rejection when it's not personally intended, but just circumstantial.

Jackel: There's going to be a lot of that for both parents in this family. In a way it has to do with the parents trying too hard to make it.

Blugerman: People in this situation have a phenomenal competency challenge. So there's a tendency to try to overperform, and they may need some soothing about that.

Interviewer: What are your predictions about how well the family will respond to the treatment plans?

Jackel: I think this family's strengths indicate a good prognosis.

Blugerman: I'm fairly optimistic. I think that this kind of work requires a skilled worker, or an experienced worker, and there's a good chance.

Jackel: I don't think that this person has to have had a personal experience with reconstituted families. Rather that he/she needs to be a skilled family therapist with an eclectic approach.

Blugerman: I'd go with that. Except for Teddy, who is going through a very mild adolescence, they all have developmental problems to look forward to. So as the parents try to pull this together, the normal age-appropriate, stage-appropriate activity for the next few years is going to be separation. I keep stressing the amount of normal craziness that there is here.

SUMMARY

The final three cases are devoted to families in which significant relationships with individuals outside the nuclear family contribute directly to a child's problem. While extended relationships are virtually always present in families, in these cases a grandparent or ex-spouse plays a direct role in a child's problem.

The Silverstein family is a single-parent family consisting of mother and her 7-year-old son. In this case the father's desertion of the family one and one-half years prior resulted in a rapid deterioration of Mrs. Silverstein. There has been a shift from a middle-class lifestyle to welfare status, and mother claims to be totally helpless in parenting and disciplining her son. She presents as an indulged, harassed, and bitter woman who does have some skill in eliciting aid from her own mother and various social service agencies. Her son appears to be dependent on his mother, uncooperative at home, and not coping well at school.

The consultants suggest that Mrs. Silverstein would be both needy and challenging in therapy and that a worker must be careful to build on her strengths rather than succumb to her passivity. An active approach would be used to assist mother in separating from her own mother and in developing skills to take responsibility for caring for herself and her son. It is pointed out that the same themes of disappointment and manipulation seem to be cross-generational. Other work would include extending the boy's activities and social contacts beyond the immediate family.

The Calderone family consists of Mrs. Lillian Calderone, her 5-year-old son Andrew, and Mrs. Calerone's mother. Mrs. Calderone is a divorced woman who feels squeezed between caring for a demanding 5-year-old and meeting the expectations of her own dominating mother, while maintaining a job and taking university courses. Her relationship with her son is close and protective, but the boy is able to intimidate her and she is helpless in controlling his aggressively defiant behavior. Contributing to Mrs. Calderone's negative self-image is her ex-husband, who drank heavily and used to abuse his wife and who now visits their son periodically and undermines her parenting efforts.

The consultants see the need for more information about recent changes that may account for the family's seeking treatment at this time. There is a clear need to focus the intervention on mother and clarify her role vis-à-vis her ex-husband and her mother. Less work would be done with Andrew since only his mother appears to have difficulty managing him. Indeed, Mrs. Calderone may be seeking help for Andrew while actually wanting something for herself. One component of treatment would probably be guidance in child management techniques to reinforce mother's parental role.

The West family is a reconstituted family consisting of two divorced parents and their four children by previous marriages. The presenting difficulties revolve around sibling relationships and tension among the children and their new parents. Mr. and Mrs. West themselves seem to have a good relationship although difficulties in coping with four children, aged 8 to 15, are exerting pressure on it.

The consultants conceptualize the Wests as a reconstituted family with confusion regarding role definition, parenting responsibilities, and sibling relationships. The consultants recommend a family therapy framework rather than individual work with the parents. One key issue is the need for the parents to join together in the executive function of the family and then negotiate individual child complaints. The children also need the opportunity to resolve their feelings about the departed parents and the new marriage. One possible additional intervention would be referral of the children, especially the 13-year-old girl, to a group for children of divorced or separated parents.

STUDY/DISCUSSION QUESTIONS

1. When is it advisable to include or exclude extended family members in treatment? What are the hazards of either course of action?

2. What are the needs and difficulties for each generation when grandparents, parents, and children share the same household?
3. What is the appropriate role for a divorced parent who is not living in the home with regard to parenting the children and participating in treatment?
4. What kinds of relationships are desirable among adults and children in reconstituted families? What kinds of feelings and problems are likely to arise in such families?
5. What are the needs of children whose parents separate or divorce?

Glossary

acting-out: the indirect expression of negative feelings through aggressive behavior rather than through direct confrontation or constructive problem-solving. Acting-out often characterizes the delinquent or negativistic behavior of children and adolescents.

aligning: the process by which therapy is structured to create alliances between two family members to allow one of them freedom and distance from a third member. Deprived of this relationship, the first and third members must now concentrate on changing other interactions. The therapist can also facilitate change by aligning himself or herself with a given family member through support and agreement.

auxiliary ego: a psychodrama technique instituted by J. L. Moreno, in which a secondary actor adopts and enacts a role that is supportive of the target actor.

behavior chart: a chart used by behavior therapists to modify their clients' behavior. The chart shows a desired behavior together with consequences (reinforcing or punishing) for its completion.

character disorder: a social diagnosis made by someone other than the person in focus. It refers to someone whose behavior others perceive as destructive, frightening, overly nonconforming, or in some other way deviant.

Children's Aid Society: a provincially (Ontario) funded organization filling the function of a child protective service. Its main duties involve providing information and counseling to families and performing the roles of supervision, removal, or care of children who are inadequately parented.

Children's Apperception Test (CAT):   a projective technique adapted for use with children from the original Thematic Apperception Test of Henry Murray. The child views a series of pictures of animals or children and is asked to tell a story of what is occurring in the picture, how the participants are feeling, and what the outcome might be. The rationale is that the child will reveal his or her own personality or conflicts by interpreting the pictures.

compulsion: the persistence of an irresistible urge or the carrying out of that urge. A compulsion has a repetitive and ritualistic nature that persists despite the individual's strong desire to ban it from awareness.

contingency contracting: a behavior-modification procedure consisting of clearly identifying the target behavior and the reinforcers that will be made contingent on its performance.

contracting: the therapeutic process by which client and therapist agree on the nature of the problem to be addressed and on the goals and procedures for change. Although the nature of the agreement may change, it must always change in a direction formed by mutual consent. See **contingency contracting.**

countertransference: the complex of unconscious feelings of a therapist in reaction to his or her client that has a bearing on the therapeutic process.

delusion: a false belief or cognition, actively defended by the bearer, that persists in spite of evidence to the contrary and in light of common sense.

disengaged family: a family that shows a type of interaction in which members function in an almost totally autonomous manner. The sense of independence is extreme, and norms for loyalty and belonging are absent.

double-bind: the core concept in the theory that schizophrenia often develops in children who are confronted by contradictory messages from their parents. The messages are sent in different ways (open statements, innuendos, or bodily gestures) at different times, but the parent always denies the contradiction. The child, however, cannot escape the contradictory demands of the parents' messages and is held to blame no matter how he or she behaves.

ego boundary: hypothetical boundaries said to exist between the individual and the outer world of reality and between the individual and his or her unconscious world. In an adjusted person, the boundaries are flexible enough to allow selective admittance of unconscious thoughts to awareness and external information that tests the person's understanding of reality.

empty-chair technique: a therapeutic tool used by Gestalt psychotherapists. Literally seated across from an empty chair, the client is asked to imagine seated in that chair a significant other with whom he or she has unfinished business. The client then role-plays a dialogue between himself or herself and the other person, in an attempt to clarify and resolve the conflict.

enmeshed family: a family characterized by such closeness and sense of belonging that the members' autonomy and individual coping are impeded.

enuresis: commonly known as *bedwetting*, enuresis refers to the involuntary elimination of urine. Although enuresis can result from physical malfunctioning, it is more commonly seen as a psychogenic problem accompanied by other signs of emotional upset.

family council: a meeting of all family members to discuss and solve a problem and/or to make a decision affecting the family. This is a practice usually recommended to families who need to improve their cohesion and communication skills.

family of origin: the family system into which one is born; it includes one's parents and siblings and describes the interrelationship patterns common to those family members.

genogram: a line diagram that conveys the identities, ages, and relationships of family members. It is especially useful as a way of tracing and illustrating family membership in reconstituted, extended, and multigenerational families.

hyperactivity: a label used to refer to a behavior disorder in children. The hyperactive child is said to be restless, to have a brief attention span, and to suffer an inability to control his or her impulses. These symptoms result in sleeping disturbance and social and educational problems. The etiology of the disorder is still being explored.

hyperkinesia: abnormally increased and often purposeless and uncontrollable muscular movement.

iatrogenic: referring to a behavior or ailment that is a negative side effect of treatment.

identified patient (IP):   a family-systems term referring to a person brought into therapy as deviant or unmanageable and considered the primary source of pain for the family. Typically, the patient's symptoms are assumed to be an expression of a family dysfunction rather than of an individual's dysfunction.

joining: the process by which the therapist, in an attempt to understand and bring about change in a family, accommodates himself or herself to the family system to the extent that he or she comes to experience the stress and pain of the family interactions. In joining the family system, however, the therapist must maintain a leadership role and guard against being emotionally drawn into the family system.

Klinefelter's syndrome: one of two abnormal sex chromosomal patterns found in males. The individual with Klinefelter's syndrome has one more X chromosome (XXY) than is found in the normal male (XY). Males with this syndrome may develop enlarged breasts and show retardation of male secondary sex characteristics. The research on Klinefelter's has centered on the controversial issue of whether this chromosomal abnormality is responsible for psychological problems such as mental retardation, impulsivity, and violent anti-social behavior reported for some of these males.

manic-depressive: one who displays a major mental disorder characterized by alternating moods of mania, extreme euphoria, and severe psychotic depression.

mental-status interview: generic term used to refer to a battery of tests or questions used by clinicians and societal authorities to identify one's mental state (contact with reality) in order to determine whether the person can stand trial, is criminally insane, or needs to be committed to an institution.

metacommunication: communication at a higher level than what is said at the surface level. It adds meaning to the message and is used to talk *about* communication rather than to communicate the content of our expressions.

minimal brain dysfunction: a term that refers to hypothetical minor neurological damage. The term is used primarily with regard to children who have below-average intelligence, who are autistic, or who exhibit hyperactive behaviors.

modeling: according to social learning theory, modeling involves imitating or learning a behavior by observing the behavior being performed by others.

neurological exam: a battery of tests designed primarily for diagnostic purposes to determine possible degrees of intellectual impairment or changes in personality due to deviation in neurological functioning.

neurosis: a psychological disorder characterized by inappropriate levels of anxiety or depression. There is no loss of contact with reality.

normalization: integrating children with special learning needs into the educational system and society at large. It often entails integrating gifted or learning-disabled children into classes with average students. The term is also used to refer to any programming that minimizes, reduces, or deemphasizes the deviance of an individual or group.

object relations: in psychoanalytic theory, it means to react to an object (human or inanimate) on the basis of its ability to provide instinctual gratification.

paradoxical intervention: specific tactics and maneuvers that appear to be opposed to the goals of therapy but that, in reality, are designed to achieve them. Paradoxical interventions have been divided into (1) *compliance-based strategies,* in which the client, by attempting to comply with the therapist, will not be able to resist the therapist's directive, and (2) *defiance-based strategies,* in which the therapist expects the client to resist the directive.

projection: a psychoanalytic term that refers to a defense mechanism involving temporary attribution of one's own unacceptable thoughts, wishes, or desires to another individual.

projective test: a personality-assessment measure using ambiguous or unstructured stimulus material (such as inkblots) for the purpose of tapping unconscious personality factors.

reaction formation: a defense mechanism in which the person acts in an exaggerated manner opposite to what he or she really feels.

reconstituted family: a family formed from two previously independent families, such as the union of two divorced adults and their respective children.

reframing: a therapeutic intervention that consists of reinterpreting a weakness or problem behavior as a strength or positive behavior. Reframing is intended to alter a client's perception of a problem and to interrupt destructive interpersonal transactions.

regression: a defense mechanism in which the individual returns to more primitive or infantile ways of reasoning or behaving when confronted by an anxiety-arousing situation.

reinforce: to follow a desired response with a stimulus that has the likelihood of increasing that same response. *Positive reinforcement* involves giving a reward contingent on performing the desired behavior; *negative reinforcement* involves terminating an aversive stimulus contingent on performing the desired behavior.

Ritalin: common name for *methylphenidate,* a central nervous system stimulant used in the treatment of depression to increase euphoria. In hyperactive children, it is said to *quiet* the overactivity.

schizoid: characterized by a life-long pattern of avoiding interpersonal contacts. Behaviors that may be representative of the schizoid personality include excessive shyness and daydreaming.

schizophrenia: a class of psychotic disorders characterized by poor contact with reality and a tendency toward unpredictable mood changes. Fantasies, delusions, or hallucinations may occur.

script: in Transactional Analysis, a life plan based on a childhood decision that was reinforced by one's parents, was justified by subsequent events, and culminates in a chosen alternative.

secondary gains: those benefits one derives indirectly from being ill, including attention and sympathy from others and exemption from work or other obligations.

separation and individuation: those processes that lead to the individual's autonomy. According to Mahler, separation and individuation occur when the child learns to exist as a separate and unique individual through the process of negotiating with various family subsystems and through interactions with others outside the family.

strokes: in Transactional Analysis, units of interpersonal recognition, such as "Hello" or "Thanks."

structural family therapy: a body of theory and techniques, developed by S. Minuchin and others, that approaches the person within his or her own social context. Any step toward changing an individual is directed toward changing the structure of the family group of which that individual is a member.

symbiotic: a type of relationship or intimate association between two individuals that works to the mutual detriment of both; according to

E. Fromm, a neurotic dependence of one individual on another. When it occurs between mother and child, it has been considered by Mahler to be a cause of childhood schizophrenia.

Thematic Apperception Test (TAT):   a projective technique designed by Henry Murray, in which the person views a series of pictures and is asked to tell a story of what is occurring, how the participants are feeling, and what the outcome might be. The rationale is that the individual will reveal his or her own personality or conflicts in the interpretations.

time-out: an operant-conditioning technique used primarily with children. It can be defined as removal of a child from a potentially reinforcing situation when the child behaves inappropriately. The child remains in isolation for a specified time limit and is allowed to return only after that time has passed and the behavior has terminated.

transference: occurs in therapy when a client directs to the therapist positive or negative feelings that he or she holds toward other significant individuals in his or her life, such as parental figures. The occurrence and resolution of transference is considered an essential step in psychoanalysis but is regarded as less desirable in other forms of insight therapy.

transsexuality: a clinical disorder in which the individual's gender identity is at variance with his or her biological sex. The transsexual person experiences the life-long belief that she or he has been born with the body of the wrong sex. Transsexuals sometimes choose a sex-change operation to correct the condition.

Uproar: in Transactional Analysis, a "game" that consists of dramatic, angry exchanges to avoid sexual intimacy, usually played between domineering fathers and adolescent daughters.

WRAT (Wide Range Achievement Test):   a test of academic achievement administered by a psychologist or psychoeducational specialist. The test yields scores that indicate the student's current grade level and standing in reading, spelling, and arithmetic.